BACKPACKING WISCONSIN

BACKPACKING WISCONSIN

Jack P. Hailman & Elizabeth D. Hailman

THE UNIVERSITY OF WISCONSIN PRESS

The University of Wisconsin Press
2537 Daniels Street
Madison, Wisconsin 53718

3 Henrietta Street
London WC2E 8LU, England

5   4   3   2   1

Printed in the United States of America

Library of Congress Cataloging-in-Publication Data

Hailman, Jack Parker, 1936–
        Backpacking Wisconsin / Jack P. Hailman and Elizabeth D. Hailman.
            pp.   cm.
        Includes bibliographical references (p.) and index.
        ISBN 0-299-16814-X (paper : alk. paper)
          1. Backpacking—Wisconsin—Guidebooks.   2. Wisconsin—Guidebooks.
        I. Hailman, Elizabeth D.   II. Title.
        GV199.42.W6 H35   2000
        917.7504'43—dc21   99-053843

For Karl and Eric,
backpacking
companions
and sons

CONTENTS

PREFACE

This book is a labor of love, but it also has some hidden agendas. A few years ago, we happened upon a backpacking guide to a sister state to the south, and it dawned on us that Wisconsin lacked such a guide. This deficiency seemed all the more deplorable when we realized that Wisconsin is a much better state for backpacking than is that other one. Because we had been backpacking all over our state, we decided to write the needed guide. The book gives us an opportunity to promote backpacking to the uninitiate, to encourage the construction and maintenance of more miles of foot trails, and to attract support for efforts to preserve more lands in their natural condition. But first, a few words about the structure of the book.

NATURAL HISTORY LISTS

People told us on questionnaires we distributed that one of their enjoyments in backpacking was natural history. Therefore, we have included in reporting our own trips the various plants and animals that we noted. Parks sometimes— annoyingly—emphasize the dramatic living things, especially animals, that have at one time or another been recorded within their boundaries. These dramatic animals (for example, Bobcat) are often the rare or secretive species that the average visitor would be lucky to see in an entire season in the park. Furthermore, lists of wildflowers and birds in particular can mislead the user because many are found only in special habitats. For these reasons we wanted to put down in black and white what we actually did see (or hear, in the case of some birds) on a specific trail. Go at a different time of year and you will see a different mix of plants in flower and birds in song, but at least our notes provide a starting place of things you really can see while backpacking at a given place.

SPECIES NAMES

We capitalized common names of plant and animal species but not groups. Thus we might write about "Nodding Trillium" but refer to "trillium" when not indicating a particular species. Scientists usually do not capitalize common names because they rely more upon the Latinized scientific names. In a work like this, however, it is useful to distinguish a blue jay (any jay that is blue, such as the Steller's Jay) from the Blue Jay (the species *Cyanocitta cristata*). We did not want to weigh down the text with unwieldy scientific names.

NAMES OF BIRDS

The relatively few species of trees and mammals we report provide no problems of nomenclature, but wildflowers and birds are another matter entirely. You want to be certain of the species mentioned—without resorting to those eminently forgettable scientific names—so you need to use standard common names of some sort. There is an easy solution with regard to birds, because the American Ornithologists' Union publishes *The A.O.U. Check-list of North American Birds,* the standard reference work used by amateur birders and professional ornithologists alike. We follow exactly the common names given in the seventh edition (1998). You do not even have to buy this tome or find it in a library; the list of species is available on the World Wide Web (http://pica.wru.umt.edu/aou/birdlist.html). If you want to know the scientific name of a bird we refer to, look up the common name in that list.

NAMES OF WILDFLOWERS

Wildflowers, by contrast with birds, present problems, because there exists no standard authority equivalent to the A.O.U.'s *Check-list.* We have relied primarily on *A Field Guide to Wildflowers: Northeastern and North-central North America,* by Peterson and McKenny, first published in 1968 and reprinted many times, in conjunction with two other popular guides, both now out of print: *Wildflowers of North America: A Guide to Field Identification* (1984), by Venning, and *Wildflowers and Weeds: A Field Guide in Full Color* (1972), by Courtenay and Zimmerman (see Further Reading). We have used the common names given in Peterson and McKenny for all but the handful of species that are not included in that guide. Where Peterson and McKenny give two names for one wildflower species, we have adopted the first name and indicated the second in parentheses. We have also included in parentheses the common name used for the same species in the field guides by Venning and by Courtenay and Zimmerman. Alternative names may refer to either all or part of the name: thus, "Fringed Polygala (Gaywings)" means that the species is called either Fringed Polygala or Gaywings, whereas "Common (Tall) Buttercup" means that the two names applied to this species are Common Buttercup and Tall Buttercup. We have ignored orthographic differences and truncations: e.g., Peterson and McKenny use "Wild Lily-of-the-valley," "Colicroot," and "Ohio Spiderwort," whereas Courtenay and Zimmerman refer to "Wild Lily of the Valley," "Colic Root," and "Spiderwort." For the few species that are entirely missing from Peterson and McKenny, we have taken the common names from Courtenay and Zimmerman. Because that book is now out of print, we give the scientific names for those species here:

Dwarf Lake-Iris, *Iris lacustris*
Jump Seed, *Polygonum virginianum*

Thimbleberry, *Rubus parviflorus*
Red Raspberry, *Rubus idaeus*
Goat's Beard, *Aruncus dioicus*
Poison Ivy, *Rhus radicans*
(Prostrate) Vervain, *Verbena bracteata*
Meadow Goat's Beard, *Tragopogon dubius*

ORDER OF TRAIL DESCRIPTIONS

This book reads Wisconsin's geography as though it were a book: starting at the top left and reading rightward, then dropping lower on the left and reading rightward, and so on to the bottom. We have divided the state into regions, and the sequence of chapters follows the left to right (west to east), top to bottom (north to south) rule. The first four chapters cover the Northwest, North Central, and Northeast regions, and the remaining regions are gathered into a last chapter, which follows the rule internally. Each chapter begins with a regional map to show the locations of trails given in the accounts. "Read" these backpacking areas on the regional map according to the same rule, and you will be following the sequence of accounts within that chapter. Within accounts that require more than one trail map, an area map provides a guide to the detailed trail maps, which are numbered west to east, then north to south. Occasionally geography fails to cooperate with our *modus operandi,* as when trails run from southwest to northeast. We have made arbitrary decisions in such cases, usually opting for west to east to take precedence over north to south.

THE MAPS

We have made trail maps for every trail included in this book. Because all of them are marked trails, our maps should be sufficient, assuming that the backpacker stays on the trail. Sometimes parks distribute separate maps for different uses, such as hiking, biking, and riding, which show only one kind of trail. The hiker using such a map may unexpectedly encounter a trail junction not on the map because it is a different kind of trail, even though hikers may be allowed on it. We have tried to include such junctions and crossings with other trails, and sometimes (for most state parks) provide the complete routes of all trails open to foot travel.

We have included a scale marker on each trail map and have also indicated trail distances between points when such information was available to us. Nevertheless, putative trail distances are often in error, so figures shown should be considered only approximate.

For each account having more than one trail map, as well as for a few that have only one trail map, there is also an area map. The area map diagrams the geographic coverage of each of the trail maps and also shows the principal access roads. Finding the trailhead is sometimes the most difficult part of a backpacking trip, so the text of each account includes directions for getting there.

TRAIL NAMES

The Ice Age National Scenic Trail is divided into named segments by the foundation that builds and maintains it. We have used these segment names in accounts devoted to the Ice Age Trail outside of state and national forest lands. In some cases our maps show only a portion of the official segment: the portion on public lands (mainly county forests) where camping is allowed.

For ski trail complexes, we have used the plural even when they bear a singular name (e.g., Penokee Mountain Ski Trails, not Trail) because these complexes always contain multiple trails. In some cases we have also shortened names, for example by omitting "ski" from the name.

WHY THIS BOOK CONTAINS ERRORS

We have produced this work during a period of unexpected change (especially during 1999) in Wisconsin backpacking opportunities. Most of these recent changes were not discovered until the completed manuscript was sent to various authorities for checking. Some of them were largely administrative, such as the amalgamation of Chequamegon and Nicolet National Forests into one forest—thereby requiring lots of textual adjustments, as well as relabeling of maps. Others were far more substantial, such as changes in policies in state forests, one of which required deleting seven maps for areas in which backpacking is no longer allowed. One state park where we have been backpacking was "delisted" by the state Department of Natural Resources in spring 1999 and was removed from the book, and another that is still officially listed as offering backpacking in fact has eliminated it and bulldozed the campsite in which we had stayed. We are aware of the following state-administered areas that were at one time in the past listed in the literature of Wisconsin's Department of Natural Resources as offering backpacking but no longer do so (1999).

> Big Bay State Park
> Chippewa Moraine State Recreation Area (a unit of the Ice Age National
> Scientific Reserve)
> Hoffman Hills State Recreation Area
> Willow River State Park

Even as the state curtails backpacking and institutes new charges where it is allowed, however, the two national scenic trails are growing and so providing new opportunities for the backpacker. We have made every effort to incorporate these many recent changes and hope that we have caught the worst of the errors and ambiguities engendered by revising an already completed manuscript. Be aware, though, that conditions may continue to change after this book has gone to press.

WE WANT TO HEAR FROM YOU

We would love for you to point out errors you find in the book and to explain where some ambiguity led to your being confused. If your favorite backpacking area was not included, tell us about it. If you find things have changed somewhere since the text and maps were finalized, tell us about that, too. Jack expects to maintain indefinitely his e-mail address: jhailman@facstaff.wisc.edu. Regular mail should be sent care of the University of Wisconsin Press for forwarding to us.

ACKNOWLEDGMENTS

We thank the many people who helped make this book possible. Mary Elizabeth Braun solicited the project while she was an acquisitions editor at the University of Wisconsin Press. Renee Callaway facilitated our survey of backpackers while she was director of recreational clinics at REI in Madison. Chapter leaders in the Ice Age Park and Trail Foundation and the North Country Trail Association—some whose names we never knew—distributed our questionnaire to their members at meetings and by electronic mail. Not to be overlooked are the nearly four dozen backpackers, most of them anonymous, who kindly took the time and trouble to fill out and return the questionnaires. William Menke of the National Park Service provided copies of unpublished maps of a new segment of the North Country Trail.

After the manuscript was completed, we continued to rely on various people for help. We sent each account to one or more trail authorities, such as the staff of the park maintaining a trail, and invited them to correct anything they found amiss. Staffs of almost all the state parks and state forests, along with some federal authorities, kindly returned the manuscript and maps with useful annotations, and perhaps those who did not reply found nothing to modify. We realize that government officials consider it part of their jobs to help get the information about their areas as correct as possible, and therefore they do not expect public thanks. (Each respondent was thanked individually, of course.) In fact, it would not be possible to thank everyone by name here because most responses were sent back anonymously, and some manuscripts and maps were obviously marked by more than one person. We are, though, very grateful to these wonderful civil servants who caught many of our mistakes; those that remain are wholly our responsibility.

Then there are volunteers, mainly coordinators and officers of organizations such as the North Country Trail Association and the Ice Age Park and Trail Foundation. We are very grateful to Ron Becker, Jim Bower, Adam

Cahow, Joe Jopek, Ken Neitzke, Peter Nordgren, and Chris Schotz. We especially appreciate the efforts of Bill Menke and Gaylord Yost in reviewing all of the material on the North Country Trail and of Andrew Hanson in similarly reviewing all of the accounts on the Ice Age Trail. In fact, we relied on Gaylord and Drew to answer many questions as they arose and to provide advice on handling certain issues.

We are especially grateful to the many people at the University of Wisconsin Press who went the "extra mile" to get this volume on a fast production track. We were delighted to have been able to begin the book under the editorship of Elizabeth (Betty) Steinberg—one of the last projects in which she had a hand before retiring from a long and distinguished career at the Press. Finally, we were truly fortunate to have Louise Robbins copy edit the manuscript; she went far beyond the usual tasks of improving the grammar and intelligibility of the text, and readers will never know how much they are in her debt.

BACKPACKING WISCONSIN

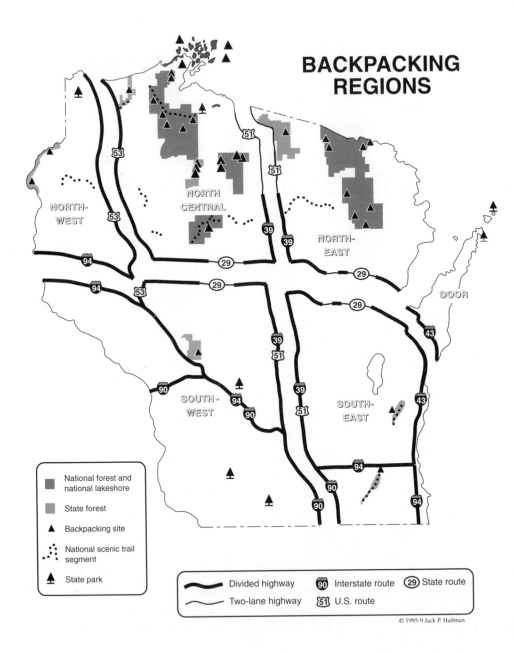

BACKPACKING REGIONS

NORTH-WEST

NORTH CENTRAL

NORTH-EAST

DOOR

SOUTH-WEST

SOUTH-EAST

Legend:

■ National forest and national lakeshore

■ State forest

▲ Backpacking site

⋰ National scenic trail segment

♠ State park

~~~ Divided highway

— Two-lane highway

🅐 Interstate route

🅑 U.S. route

Ⓐ State route

© 1995-9 Jack P. Hailman

WISCONSIN COUNTIES

	Divided highway	🛡90 Interstate route	⑳ State route
	Two-lane highway	🛡51 U.S. route	

© 1995-9 Jack P. Hailman

3

Introduction

Wisconsin is a truly wonderful backpacking state, even though it does not have the lofty grandeur of the Colorado Rockies, the teeming wildlife of Wyoming's Yellowstone, or the awesome wilderness of Alaska. What Wisconsin does offer is a plethora of backpacking opportunities in the north woods, on the shores of two Great Lakes, along scenic rivers, and in many other environs. Wisconsin sports two national scenic trails and contains extensive wild areas within a large national forest. The many trails cut for cross-country skiing lie almost unused when the snow is gone, beckoning the hiker to walk into solitude. If there exists in the eastern two-thirds of the nation a manifestly better state for weekend backpacking trips, it has escaped our attention.

WHAT IS BACKPACKING?

Backpacking combines two of the oldest and most popular forms of outdoor recreation: hiking and camping. The backpacker carries all of life's essentials in a large "pack," which among enthusiasts preempts the name "backpack." Day hikers may also carry packs on their backs, but these are called "day packs" in the lingo. Backpacking is more than the sum of its hiking and camping parts: it can be an experience of wilderness, solitude, and self-reliance.

Backpacking is recreation for almost all ages. Children can begin when very young, if their parents will carry some added weight, and seniors in good health and physical shape can often continue shouldering their backpacks into their seventies. As campgrounds are becoming more crowded and noisy, many former car campers are taking to the trails for their camping experiences.

What backpackers seek

In order to document some of the diverse reasons that people go backpacking, we devised a straightforward questionnaire and asked people to fill it out, anonymously if they wished. We put a notice on the web site of the North Country Trail Association, and anyone who wanted to respond requested an e-mail questionnaire to fill out. We also sent forms to leaders of the North Country Trail Association and the Ice Age Park and Trail Foundation and requested that they make them available to backpackers in their membership. Finally, we took questionnaires to several free backpacking clinics at REI in Madison and invited people to fill them out after the presentations. We received 45 responses, a sample that, although not scientifically stratified, did include a good mix of both sexes, various ages, and different levels of backpacking experience. We asked people to rate whether various factors were very important (two points), important (one point), or unimportant (zero) to their backpacking enjoyment. Here are the summarized results ordered by the mean score over the entire sample:

1.8 Scenery: experiencing scenic beauty (waterfalls, autumn colors, etc.)

1.7 Escape: getting away from everyday hassle (from phone, job stress, whatever)

1.7 Quiet: quiet camping (no radios, no traffic noise, etc.)

1.5 Comradeship: being with special people

1.4 Solitude: encountering few other people

1.3 Exercise: walking long distances

1.2 Nature: studying natural history (wildflowers, birdwatching, etc.)

0.9 History: seeing sites of local/regional history (logging, settlements, lighthouses, etc.)

0.8 Circuit: hiking a circuit route, no retracing of steps

0.8 Cost: low cost (entrance and camping fees, etc.)

0.4 Nearness: proximity of trail or area to hometown

Averages disguise the fact that every item was rated as "very important" by at least one respondent. Backpackers are a diverse lot, and different people value a slightly different mix of factors.

Backpackers have spoken and we have listened. We have tried to include in each trail account the kind of information that backpackers need in order to plan trips that will maximize factors important to them. We have also devised a rating system (more about this later) to reflect the potential quality of a trail from the viewpoint of an average backpacker.

BACKPACKING IN WISCONSIN

Wisconsin is mainly, albeit not exclusively, a place for backpacking trips of one to three nights. Opportunities for longer trips are fewer, but you can easily spend a week on the North Country National Scenic Trail, for example. To aid your planning of Wisconsin backpacking trips, we discuss here seasons; types of trails; locations; types of camping; permits, fees, and reservations; and our rating system.

Three-season backpacking

Our focus is spring-to-fall backpacking. Winter hiking and camping in Wisconsin require special skills and equipment beyond the scope of this book. Many people enjoy winter backpacking, but we find that the cold and darkness dim our spirits, and fewer facilities are available in the winter. Public water supplies may be shut down even before the cold sets in, and once snow is falling, many of the trails in this book will be devoted to skiing. Hardy three-season backpackers may venture out as early as March in a warm year, but we usually await full snowmelt and the warmer weather that comes in the latter part of April or later in most years. Backpacking is generally good through October, but once the nights get shorter and colder in November, some measure of fun slips from the experience.

Backpacking on trails

In Wisconsin, it is best to backpack on marked trails. In the western United States, cross-country trekking is feasible in many places because sparse vegetation allows for easy walking and unimpeded vision. By contrast in most of the eastern United States, including Wisconsin, the forests are remarkably dense. Lost hikers have died of exposure in eastern mountains just a few yards from the Appalachian Trail, which they could not find. This guide is restricted to marked trails, with one situation that nearly qualifies as an exception: designated wilderness areas in the national forest lack the usual reassurance markers along the trails and have only cedar posts at trail junctions.

We recommend that you stay on established trails when backpacking in Wisconsin unless you are very experienced in using a map and compass and in practicing wilderness survival skills. Much of Wisconsin is glaciated terrain, especially in the north, so the surface contains enormous numbers of spruce bogs and other wetlands that no person on foot can cross except when the water is frozen. Stay safe—stay on marked trails.

Types of trails

There are, by and large, three kinds of trails suited to backpacking in Wisconsin: sections of national scenic trails on public lands, hiking trails maintained within parks and forests, and public cross-country ski trails. All three kinds are represented in this book.

Wisconsin has two national scenic trails: the North Country Trail, which originated in Wisconsin and now stretches from North Dakota to New York, and the Ice Age Trail, wholly confined to our state. Both trails are only partially completed, and both run over land owned by various public and private parties, some of which prohibit camping. The second type, traditional hiking trails, exist in virtually all public recreation lands, but not all are well marked or well maintained. The third kind of trail, the cross-country ski trail, is a sort of mixed blessing. Good foot trails are laid out like railroad beds—with gentle grades. The specifications for the North Country Trail, for example, restrict climbing of hills to 10 percent, which means the trail can gain no more than a foot of altitude for every 10 feet walked forward. On a topographic map, well laid out foot trails cross contour lines obliquely with maximum spacing between crossings. Ski trails, by contrast, purposely cross at right angles to dense contour lines, often following the steepest route possible. So hiking ski trails can require physical exertion out of proportion for the terrain. Still, the popularity of cross-country skiing in Wisconsin has opened untold miles of trails that often form excellent backpacking areas when the snow is gone. Thank you, skiers.

Types of jurisdictions

Two types of jurisdictions affect trails: who owns the land they cross and who is responsible for maintaining them. Public landholders with backpacking trails on their properties include the National Park Service of the Department of the Interior (Apostle Islands National Lakeshore), the U.S. Forest Service of the Department of Agriculture (Chequamegon-Nicolet National Forest, formerly two separate national forests), the Wisconsin Department of Natural Resources (state parks, state forests, and some other kinds of lands), and county forestry departments. All these agencies maintain trails that are in this book, and, in addition, national scenic trails are made and maintained by volunteers from trail organizations. In some cases, trails in this book have been created and maintained by local organizations, especially for cross-country skiing. The rules of different landowners differ, and the quality and type of trail marking and maintenance varies among responsible organizations. Expect diversity; it is part of Wisconsin's backpacking charm.

Types of campsites

Different trails offer different kinds of camping places, which we divide into designated (or mandatory) campsites, established (or optional) campsites, wilderness campsites, traditional camping places, and trail shelters. In general, the jurisdiction of the trail determines the type(s) of camping allowed; as a rough generalization, designated campsites characterize parks, and other types characterize national, state, or county forests.

Designated campsites are required camping places. You cannot camp anywhere else on the trail and must have a permit for a specific campsite for each night. These permits are, regrettably, overpriced in Wisconsin. Apostle Islands National Lakeshore instituted a whopping fee in the mid 1990s, making it by far the most expensive place to backpack in the state, and the state parks charge the same fee for designated campsites as they do for campgrounds with all the conveniences. The national lakeshore campsites usually provide nothing but a picnic table (which may be missing); the state park campsites usually have an outhouse nearby in addition to a table.

What we call established campsites are generally found only in the national forest. They are optional, not required, camping places. Use of these campsites is free, and you do not require a site-specific permit; they are occu-

7

pied on a first-come, first-served basis. An established campsite may offer no more than a place to pitch your little tent and an open throne toilet off in the nearby woods; some also have tables.

Wilderness camping is the term we use for making camp other than at a designated or established campsite. This type of camping is most common in national, state, and county forests. State forests require you to obtain a free backpacking permit, which usually must specify the general area in which you will set up your wilderness camp. Rules on placement of wilderness camps are based on common sense: you must place your tent well off trails and well away from water features such as lakes, rivers, and creeks. (The minimum distances vary among jurisdictions.) A subtype of wilderness camping is what we call use of traditional camping places. Along the North Country Trail, and in a few other locales we know of in the national forest, a particular spot has been used by generations of campers. These traditional camping places usually overlook lakes or other scenic features.

Trail shelters resemble designated campsites in some cases and established campsites in others. Most trail shelters are of the so-called Adirondack type, which is open on one side. (A few we have encountered are completely enclosed.) Some were built along national scenic trails for "through hikers," and others were erected mainly to serve skiers in winter. Sometimes these shelters have a picnic table, and sometimes not; sometimes there is an outhouse nearby, and sometimes not; sometimes they have built-in benches on which one could sleep, and sometimes not. In Kettle Moraine State Forest (both North and South Units) backpacking is allowed only at the trail shelters, and campground fees are charged, so the shelters are in effect designated campsites. Nearly everywhere else trail shelters are for optional, free use, and hence are the equivalent of established campsites. In some state parks, however, trail shelters are for skiers only and no camping at them is allowed.

We need to add a few words about camping at shelters. A trail shelter is a great place to cook a meal in driving rain. As a sleeping place, though, it is a mixed blessing. In the cool of autumn you will stay warmer in your tent, and in summer you will appreciate your tent's built-in mosquito netting. Above all, what trail shelters mean to us is summed up by one of those nasty four-letter words: mice. Even if your food is strung high in trees outside the shelter, the little rodents may scamper across you all night long in search of something to snitch.

Finally, the term "walk-in" campsite is used variously by different jurisdictions. The state uses it mainly to designate campsites within campgrounds—sites where you must park your vehicle by the road and walk a short distance to the table and clearing. Use of the term by the U.S. Forest Service is similar, but the so-called campground is composed wholly of the walk-in sites, and the walking distance is on a vastly different scale—measured in tenths of a mile rather than feet. We use "walk-in" to refer to any campsite within 100 feet of a parking place, regardless of whether or not it is within a campground.

Criteria for inclusion and the geography of trails

We define a backpacking area as a site that has at least 5 miles of foot trails with trail-accessible camping in one or more places where vehicles cannot be parked within 100 feet. Furthermore, the trail must offer reasonable natural surroundings; for example, city walking tours would not qualify even if they somehow met the other criteria. The only exceptions we have tolerated are a few state parks that the Wisconsin Department of Natural Resources advertises as offering backpacking but which fail to meet one or more of the criteria. (Mainly, these exceptions either have campsites not accessible from the trails, or walk-in rather than true back-country campsites.)

We have let major, divided-lane highways conveniently divide the state into six geographic regions (see the map near the front of this book). A glance at the map reveals that the epicenter of Wisconsin backpacking lies in the North Central region, which is dominated by the Chequamegon side of the Chequamegon-Nicolet National Forest. The organization of the book reflects that predominance: we have devoted one chapter to the Northwest region, two to the North Central region (one just for Chequamegon), one to the Northeast region, and one to the Door, Southwest, and Southeast regions. In each account a backpacking trail is geographically specified in three ways: by the region in which it lies, by the county or counties in which it lies (see map near the front of the book), and by the coordinates on the official state highway map, which is available free to residents and out-of-state tourists alike.

There are places in Wisconsin that do not meet our criteria for inclusion as backpacking sites, but at which you could have a minimal backpacking experience. The sacrifice here is that you must camp in a campground. We use the term "quasi-backpacking places" for linear trails of at least 10 miles with campgrounds on or near them and for parks with a campground and a trail system that totals at least 10 miles. We do not give them separate accounts but do list them in Appendix A, which specifies their location by region and by county and indicates how to contact the jurisdiction for more information.

For backpacking and quasi-backpacking trails alike we have used further criteria for inclusion based on type of multiple use. In no case have we knowingly included a trail that is open to horses or to motorized use when not snow covered. (Snowmobiles are allowed on some of the quasi-backpacking trails, but the trails included in the main body of the book do not allow motorized vehicles at any time.) We have hiked trails open to equestrian use and found that besides having to watch where you step, the flies along the trail drive you batty—even if you never actually see a horse. We have, however, included trails shared with bicycles. Some hikers and backpackers object to mountain bikes for several reasons, principally because bicycle traffic erodes trails. Cyclists also decrease the wilderness experience in that they often shout to be heard by others within their group, so the hiker may hear cyclists coming long before seeing them. Nevertheless, the distinctions among trails that encourage, allow, and prohibit mountain bikes are blurred, and many trails have no stated policy with respect to bicycles. If we know that you are likely to encounter bicycle traffic on a given trail, we have tried to say so explicitly in the accounts.

Permits, fees, and reservations

Fees for backpacking range from free to outlandish. Curiously, it seems that the lower the cost of a trip, the higher the quality of the experience (at least in terms of solitude). In some cases the backpacker has to pay both entrance and camping fees; some explanation may help the reader through the maze of charges and permits.

Backpacking is usually free in all county forests. The trails we have included are sections of the Ice Age and the North Country National Scenic Trails and certain ski trails on county forest lands. These trails are usually completely deserted, unless near a county park or providing access to a fishing spot, so they provide maximum solitude at absolutely no cost.

Backpacking in the national forest is almost free, but during the 1990s a moderate vehicle sticker fee was instituted for use of certain parking lots and other forest facilities. Senior discounts apply for holders of the federal Golden Age Passports (obtainable at age 62). In lieu of the annual vehicle sticker, you can purchase daily passes, mainly something only cross-country skiers or snowmobilers do for one weekend trip in the winter. Although purchasing daily passes may be cheaper for a short trip, it can be inconvenient because they must be obtained during weekday working hours. Use of trails and campsites is free; only the campgrounds have camping fees.

Permits and fees for most state forests are similar to but not identical with those for the national forest. You need an annual vehicle sticker (or daily pass) to use parking lots or any other state forest facility. These state stickers are also valid for state parks. Seniors get a discount, but the minimum age (65) is higher than for federal stickers. Backpacking in state forests requires a permit, which is free in the forests offering wilderness camping (all except Kettle Moraine). This policy is under review and might change.

All state parks plus Kettle Moraine State Forest require the state annual sticker (or daily pass), and all restrict camping to designated campsites. In the North and South Units (but not the Lapham Peak Unit) of Kettle Moraine, the designated campsites are trail shelters. Permits for designated campsites cost the same, inappropriately we think, as those for family campgrounds. Designated campsites can be reserved in advance, but the cost is horrendous because, beginning in 1999, the state subcontracted the procedure to a commercial reservation service. State legislators are currently probing the situation, so perhaps changes in cost or procedure are on the horizon.

The Apostle Islands National Lakeshore instituted in the late 1990s a camping fee that is unfair in at least three ways. First, there is no entrance fee or any other charge for anything else in the national lakeshore, so the park is being run off the backs of campers. Second, the permit required for camping is good for two weeks, making it a reasonable cost for a fortnight's vacation but unconscionably high for the one- or two-night weekend backpacker. Last, camping fees in units of the National Park Service are supposed to be discounted by half for holders of the Golden Eagle and Golden Age Passports. The national lakeshore changed its terminology in 1998 and began calling its camping permits "special use permits." This trick of terminology enabled it to take advantage of a loophole exempting special use permits from the discounts. It is clearly a violation of the spirit of the law, and possibly the letter as well, but likely to stay in place unless someone bothers to drag the national lakeshore into court.

Fees change, and we all know the inevitability of the direction. Therefore, rather than citing specific figures in the accounts, we state only the types of permits and fees required. In Appendix B, we give the 1999 fees. As fees rise in coming years, the reader can pencil in the new values.

Quality ratings of trails

Each trail is rated by criteria that indicate the potential quality of a backpacking experience on it. You might wonder why we do not also rate the difficulty of trails, as is commonly done in hiking guides. The reason is simple. Because hiking guides are used by a much wider variety of people than are backpacking guides, it is appropriate to rate hiking trails so that people who are aged, overweight, or disabled can decide whether or not to attempt a given walk. You certainly do not have to be an Arnold Schwarzenegger to go backpacking, but in all frankness the trails in Wisconsin would all be rated as easy by any experienced backpacker. If you backpack on the Appalachian Trail, you will certainly find difficult sections. In Wisconsin, however, hills are sufficiently small that even if the trail is steep, the climb is short. The difficulty of a backpacking trip here is mainly a function of how much weight you carry, how far you go, and what kind of shape you are in; the relative ruggedness of the trail is too minor a factor to be noticeable.

Our quality scale is represented by conifer symbols, much as restaurants are sometimes rated by stars. A trail can earn a tree (or half tree) in five categories that were devised to reflect the factors considered important in a backpacking experience by the respondents of our survey. These are the categories:

🌲 Scenery: special scene (e.g., waterfall) or trail itself is scenic (e.g., along coastline)

🌲 Quiet: camping possible at least 1 mile from the nearest paved road and from water courses with powerboats, and no industrial noise (as from railroad switching yards)

🌲 Trails: a combination of factors reflecting potential exercise and varied trip experience; at least 10 miles of trail accessible from

11

the camping place, or can camp on a circuit route of at least 5 miles

🌲 Solitude: unlikely to encounter more than 2 other parties per day on the trail itself (not counting fishing lakes or other places passed by the trail)

🌲 Interest (nature or history): special birds, wildflowers, geology, or other natural history or sites of local/regional history (past logging, old homesteads, lighthouses, etc.)

Half credit (represented by 🌲) is awarded for approaching a criterion. For example, solitude is rated one-half if you are likely to encounter more than two but no more than six other parties in a day on the trail.

Furthermore, keep in mind that the quality ratings are for trails that already meet basic standards for inclusion. These standards include at least 5 miles of trail, trail-accessible camping places away from roads, natural surroundings, and exclusion of horses and motorized equipment. A trail could score zero in the rating system and still offer a minimal backpacking experience.

We realize that the rating system—based as it is on the wants of a mythical average backpacker—might not be right for you. Our survey documented a variety among people as to what they value in a backpacking experience, so feel free to disagree with our quality assessments. The rating system may be a crooked wheel, but if it's the only wheel in town, it may be of at least some use.

EQUIPMENT

To help demystify backpacking for the beginner, we offer here brief comments on the most important types of equipment and how to use them. Remember: any suggestion we make is just one opinion, which may differ from that of other equally experienced backpackers. (See Appendix C for a checklist of items to take on your trip.)

Try before you buy

Backpacking equipment is generally not cheap, but the cost is mainly the initial investment, and good products will last for decades. Therefore, do not make purchases in a hurry unless you have excess disposable income. Visit stores specializing in outdoor equipment, peruse catalogs, and talk with other backpackers to get a sense of what factors are important in choosing various items—and if at all possible, try equipment before you buy it.

There are at least three ways to try out equipment. Sometimes local outing clubs lend out gear such as packs and tents to members on a short-term basis. Student outing clubs are common at colleges, but finding other local clubs may require some detective work. A second possibility is to borrow from friends, neighbors, and relatives, who are usually delighted to have *somebody* use their equipment, helping to justify their investment. Finally, it is possible to rent equipment from outdoor stores like REI (Recreational Equipment Incorporated).

Boots and socks

There was a famous "little old lady" who walked the Appalachian Trail in tennis shoes, but most backpackers prefer sturdy boots. You probably cannot borrow or rent boots to try out, so you should research your purchase thoroughly in advance. We are not keen on buying shoes of any kind from mail-order catalogs, but must admit that the one experience of acquiring boots sight unseen was a completely satisfactory one. Still, it is probably best to go to stores and try on several brands and styles of boots before plunking down your hard-earned cash. Then walk around the house in them to be sure they fit; stores usually will not accept return or exchange of shoes worn in the out-of-doors.

There are only a couple of substantive differences among boots, apart from trivia such as style and color. One difference is in height. Nearly everyone agrees that hiking boots need to be only high enough to support the ankles; taller boots are more a hindrance than a help. The other main difference is in materials. Leather was the mainstay of hikers until the invention of boots made partly of breathable, waterproof fabric such as Gortex. The latter now dominate the market and can be cooler than all-leather boots, but they probably will not last as long. We have both used both kinds and have developed no preferences.

We recommend wearing two pairs of socks with boots: a heavy, thick outer sock that cushions your foot, and a thin inner sock. The two-sock technique focuses the main slippage of the foot relative to the boot between the socks, thus helping to stave off blisters. We confirmed this the hard way. A young, supposedly experienced clerk in an outdoor store in Montana swore that a new type of sock was sufficient by itself. Jack bought a pair but continued to wear thin socks beneath, until a year later back in Wisconsin when he decided to do the critical experiment—and blistered up in less than a mile (carrying only a small day pack). The heavy, outer socks can be of wool or synthetic material (we prefer wool), and the thin, inner sock can be of cotton or synthetics. There are newer, thin socks of polypropylene, which wicks moisture away from your foot. Jack loves these socks and Liz detests them because they melt in the dryer—try to remember to line dry them.

Finally, break in your new boots. Modern leather-and-fabric boots require less breaking in than do all-leather boots, but setting off on a trip with untried boots is to invite disaster. Jack spent two years breaking in his beloved, all-leather Vasque boots by frequently walking 2 miles to work carrying a day pack. Even so, on the first backpacking trip with these boots, Jack's feet blistered up within an hour. The only alternative footwear he had was leather moccasins with no insole, which proved that you really do not absolutely require boots for backpacking. Still, your feet hurt a lot less if you wear properly broken-in boots. If stiff boots stubbornly resist breaking in, wear them around the house with soaking wet socks to hasten the process.

Backpacks

In his hilarious book *A Walk in the Woods*, Bill Bryson reported that when someone asked him why he had bought such-and-such a brand of backpack, he wearily replied that it seemed preferable to carrying everything in his arms. You can go backpacking in tennis shoes or moccasins instead of boots, sleep in the wild without tent or sleeping bag, build a fire instead of taking a stove, and get wet and cold without proper clothing—but it's hard to imagine backpacking without a backpack. There are two principal issues to consider when choosing this essential piece of gear: internal versus external frame, and the arrangement of compartments.

We attended, within months of one another, two free clinics at REI given by their young, enthusiastic sales personnel. One chap advised against even considering an external-frame pack; they were old fashioned, he asserted. His colleague giving the other clinic, when asked his choice (by Jack), said he owned one external-frame and three internal-frame packs and used the former far more than the other three combined. On this much Liz and Jack agree: internal-frame packs may be great for cross-country trekking in the cool, dry western mountains, but they are hot as hell to wear on humid eastern trails. We will stick to external-frame packs that allow air to circulate on our sweaty backs, thank you.

We disagree violently on the geometry of packs, however. Jack loves packs bristling with little pockets, compartments, and attaching straps. He claims without a shred of proof that he can go directly to anything in pitch darkness. Liz prefers the flexibility of a few large compartments, which can easily be packed differently for different kinds of trips, and where fitting everything in is not a major undertaking in three-dimensional geometry.

Backpacks cannot be made waterproof: they have too many flaps, zippers, and seams. Therefore, consider buying or making a pack cover. We bought covers, and Liz enlarged them and tailored them using extra cloth ordered from the retailer's supplier. It was a lot of trouble, but our packs stay bone dry in the worst of storms.

Tents

Backpacking tents need to be lightweight, which means they are cozy in size. That turns out to be an advantage, though, because a small tent keeps you warmer in cold weather. Furthermore, it is easier to situate because it requires only a small patch of flat ground. Virtually all backpacking tents are built on the same general principle of having a tent supported by a frame external to it and a rain fly over the frame. For Wisconsin trips, we think a backpacking tent needs to be self-standing, absolutely bug-proof, and absolutely rainproof. Beyond those characteristics everything else about a tent is pretty much a matter of personal preference.

Here is how we picked out the tent we are now using. We were weary of threading poles into sleeves on the tent's exterior, as required by our previous tent, so we restricted searching to models that were held on the pole framework by external clips. We also wanted some kind of a vestibule where we could set our boots out of nocturnal rains, a feature lacking in our previous tent, which required us to drag the often muddy boots inside with us. Finally, Jack's troublesome back makes it hard for him to dress in a supine position, so we measured his height while kneeling and sought a tent that high on the inside at its tallest point. Then we looked at specifications in every catalog we could find and discovered that (at that time) there was exactly one make and model of tent that met our needs—so that is what we bought, and we have been pleased as punch with it.

Now, about floors. Floors wear out because they move over the ground when people inside the tent scrunch around. Therefore, to extend the life of the floor, you can put a plastic sheet either on top of it within the tent or below it under the tent. That sheet focuses the main slippage between the floor and the sheet instead of the floor and the ground. You might think that the outside, ground-cloth type of sheet would be superior, and maybe it is under some conditions. We use the inside sheet, though, because a ground cloth under a tent must be smaller than the tent floor and so does not seem to do quite as good a job of protecting the floor from abrasion (especially near the door). If a ground cloth sticks out beyond the edge of the tent fly, it collects the water running off the fly and channels it directly below the tent.

Finally, tent pegs. Some tents come with those yellow, plastic pegs that you see fragments of littering campgrounds. That kind of peg is just what you need for beach camping in loose sand, but it's nearly worthless everywhere else. Backpacking tents should come with simple wire pegs that will slip between rocks in our glacially bulldozed Wisconsin soils. If your tent does not come with such metal pegs, buy them and throw away the useless plastic pegs (or save them for your next beach camping trip). In fact, buy a few extras anyway because tent pegs are the item most frequently lost by backpackers.

Sleeping bags

Sleeping bags differ in size, cut, and fill. To keep down the weight and minimize the air space that your body must heat, you want a bag that is no larger than it needs to be for you. Types of cut vary from inefficient rectangular bags, rarely carried by backpackers, to body-hugging mummy bags, the traditional choice. Today, bags of intermediate cut ("semi-rectangular") are being marketed, and there are even mummy bags that are cut differently for women and men. We actually have two sets of backpacking sleeping bags: lightweight, rectangular bags for summer and mummy bags for colder times; our rectangular bags zip together.

It is the insulating fill of sleeping bags that has changed most over the years. Traditionally, the fill of choice was goose down. When synthetic fiberfills were first developed, they were poor insulators for their weight and bulk. That situation has changed in recent years as improvements in polyester technology have produced lighter, more insulating fibers for bags rated as low as −20°F. (If you are a winter camper in Wisconsin, even that is not enough; you had better buy a down bag.) The main concern about fiberfill now is compressibility, for even though the polyester-filled bags are sufficiently warm and lightweight, they remain bulky. So why even consider an alternative to goose down? Two reasons: down is more expensive, and it loses its insulating ability if it gets wet. We use only down bags, but we are paranoid about keeping them dry.

Stoves

Jack had always been confident of his ability to build a fire using no more than two matches. Then one autumn alone on the Appalachian Trail in rain that later turned to snow, he worked for a very long time before getting his dinner fire going—and even failed to locate his fire ring beneath the snow the next morning. That is when he decided to buy a backpacking stove. Years and stoves later, we always carry one because many jurisdictions now prohibit campfires, either permanently or temporarily when the forest is very dry. And let's face it, lighting a stove is always quicker and easier than building a fire.

Stoves, like other outdoor gear, have improved markedly over the years. One aspect of stoves that books never seem to mention is the noise they make. Our old Swedish stove hissed like a 19th-century steam locomotive, and we had to shout at each other while cooking dinner. Although all modern stoves are quieter now, those using canned butane or propane are usually completely silent.

Mention of fuel raises a major consideration in choosing a stove: does it burn white gas, kerosene, butane, propane, unleaded auto fuel, or vodka? Well, actually, we have never seen a stove claiming the last, but all the other fuels are in common use, along with isobutane, diesel fuel, aviation gas, naphtha, and even something called Stoddard Solvent. We use white-gas stoves, and they are the only kind we have ever used. Most backpacking stoves on the market will burn white gas, even if they also accept various other fuels. Coleman fuel is white gas, and cans of it can be found in all kinds of general, hardware, outdoor, and even grocery stores everywhere in the United States. Unleaded auto fuel is similar, but some kinds have additives that might clog your stove or promote corrosion of some parts. (If you want to go backpacking in Europe or elsewhere, better look into stoves that burn bottled butane or similar fuels, because white gas is rare outside of the United States.)

Even if you know what kind of fuel you want your stove to burn, all kinds of other considerations may influence your choice of models: weight (usually the backpacker's first concern about equipment), size and shape, cost, fuel capacity, how long it burns without refueling, how long it takes to boil water, how stable it is, and how easy it is to use. In all honesty, the backpacking stoves on today's market are actually pretty similar to one another in all those aspects. There is one feature, though, that we think important and that does vary notice-ably among models of stoves: the adjustability of the flame. If you just want to boil water for a freeze-dried dinner, any stove will do; but if you want to simmer a concoction on low heat, make sure the stove you buy is up to the task (check the product manual for this information).

Pots and pans

So what is there to say about pots and pans? A pot by any other name looks just as black, right? Actually, there *is* a little to say about backpacking cook kits of nesting pots and pans, mainly about the metal of which they are made. Steel is generally the cheapest but heaviest, and its properties most resemble what you are used to cooking with at home. Aluminum is lighter, tends to cost a little more (although sometimes less), but is not an ideal metal for pots because it does not conduct and hold heat readily. Also, aluminum dents fairly easily. And then there is the super metal, titanium—lighter than aluminum, more durable than steel, and able to leap tall buildings in a single bound. We found that tita-nium conducts heat even faster than steel and retains it to keep our food warm. Jack had coveted titanium cook kits for so long that when they went on sale, he was in the store in a flash. Be warned, though, that, even on sale, titanium is very expensive compared with steel and aluminum.

If you want to try baking, you can use an Outback Oven. It works on a backpacking stove and consists of two pans that fit together plus some reflec-tive material to surround them. It is crazy to carry that much extra weight backpacking, but we sometimes do it because you can make a pizza with it, and Jack can be bribed to do almost anything for pizza.

Clothing

We don't want to get bogged down in the morass of outdoor clothing, but four topics seem worth mentioning. First, cotton is nice, but when it gets wet it seems never to dry out again. Instead you can wear synthetic shirts and pants, and even underwear. Synthetics are hot, so specialized outdoor clothing has wick-away properties, vents where you might not expect them, and other tricks to make them tolerable. Still, we admit to wearing a lot of cotton.

Second, we have found convenient those special pants with zip-off legs that allow you either to cover up to keep off the bugs or to hike in shorts. Liz's pants, bought years before Jack finally saw the light and bought a pair, had removable legs that would not fit over her boots, so she copied Jack's pant legs by sewing zippers in hers.

The decision to make about rain gear is basically whether to use a poncho or a raincoat. A poncho fits over your backpack (one too small to do that would be useless) and so obviates the need for a pack cover. At night, use it to cover your pack. We prefer raincoats; we don't know why, but we do. A longer raincoat is better than a waist-length one for backpacking and hiking because if you are wearing shorts the raincoat will cover them. Nowadays, the only raincoats seriously considered by backpackers are made from breathable synthetics like Gortex. Rubberized coats are too heavy, and treated nylon wears out fairly quickly.

Finally, how about coats for warmth? For years, we have carried our nicely compressible down jackets in our backpacks wherever we go in every season. The young whippersnappers warn that down loses its insulation when wet, a problem we solve by donning raincoats over our down jackets when it rains or snows. Still, we admit to each having purchased both a fleece jacket and vest in recent years. The fleece garments are lightweight, more insulating than we expected, and of course they keep their insulating qualities when they get wet. The original synthetic fleece was like a sieve when the breeze stirred, so you had to wear a windbreaker over it, but now some fleeces incorporate a wind-blocking layer. Liz's fleece jacket is of the former type, Jack's of the latter. The advantage of her material is that you get more insulating value for the weight (not counting the windbreaker you have to wear over it).

DANGERS

Continuing our quest to demystify backpacking for the uninitiate, we discuss here how to deal with real dangers and distinguish them from the imagined ones. Beginners may fear the unfamiliar, but actually backpacking is a very safe form of outdoor recreation—especially in Wisconsin, where there are no mountains to fall off and no mountain lions to pounce on you. Indeed, you are in far greater danger when driving to and from the backpacking site than you are when actually on the trail. So here are some comments about such things as bears, poison ivy, injuries, sunstroke, *Giardia,* and getting lost in the woods. The same caveat applies here as elsewhere: our word is not gospel, but merely one of many possible opinions.

Bears

Apparently, a great fear of many beginners is that they will be attacked by a bear. Let's start by dispelling that myth. Grizzly Bears are unquestionably dangerous, but they do not occur east of the Rocky Mountains, so forget about them in Wisconsin. Black Bears are all over northern Wisconsin, and you can consider yourself fortunate if you ever catch a glimpse of one while you are backpacking; we never have. The only time either of us has ever met a bear on a trail was when Jack was hiking alone in Florida and in rounding a bend came suddenly upon a Black Bear foraging. The bear bolted away and disappeared into the woods in a wink.

Except in state parks where hunting is prohibited, Black Bears are hunted throughout northern Wisconsin. That fact exacerbates their natural fear of humans. They usually hear or smell you coming and go the other way long before you have any chance of catching sight of them. You are far more likely to see a bear rummaging in a roadside Dumpster than to see one in the wilderness.

If you do encounter a bear on the trail, back off until you can just see the animal, then hope that it ambles off in a reasonable time. Or, terrain permitting, you can make a large semicircle around the bear. Hikers should keep together to present a large image; that alone will inhibit Black Bears (but not Grizzlies) from attacking. Black Bears seem not as deterred by noise as many books say. We've banged pots until blue in the face when encountering bears in a campground, and the noise has seemed to have little effect.

If you are really intent upon precipitating a bear encounter, take a dog on the trail with you. Black Bears consider dogs to be prey. Two bear-human encounters took place in Wisconsin in the spring of 1999. Both were near areas where bears may have been attracted to garbage and become habituated to people. In both cases, a man was with a dog that ran ahead of him. A bear gave chase, the dog turned and ran, passing by its master, and the pursuing bear collided with the person.

You don't want to invite bears into your camp at night, though, so string up your food. That means every scrap of food including the candy bar you absentmindedly stuck in your shirt pocket, as well as anything else (food or not) that might have an odor detectable by sharp-nosed mammals. Raccoons and Porcupines are far more likely to amble by than is a bear, and you deter them as well when you string food out of reach of bears. We put the food in a stuff sack dedicated to food, augmenting that with a plastic garbage bag when needed, and tie two long pieces of nylon line to the bag(s). Jack ties the other end of one line to the ring on his Swiss Army knife and heaves it over as high a branch as possible, and then does the same with the other line on a tree 20 feet or more away from the first one. We pull on the lines and tie them off, and voilá—food levitating a dozen or more feet off the ground between two trees, well out of reach even of a bear standing on its tiptoes.

Other critters

And then there are poisonous snakes: forget them. There are no species of venomous snakes in northern Wisconsin where most of the backpacking occurs: not cottonmouths, coral snakes, copperheads, or any sort of rattlesnake. There is probably no other state that is as free of poisonous snakes as Wisconsin. Even Hawaii has highly venomous sea snakes. The range of a very small rattlesnake called the Massasauga extends into the southern part of Wisconsin, but this retiring, unaggressive reptile is never seen except by herpetologists searching for it in its special habitat. In the Mississippi River bottoms, and similar habitat along the lower part of the Wisconsin River, Timber Rattlesnakes have been reported occasionally. They don't live where any backpacking trails go, though. A herpetologist told Jack many years ago that there was no authenticated case of a rattlesnake biting a person in Wisconsin, and likely that remains true today.

With few bears and no venomous snakes to worry about, Wisconsin is a backpacker's paradise, but there are leeches, black flies, mosquitoes, and ticks. Leeches are in the northern lakes and sufficiently repulsive to us that we rarely swim on a backpacking trip. But if you do, pull off the leeches when you get out of the water and expect to see a little blood run. They come off more easily if you hold a flame from a match or lighter to them first. Deter mosquitoes (and black flies in their short season in early summer) with a repellent containing 20% DEET. A higher concentration of DEET is unnecessary, and indeed undesirable, as studies have demonstrated that at higher concentrations so much is absorbed through your skin that it begins showing up in your blood.

Ticks are probably the animals that pose the greatest potential threat to Wisconsin backpackers, because they are common in some places and they can carry serious diseases. Ticks are commonest in the northwestern part of the state, especially in the St. Croix River valley. It is the larger Wood Ticks that you notice, but they can generally be picked off with your fingers, and the diseases they can carry appear to be rare or completely absent in Wisconsin. The tiny Deer Tick, however, is hard to see and can carry Lyme disease, a serious bacterial infection named for Lyme, Connecticut, where it was discovered. The tick is no larger than a pinhead and therefore hard to find on your skin and hard to remove. Signs of Lyme disease are many, the most reliable one being an irregular reddish spot with a whitish center on the skin. If you have been hiking in northwestern Wisconsin during the height of the tick season (spring and early summer) and subsequently suspect you have a health problem, see a doctor immediately. If treated early, Lyme disease is not dangerous, but if let go it can cause severe health problems and even death.

Enemy #1

The living thing most likely to give the Wisconsin backpacker grief is not an animal but a plant. "Leaves of three, let it be" will cause you to avoid a host of harmless plants besides Poison Ivy, but in this case it is definitely better to be safe than sorry. Poison Ivy is highly variable in form, but once you get the hang of it, it is fairly easy to spot. The often shiny (but sometimes dull) leaflets often have smooth margins but may have sparse, irregular teeth (or notches). The center leaflet is often vaguely bilaterally symmetric in the sense that if the left margin is toothed, the right one usually is as well. The lateral leaflets are asymmetric, usually being untoothed on the side of the middle leaflet but sometimes toothed or notched on the side away from the middle leaflet. If one of the lateral leaflets is toothed on the outside margin, the other usually is too. Poison Ivy as a vine hugging a tree trunk is very hairy. As an herb it is a sun-loving plant that prefers edges of fields and the sides of broad trails such as the widest of old woods roads. It virtually never grows on a shady trail. Its spring flowers are inconspicuous and later transform to white berries; in fall, the leaflets turn to brilliant yellows, oranges, and reds, thus forming a delight to the eye but not to the skin. The plant is toxic at all seasons. If in doubt, don't touch!

Poison Sumac also occurs in Wisconsin, in wet areas. It is a shrub or small tree whose nine or so leaflets are always without teeth and resemble those of Shining Sumac. (The larger Staghorn Sumac has toothed leaflets but is otherwise similar.) Poison Sumac is a close relative of Poison Ivy and just as toxic. Like Poison Ivy, it has white berries, whereas the so-called harmless sumacs, such as Shining and Staghorn, have bright red berries. Nevertheless, all of the sumacs are in the cashew family, and some unfortunate people are sensitive to the oils of even the "harmless" species.

If you do have a brush with Poison Ivy or Poison Sumac, wash thoroughly as soon as possible to inhibit absorption of the oil into your skin. Potential antidotes in the woods are rare. The juices of jewelweeds—two species of common Wisconsin flowers that grow in damp or wet areas—are said to help.

Injuries

The local outdoor store will happily sell you an elaborate first-aid kit for dealing with all those injuries you imagine befall backpackers, but most of the time you can get by on some Band-Aids—plus soap and water. In fact, you can do nothing for the commonest injury of backpackers: jammed fingers sustained while cramming a sleeping bag or other item into a stuff sack. Blisters from boots that you should have broken in more thoroughly can be covered with a miracle product called Spenco. Actually, Spenco is nothing but a moist pad held to your skin with a piece of adhesive, but if you put it on a hot spot immediately, you will avoid a blister. We have been told that covering incipient blisters with a piece of duct tape also works well. Opinions differ on what to do about a full-fledged blister. We drain it at the edge with a needle sterilized in a match flame, and then cover it with Spenco (or at least a Band-Aid). Another technique we have used is to cut a blister-sized hole in a piece of moleskin, and then to place the moleskin on the area surrounding the blister (undrained if small or drained if large). The raised surface prevents the blister from rubbing further against the sock.

Turning an ankle is no fun, and spraining an ankle is serious when you are out in the wilds. Turned ankles recover with a little rest (minutes to hours), but sprained ankles usually require weeks or months to heal. Neither of us has ever sprained an ankle while backpacking, but Jack did sprain an ankle while jogging at night. He could hardly walk for nearly a week and required three months to heal completely. Being the cautious wimp that he is, he now carries in his backpack an elastic wrap to bind an ankle he will never sprain while backpacking. If you should be so unfortunate as to sprain an ankle on the trail, your trip is over and it is going to be painful walking out. Your ankle will probably swell alarmingly, and if you remove your boot, you may not be able to get it back on. Your boot provides the best support, but leaving it on runs the risk of not being able to get it off, so some judgment is required. If you don't carry a walking stick (we always do while backpacking), fashion one from the best available branch that won't break when you are leaning on it. Put that walking stick or makeshift cane *in the hand opposite to the sprained ankle.* That's the counter-intuitive part, but if you don't trust us on this point, ask your doctor.

You might accidentally cut a finger or something with your pocket knife. To lessen the chances, obey the two rules that should become second nature to any outdoors person: always cut away from your body rather than toward it, and always keep your knife edge sharp. A dull knife is more dangerous than a sharp one because you tend to press too hard and can lose control of it. We carry a small whetstone to sharpen knives in the field. If you do cut yourself, wash the wound thoroughly with soap and water, then apply a Band-Aid to keep out the dirt.

Heat and cold

Don't let weather spoil your trip. Sunstroke and heat exhaustion are different but equally serious reactions to a body temperature of 105°F or above. Avoid them in hot weather by wearing a hat, covering arms and legs, staying in the shade, slowing down, and drinking plenty of water. Recognize sunstroke by redness of skin; heat exhaustion (essentially a form of fainting) by pallid skin. Sufferers from both exhibit hot and dry skin, rapid breathing, dizziness, nausea, and weakness, or more serious behavioral manifestations (confusion, seizures, or unconsciousness). Act quickly; delay could mean irreversible brain damage. A smitten person should be lain down in the shade, undressed, and mopped with a damp cloth or completely doused with water if that much water is available. Fan the sufferer to promote cooling, and put her or him completely in water if there is a creek or lake close at hand. Do whatever is possible to bring the body temperature down to 102°F or lower.

Sunburn is also bad news, so keep the skin covered during the day and use sunscreen liberally. Sunburn is caused by the ultraviolet component of the sun's rays, and this UV light goes right through clouds, which absorb the visible light. You can still get a bad burn on an overcast day.

Probably the greatest risk of chill comes when the temperature drops to near freezing and rain begins. Assuming that you are properly equipped, the major thing is to stay dry by donning your raincoat when the first drop falls— not when you are already wet. Getting cold at night is something else you want to avoid because you won't get much sleep, thus making the next day all the more trying. Again, assuming that you have a sleeping bag adequate for the climate, avoid getting damp: remove all of your clothing at night, including under-wear. The clothing is moisture-laden from your day's perspiration, and moist clothes will cool you rather than help keep you warm. Put on dry clothes or nightclothes, or sleep in the altogether. As this book is aimed at three-season backpacking, we don't discuss frostbite, but if you are to be a winter camper, you should learn about it.

Water

Dehydration is serious and can bring on or exacerbate sunstroke and heat exhaustion. Drink more water than you think you need, and drink a little even when you are not thirsty. The human body can go about a week without food (not that it would be pleasant to do so), but effects of water deprivation occur within a day or less.

It was only a few decades ago that you could drink safely from any moun-tain stream in the nation, and a lot of other natural water supplies as well. Today, you would be absolutely crazy to do that because a nasty protozoan called *Giardia* has invaded virtually all natural waters everywhere. It is therefore mandatory to make your drinking and cooking water safe from this and other microorganisms, and there are three ways to do that: boiling, filtering, or treat-ing. Bringing water to a round boil for a couple of minutes works well for cooking, but who wants to fill a water bottle with boiling water? You can treat water with chemicals, but do not rely on older kinds of treatments that may not be effective on *Giardia*. Buy treatment pills or liquids that say explicitly on the label that they kill *Giardia*. Filtering is great because it does not heat up your drinking water or leave a taste in it as some treatment chemicals do. Proper filters are ceramic, micropore filters whose holes are far too small for you to see—small enough to exclude *Giardia* and its friends. Portable filters come in bewildering sizes and configurations, and they seem to be unnecessarily expen-sive, but grit your teeth and buy one.

Getting lost

Losing the way is probably the main thing that beginners fear, and justifiably so. We repeat our earlier recommendation to stay on marked trails. Carry a map of your trail and know how to read it. Never rely on trail signs, which get turned the wrong way, chewed on by animals, and vandalized by animals of our own species. Buy a good mapping compass and learn how to use it. If there is any chance that you must go cross-country using a map and compass, be certain you find out in advance the corrections for variation and declination in the area and know how to apply them.

For all you technophiles out there, here is why we think you should not depend upon the Global Positioning System (GPS) for finding your way. Even the best of hand-held, affordable (under $200) GPS units are not accurate enough to help you, and some are pure junk. Jack went through five units of three models from two manufacturers before finding one that did not blatantly malfunction. GPS is supposed to give an accurate position within 100 yards, which is not very precise by trail standards, and is rarely achievable with these units anyway. We took the functional one on a section of the Ice Age Trail and stopped frequently to let the unit average satellite signals before we marked a waypoint. At the end of our journey the gadget gave us three assessments of the same trail distance: the final value of the continuously recording odometer, the unit's summation of the segments marked by waypoints, and all the individual segments, which we totaled. Those three values should have been the same, but they were all different from one another. We then turned around and walked back, again marking waypoints as we went, and thereby collected three more different values for exactly the same trail distance as before. Six different assessments for the same distance, the closest two of which were 0.1 mile apart! Knowing where you are or how far you have walked within a half mile just isn't sufficiently precise for the hiker.

What should you do when you get lost? We say "when" rather than "if" because anyone who spends much time in the great out-of-doors will probably become lost sooner or later. Jack, who has a better than average sense of direction, got lost once, and this is how he got out of it. He was with a colleague in a state forest in Maryland where Jack had never been before. The colleague was doing serious field work, so Jack left him alone and went for a hike on unmarked trails in an unfamiliar forest for which he had never seen a map. (Well, sometimes he isn't too bright.) After a couple of hours, he came to a trail junction that was strikingly familiar, and it quickly dawned on him that he had performed the classical lost act: he had walked in a circle. He sat down immediately and evaluated all the evidence available. He could not be absolutely certain how to retrace his steps to get back to where he had left his colleague at work; there were too many trail segments with too many junctions. He was probably much too far away from his colleague to be heard, but he shouted a few times anyway (to no avail). They had seen no one else in this forest, either on the road driving in or on the trails, so the chances of somebody's happening by were slim. Jack would be missed by the end of the afternoon, and eventually a search party could find him, but why call out the Marines when you should be able to get out of a jam of your own making?

Jack remembered that they had driven in on a very long dirt road almost directly southward and had then walked together roughly eastward down a slope from the parked car. Jack was pretty sure that he had headed off to the north when leaving his colleague. Although turned around at the moment, he had probably come basically north for a pretty long way. Therefore, if he could now walk directly westward, holding a straight course by the sun's position, he should cross that dirt road. So he set out, keeping the sun obliquely to his left, and within 15 minutes he hit the road. The lesson is: when you know you are lost, sit down and review everything you know in order to devise the best strategy for action.

Please don't bring that cell phone into the woods; it's of little potential help. It won't bring anyone to you unless you know where you are—and if you knew that, you wouldn't be lost. At best you can just tell somebody that you are lost, but if you left word with someone before you set out (as you should), that person will eventually figure out you are lost and come looking. You are probably backpacking to escape telephones and the like in the first place, so why should you ruin your trip with stressful calls? Furthermore, those batteries are going to drain sometime, and that will be before your return from a trip if it is a long one. Do not depend upon gadgetry, especially battery powered gadgetry, to get you out of a pickle. Learn the simple skills necessary to save your own hide, or else stay home.

If you are really hopelessly lost while backpacking, it's no big deal. You have your life-support system on your back. Build a fire to lead rescuers to your position, set up your tent, and hope that you don't grow old waiting to be rescued. Oh, yes—be prepared to pay the cost of the rescue, which could run into the thousands of dollars if helicopters are employed. It is much better not to get lost in the first place.

MAKING LIFE EASIER

We add some random tips on what we have found to make our backpacking trips go a little more smoothly. Talk to other backpackers to pick up more tips like these, and then sort through them to see what works for you.

How much weight to carry

A rule of thumb is to carry between a quarter and a third of your body weight. Aim for the lower value. A certain minimum amount is needed to support life, or at least the backpacking lifestyle to which you would like to become accustomed. This fact means that small people may have to carry a greater proportion of their body weight than do big people. Who said life was fair?

How to weigh your pack

The easiest way to weigh your pack is with a suitcase scale, although they are hard to find in stores. We hang our scale from a large nail pounded into a rafter in the garage, and then hang the fully loaded pack from the spring scale. Lacking that, weigh yourself on the bathroom scale with the pack on your back and then without it, and do the subtraction.

Walk properly

Some city folk fall into a bad walking habit in which they pivot the foot outward on the heel with each step. That pivoting action unnecessarily strains certain muscles, and also makes you less stable. Practice keeping your feet pointed straight ahead when walking. If you initially feel as though you're walking pigeon-toed, then you know you have been walking poorly and need to realign those muscles with a better gait. Walking properly when carrying a backpack will be less tiring, and the more stable gait will help to keep you from falling.

Know your stride length

Sometimes you need to walk a specified number of feet or yards when following written or oral directions to something such as an inconspicuous side trail to a viewpoint. So walk 10 steps with your backpack on, measure the distance traveled with a yardstick, and do the division. The average stride length of most people carrying a full pack falls somewhere between 2 and 3 feet.

Know your pace

Even more important than stride length is pace. Not only can you plan a trip better if you know the average pace at which you walk, but it can help you find things. Say you are supposed to find a specific campsite 1 mile after a trail junction. If you generally cover a mile in 30 minutes but have not found that campsite after walking 40 minutes, you know to turn around because you surely missed it. Time how long it takes you to cover a known trail distance with a full pack. It will probably be about half again as long as your hiking pace without a pack. For example, if you hike unencumbered at 3 miles an hour (20 minutes to cover a mile), you will probably walk at about 2 miles an hour (30 minutes per mile) with a full pack.

Walking sticks

We never use walking sticks when day hiking but always use them when backpacking. It is nice to have that third support when the trail crosses a creek on a beaver dam. (Yes, even the Ice Age National Scenic Trail resorts to that in at least one place.) You will also appreciate the added stability on hills, especially when going downhill. Good walking sticks are adjustable in height; set yours so that your forearm is parallel with the ground when your elbow is at your side and your lower arm projects forward.

Snug up your boots

Usually, when you first put your boots on, you cannot tighten them up enough to prevent your foot from slipping around in them. That's a syndrome that leads to blisters. After you have been on the trail for 5 or 10 minutes and everything has sort of settled down inside the boot, stop and snug up the laces to the tightness that feels right.

Don't change your diet

A backpacking trip is not the time to experiment with new foods. Stick to the kinds of things you know and like, and make no dramatic changes in your diet. We at first got pounding headaches on backpacking trips, and eventually realized it was because we were not bringing coffee and were suffering from caffeine withdrawal.

Backcountry sanitation

Carry a plastic trowel (lighter than metal) and, imitating a house cat, scratch a hole a few inches deep, covering it over when you're through. Soil bacteria break down mammalian feces within days. For more on this topic, read Kathleen Meyer's book *How to Shit in the Woods*. Tampons and sanitary napkins must be packed out (in plastic bags) because they will not degrade if buried.

Toilet paper

A whole roll is a bit much for two people on a weekend trip, and you don't want to carry more bulk or weight than you need to. Yet having to fold or roll paper taken off the full roll is an annoyance. So we just remove a roll from the bathroom before it is completely used up and stash it away in a drawer for backpacking.

Zippered plastic bags

Everyone thinks to take foods in those various sizes of plastic bags that seal with a zipper-like strip. We also use the larger ones for items like underwear and socks. The bag keeps them together (easier to pack, easier to find) and keeps them dry. And we go one better by using the type that has a zipper pull. Those cost a little more than bags without the pull, but they are so much easier to seal reliably that we love them.

Garbage bags

Sure, use those large, dark, plastic bags to pack out your garbage; they also have other uses. It is convenient to keep all your food sealed up in a garbage bag within your pack so that the smell of food does not permeate into the pack cloth. Then you can string the food up for the night right in that bag. Garbage bags can also be used as pack covers for the night, and even (in a pinch) as a poncho if you poke a head-hole into one. Just don't use the food bag for anything else.

Nylon line

Nylon line is great for tying down tents, making clotheslines, stringing up food between trees, and so on. We like nylon better than cotton line because it is stronger and resists abrasion, rotting, and unraveling. Woven nylon line, such as parachute cord, is easy to tie knots into, but braided line comes apart and will not hold knots well. We carry lots of woven nylon line. We like subdued colors for gear such as tents and backpacks. Some national parks in the west even request that hikers do not wear bright clothing, which spoils a wilderness aura. But when it comes to nylon line, which you can trip over at night, white is better than green or brown.

Clothespins?

OK, maybe clothespins are a luxury on a backpacking trip, but they sure come in handy when you need to dry out clothes on a nylon line. Full-sized clothespins are, however, awkwardly bulky for what they do, if not heavier than they really need to be. You can buy a set of small clothespins in travel shops, paying about 10 times what they are worth. Or you can do as we did and saw the bottom half of the "handle" part off some plastic, spring-type clothespins.

"LEAVE NO TRACE" BACKPACKING

We close on this note: the sign of a good camper is no sign at all. Wisconsin has always been in the forefront of environmental awareness. Our state was the boyhood home of John Muir, who perhaps more than any other person promoted the cause of setting aside wild lands in national parks and preserves. Here is where Aldo Leopold—founder of the University of Wisconsin's Department of Wildlife Ecology (one of the first such departments in the country)—developed the concept of land ethic in his classic *A Sand County Almanac*. And it was here that the state's Department of Natural Resources held hearings which, along with Rachel Carson's *Silent Spring,* led to the banning of DDT in the United States. Wisconsinites treasure an unspoiled environment; we backpackers must do our part to ensure that we don't love it to death. Here are some suggestions.

Plan, prepare, protect

Plan your trip and the belongings you take to minimize ecological impact. Prepare, for example, by packaging food to avoid unnecessary trash. Protect by never digging ditches around your tent or otherwise marring the environment. Do not build structures such as makeshift tables. Never drive nails into trees or otherwise assault plants. Should you come across Native American mounds or other cultural artifacts, make sure no one in your party disturbs them.

Where to walk and camp

Stay on trails, and don't make shortcuts. We think it preferable to choose an established campsite in high-use areas rather than to disturb a new place. Environmentalists are divided on the advisability of using traditional camping places. Some feel that places showing human impact should be put off limits until ecological recovery has taken place, whereas others believe that because rotating camping spots ultimately spreads damage over a larger area, campers should actually be urged to use traditional places. If you do camp in a pristine area, spread out use—for example, by cooking in one small area and sleeping in another some distance away. Avoid crushing fragile vegetation. But if you notice a place where a pristine area is beginning to show evidence of use, avoid camping there.

Pack it in, pack it out

The rule of thumb is easy: if it isn't found there naturally, don't leave it there. Even disposing of some biodegradable items should give you pause. What if some of the seeds are not eaten by the mouse that finds that apple core; do you want to be responsible for planting an apple tree in the wilderness?

Sanitation

After using your 7-inch-deep cat hole, bury the feces and toilet paper, and then camouflage the site. Wash with biodegradable soap, and carry water well away from sources such as creeks and lakes to do your washing.

Read

Learn more about no-trace outdoor recreation by talking with experienced people and reading. Some helpful and interesting books are those by Harmon, Hodgson, and the Watermans (see Further Reading).

NORTHWEST REGION

The Northwest region of Wisconsin provides a good cross section of backpacking in the state. Pattison State Park has one of the highest waterfalls in the eastern United States. For the backpacker who wants to spend more than one night on the trail, both the northern and southern parts of Governor Knowles State Forest have reasonably long trails that run along the scenic St. Croix River. Finally, not to be overlooked are segments of the Ice Age National Scenic Trail that run through county forests and other public lands. These backpacking areas, which are scattered throughout the Northwest region, are readily accessible from population centers in western Wisconsin and eastern Minnesota.

NORTHWEST REGION

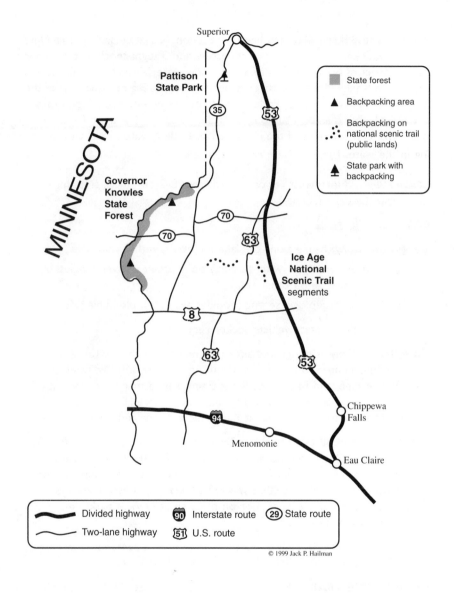

Pattison State Park

What do these three waterfalls have in common: Niagara in far western New York, Fall Creek in east-central Tennessee, and Taughannock in the Finger Lakes district of New York? They are the only waterfalls in the United States east of the Rocky Mountains that are higher than the Big Manitou Falls of the Black River in Pattison State Park. (In case you are wondering, Niagara Falls is but 2 feet higher than Big Manitou.) In Pattison State Park you can fall asleep in your tent to the sounds of the more sedate Little Manitou Falls, also on the Black River.

LOCATION. Northwest region, coordinates B-2 on official state highway map (Douglas County).

RATING. 🌲 🌲 🌲

🌲 **Scenery:** hiking along the lake and river, with 2 waterfalls

🌲 **Trails:** can camp (with detours) on a circuit of over 5 miles; more mileage on other trails

🌲 **Interest:** geologic setting (booklet available), old mining site

ENTRANCE FEE. State vehicle sticker required.

CAMPING. Only at designated sites (see map). The three sites, at the southern end of the park, are (from north to south) White Birch, White Pine, and Balsam. Each has a tent site, a metal fire ring with grate, and a picnic table; nearby outhouses serve all three campsites. Drinking water is available at the picnic grounds and campground.

PERMIT AND RESERVATIONS. Camping permit required for a specific campsite. Obtain the permit at the park office (HQ on the map). Advance reservations of campsites are accepted by the state's phone reservation service at 888/947-2757 (9 A.M. to 10 P.M. weekdays and 9 A.M. to 6 P.M. weekends) or on the web at www.wiparks.net; reservation fee charged.

CONTACT INFORMATION. Pattison State Park, 6294 South State Road 35, Superior, WI 54880; phone: 715/399-3111 (no fax).

FINDING THE TRAIL. Pattison State Park is on State Highway 35, about 13 miles south of Superior. Probably the most convenient way to get to the trail is to leave your vehicle in the small lot on the western edge of the campground (see map) and walk toward the lake to find the **Beaver Slide Trail** along the shoreline. In about three-tenths of a mile the **Logging Camp Trail** splits off to the left and climbs for

Pattison State Park

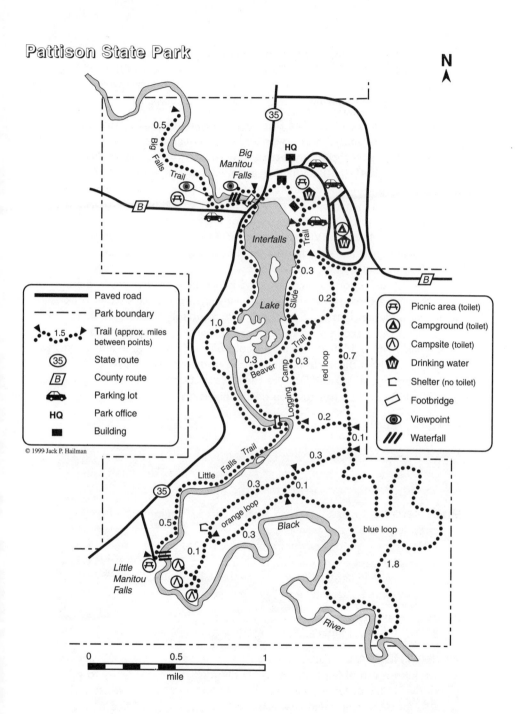

N

Legend

▬▬▬	Paved road
─ ∙ ─	Park boundary
●●● 1.5 ●●●	Trail (approx. miles between points)
(35)	State route
[B]	County route
🚗	Parking lot
HQ	Park office
■	Building

© 1999 Jack P. Hailman

🚻	Picnic area (toilet)
⒜	Campground (toilet)
⒜	Campsite (toilet)
W	Drinking water
⊏	Shelter (no toilet)
▱	Footbridge
◉	Viewpoint
///	Waterfall

Big Falls Trail

Big Manitou Falls

0.5

Interfalls Lake

Slide Trail

0.3

0.2

1.0

Beaver Trail

Logging Camp Trail

red loop

0.3

0.3

0.7

0.2

0.1

0.3

Little Falls Trail

0.3

0.1

0.5

orange loop

0.1

0.3

Black

blue loop

1.8

0.1

Little Manitou Falls

River

0	0.5	1
mile

about an equal distance to overlook the Beaver Slide Trail's footbridge over the Black River. You could also start on the red loop of the ski trail, accessible from the south end of the campground (see map), but walking along the lake is more pleasant.

BACKGROUND NOTES. The Black River flowing through Pattison State Park is different from the river that gives its name to Black River State Forest in the Southwest region. The park is named for Martin Pattison (1841–1918), a lumber and mining baron who in 1917 secretly bought up the land along the river when the area was threatened by a proposed power dam that would have destroyed the falls. He gave the land to the state for a park in 1918. Fairlawn—Pattison's 42-room, Victorian-style mansion on Lake Superior in the city of Superior—now houses the Douglas County Historical Museum and is open to the public.

A billion or so years ago, lava issued up from fissures in the earth and spread over this area, solidifying into the dark basalt rock that underlies Pattison State Park. Later, but still more than half a billion years ago, a huge sea covered this area and deposited sand grains, which lithified into a light-colored sandstone. Soon afterward, forces within the earth pushed up the land south of today's Lake Superior, creating the Douglas Fault; watercourses such as today's Black River then had to drop off the highlands in waterfalls. Things

Liz at backpacking site, Pattison State Park

34

remained more or less the same until the great continental ice masses of the Pleistocene era came and then retreated, the last disappearing only 10,000 years ago. These huge glaciers tended to scrape the sandstone off the basalt of the highlands; thus today the surface rock is basalt above the Douglas Fault but still sandstone below it. Because the hard basalt is so resistant to erosion, Big Manitou Falls—165 feet high but almost a series of cascades rather than a vertical fall—has retreated back from the fault line only a relatively short distance.

OUR TRAIL NOTES.   What should have been a quiet night in mid-September when we camped on the Black River, listening to the soothing sound of nearby Little Manitou Falls, was repeatedly disturbed by overwhelming noises from the railroad yards about 2–3 miles to the northwest. Interfalls Lake had been drained for repairs to the dam, mosquitoes had not yet been killed back by a good frost, and rain fell on us during the hike down to the Black River's gorge below Big Manitou Falls. Fortunately, the little kid in Jack loves trains, and he was able to forgive the interrupted sleep; we saw some interesting birds on the lake bottom mudflat; and any view of Big Manitou Falls, rain or shine, is one of Wisconsin's finest sights. In fact, if it had not been for the trains, Liz might not have been awake to hear the Canada Geese flying over during the night. It is difficult to find redeeming features in mosquitoes, though.

    Flora. Conifers predominate in this north woods park; we noticed Eastern White Pine, White Spruce, Northern White-Cedar, and Balsam Fir. Sweet clover and asters were the last wildflowers of the year. Among the nonflowering plants we saw were at least two (probably three) species of lycopodium and diverse kinds of ferns. And we found many fungi: puffballs, bracket fungi on the tree trunks, and large mushrooms.

    Fauna. Spring Peepers were peeping in the autumnal rain; we also found along the trail a *Rana* frog and a baby American Toad. Eastern Chipmunks still scurried about, while Red Squirrels trilled in the conifers and Gray Squirrels searched the ground in the picnic areas. Birds, as usual, were our most numerous companions: in addition to the Canada Geese, we found a Great Blue Heron and Killdeers on the drained lake, and several other species in the woods and along the trails: Downy Woodpecker, Northern Flicker, Eastern Wood-Pewee, a vireo, Blue Jay, American Crow, Common Raven, Black-capped Chickadee, White-breasted Nuthatch, Golden-crowned Kinglet, and Yellow-rumped Warbler.

Governor Knowles State Forest

With Part of St. Croix National Scenic Riverway

If you ever wanted to *hike* a national scenic riverway rather than canoe it, here is your chance. Governor Knowles State Forest maintains a trail along the river in two different sections contiguous with the St. Croix National Scenic Riverway.

LOCATION. Northwest region, coordinates A/B-3/4 on official state highway map (Burnett and Polk Counties).

RATING. 🌲🌲🌲🌲

🌲 **Scenery:** the St. Croix River

🌲 **Quiet:** more than a mile from paved roads (some campsites)

🌲 **Trails:** at least 10 miles of trail accessible from campsites

🌲 **Solitude:** trail likely to have few hikers but river often has many canoeists

🌲 **Interest:** excellent natural history, especially wildflowers and birds

ENTRANCE FEE. State sticker required to use parking areas or any other recreational facility of the state forest.

CAMPING. Only at designated sites. The state forest intends to develop its own sites, but in the interim directs backpackers to use the canoe campsites established by the National Park Service (see trail maps), where camping is limited to one night. Each campsite has a tent site, a metal fire ring with grate, a picnic table, and an open throne toilet. Drinking water is available at several river landings and at a wayside on State Highway 70, where it crosses the river (see trail maps).

PERMIT AND RESERVATIONS. A free camping permit from Governor Knowles State Forest is required. You may request this permit in advance by letter or phone and have it mailed to you. You may also pick it up at the forest headquarters in Grantsburg, but be aware that the office is open only during working hours on weekdays and is closed on weekends and holidays. You can phone to inquire about current office hours.

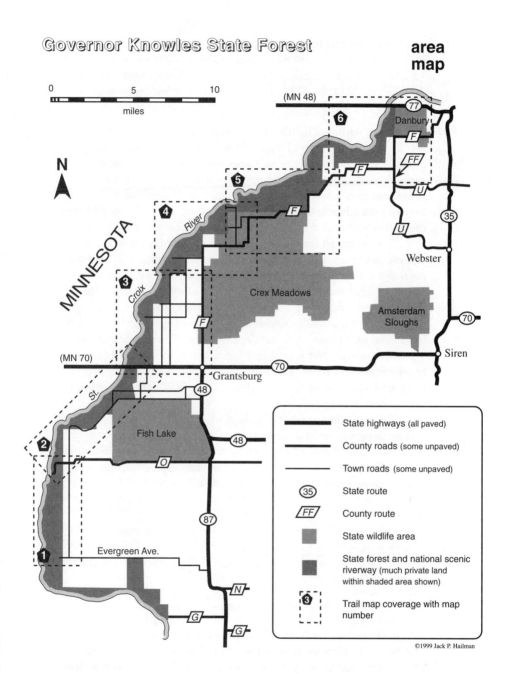

Governor Knowles State Forest

area map

0   5   10
miles

N

MINNESOTA

(MN 48)

Danbury

Webster

Crex Meadows

Amsterdam Sloughs

Siren

(MN 70)

Grantsburg

Fish Lake

Evergreen Ave.

Legend:

State highways (all paved)

County roads (some unpaved)

Town roads (some unpaved)

(35)   State route

FF   County route

State wildlife area

State forest and national scenic riverway (much private land within shaded area shown)

3   Trail map coverage with map number

©1999 Jack P. Hailman

37

CONTACT INFORMATION.   Governor Knowles State Forest, P.O. Box 367, Grantsburg, WI 54840; phone: 715/463-2898; fax: 715/463-5806. To contact the St. Croix National Scenic Riverway, write to National Park Service, P.O. Box 708, St. Croix Falls, WI 54024; phone: 715/ 483-3284 (no fax).

FINDING THE TRAIL.   The hiking trails are in the southern (trail maps #1–2) and northern (trail maps #4–6) parts of the state forest, often closely paralleling the St. Croix River, but sometimes drifting away from it, especially in the northern area. Between these two linear trails is a break of roughly 10 miles, with only the Park Service's **Sandrock Cliff Ski Trails** (trail map #3). Through-hiking the entire length of the state forest is therefore impractical.

The southern trail is divided into two "routes" called **Lagoo Creek** (trail map #1) and **Benson Brook** (trail map #2), and the northern trail is divided into three continuous routes: **Foxes Landing** (trail map #4), **Kohler-Peet** (trail map #5), and **Sioux Portage** (trail map #6). State forest literature gives the trail distances of these five routes as 9, 7, 9, 7, and 6 miles, respectively, for a total of 38 miles. We believe the Lagoo Creek route cannot be 9 miles, however, and is probably more like 6, lowering the total to approximately 35 miles. The forest staff agrees with us and suggests using 6–7 as the value for the Lagoo Creek Trail until the distance can be remeasured.

The trails are accessible at numerous points, which you can find by using the general area map and specific trail maps together. The only major trailhead likely to be confusing is the southernmost access point at the western end of Evergreen Ave. (trail map #1). The unpaved town road ends about half a mile west of 340th St., but the way continues as a primitive state forest road for a quarter mile or so. You can leave your vehicle at the end of Evergreen Ave., where there is a sort of turning circle, or you can continue on the primitive road (state forest signboard at the entrance) until you come to a small parking area (and another signboard) at the trailhead proper.

BACKGROUND NOTES.   The upper part of the St. Croix River (together with the Namekagon) was one of the eight rivers designated under the National Wild and Scenic Rivers Act of 1968. The lower St. Croix was added in 1972. The St. Croix River State Forest was created in 1970, then renamed in 1981 for popular three-term Wisconsin Governor Warren P. Knowles (1908–1993), an avid outdoorsman.

The St. Croix once drained mammoth Pleistocene Lake Duluth, the predecessor of today's much lower and smaller Lake Superior (which drains to the east through the other Great Lakes and the St. Lawrence Seaway). The St. Croix still carries an impressive annual flow from a large watershed and continues to carve a scenic valley into bedrock that is at least half a billion years old. The valley is steep sided throughout most of Governor Knowles State Forest, forming a decided escarpment (see trail maps). Layers of glacially deposited clay prevent groundwater from filtering all the way down to bedrock, so the water flows on top of these layers and emerges as seeps or springs, which create numerous small streams that run from the escarpment into the St. Croix.

OUR TRAIL NOTES. July is usually warm in Wisconsin, but the mid-July of our backpacking trip here was downright sweltering. We negotiated many downed trees across the Lagoo Trail as it descended the escarpment, lost the trail once, and walked right past the campsite situated on an embankment above us, then had to turn around and hunt for it once we knew we had walked too far. This was one of the buggiest backpacking trips in our experience with ticks as well as mosquitoes; appropriately, one of the commonest wildflowers we found was the Pointed-leaved Tick-trefoil. And the campsite, when we finally found it, was ringed with Poison Ivy. Dinnertime was already upon us, but Jack's trusty thermometer proclaimed the temperature to be 86°F, so instead of setting up

Tent, table, and pack, Governor Knowles State Forest

Jack on a bridge, Governor Knowles State Forest

camp immediately, we donned our swimming suits and waded into the St. Croix for welcome relief. An adult Bald Eagle flying low up the river failed to notice us until it was directly overhead, providing its human admirers with a breathtaking view, and then the huge bird veered sharply out across the river. Barred Owls along the valley began calling single "hoos" as we cooked dinner, and later a Whitetail doe brought her fawn to drink from the river across from our campsite. After dark, the still-calling owls were joined by Whip-poor-wills to lull us to sleep. The temperature dropped to a merciful 65°F overnight, and in the morning our enthusiasm for hiking was renewed.

Flora. We noticed Jack Pine, Sugar Maple, Paper Birch, American Hornbeam, American Basswood, Bigtooth Aspen, Bur Oak, and Pin Oak trees. No northern conifers on this trail: they are all above the escarpment. The wildflowers were far more engaging: Ohio Spiderwort, Pale Plantain, Evening Lychnis (White Campion), Hoary Alyssum, Goat's Beard, Pointed-leaved Tick-trefoil, Fireweed, Wild Carrot (Queen Anne's Lace), Wild Bergamot, a mint, Culver's-root, Common Mullein, Butter-and-eggs (Toadflax), Wild Lettuce, Ox-eye Daisy, Yarrow, Gray-headed (Prairie) Coneflower, (Woodland) Pale-leaved Wood Sunflower, a yellow composite, and an early goldenrod. The saprophytic Spotted Coralroot and Indian-pipe were perhaps our favorites of the trip: these specialized plants live on decaying organic matter. Several kinds of ferns grew in the moist bottomlands. There was also a mushroom of a beautiful purple color, which we had never before encountered, a very pretty bracket fungus, and a curly white fungus, which we nicknamed Baroque. The most "useful" plant, though, was Red Raspberry in berry.

Fauna. Lest we forget that not all insects are mosquitoes, we should mention that the dainty, jet-black damselfly we found was a miniature highlight of the trip. The amphibian clan was represented by a tiny American Toad, doubtless only recently metamorphosed, and a small, striped (Garter?) snake was the exemplary reptile. Aside from Whitetail Deer, we saw Eastern Chipmunks and Red Squirrels. By mid-July, many birds have ceased their singing, yet we heard or saw an impressive array of species: Yellow-billed Cuckoo, Barred Owl, Whip-poor-will, Ruby-throated Hummingbird, Yellow-bellied Sapsucker, Downy Woodpecker, Hairy Woodpecker, Eastern Wood-Pewee, Red-eyed Vireo, Blue Jay, American Crow, Common Raven, White-breasted Nuthatch, Wood Thrush, American Robin, Cedar Waxwing, Northern Parula, Ovenbird, Common Yellowthroat, Field Sparrow, Indigo Bunting, and American Goldfinch.

Governor Knowles
State Forest
trail map #1

Lagoo Creek Route
Evergreen Avenue to
County O Landing

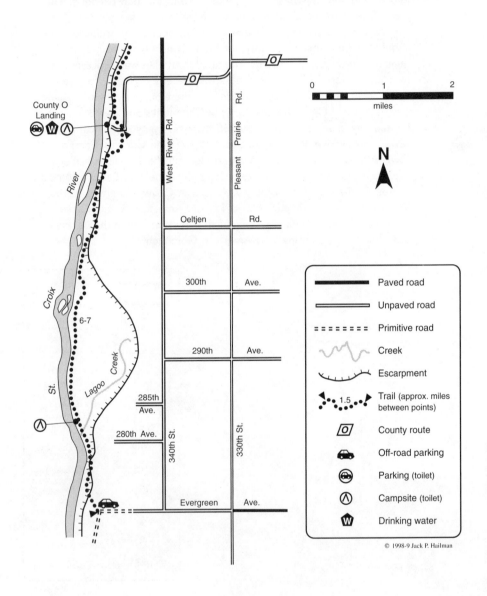

© 1998-9 Jack P. Hailman

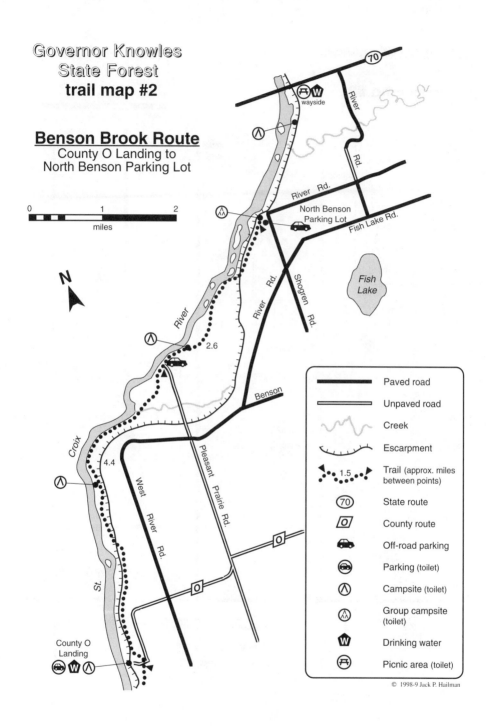

Governor Knowles State Forest
trail map #2

Benson Brook Route
County O Landing to
North Benson Parking Lot

0   1   2
miles

N

70

River

wayside

River Rd.

River Rd.

North Benson
Parking Lot

Fish Lake Rd.

River Rd.

Shogren Rd.

Fish
Lake

River

2.6

Croix

Benson

4.4

West

River

Rd.

Pleasant Prairie Rd.

St.

O

O

County O
Landing

Legend

▬▬▬	Paved road
▭▭▭	Unpaved road
∿∿∿	Creek
⌣⌣⌣	Escarpment
◄••1.5••►	Trail (approx. miles between points)
(70)	State route
◇O	County route
🚗	Off-road parking
🚗	Parking (toilet)
Ⓐ	Campsite (toilet)
Ⓐ	Group campsite (toilet)
W	Drinking water
⊖	Picnic area (toilet)

© 1998-9 Jack P. Hailman

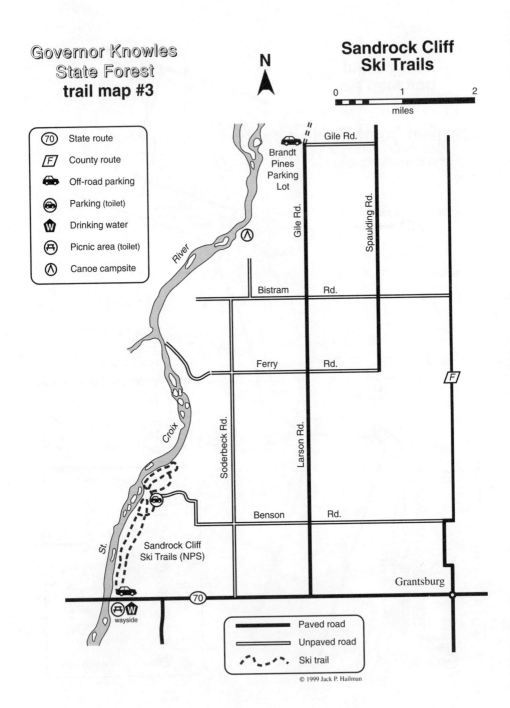

Governor Knowles
State Forest
trail map #3

N

Sandrock Cliff
Ski Trails

0   1   2
miles

70	State route
F	County route
🚗	Off-road parking
🚗	Parking (toilet)
🚰	Drinking water
🏠	Picnic area (toilet)
🛶	Canoe campsite

Gile Rd.

Brandt
Pines
Parking
Lot

Gile Rd.

Spaulding Rd.

River

Bistram   Rd.

Ferry   Rd.

F

Croix

Soderbeck Rd.

Larson Rd.

Benson   Rd.

Sandrock Cliff
Ski Trails (NPS)

St.

Grantsburg

70

wayside

▬▬▬▬	Paved road
▭▭▭▭	Unpaved road
⌇⌇⌇	Ski trail

© 1999 Jack P. Hailman

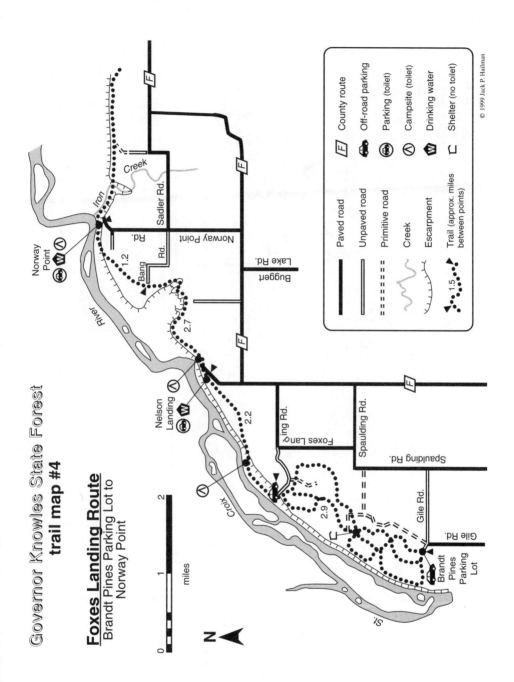

Governor Knowles State Forest
trail map #4

Foxes Landing Route
Brandt Pines Parking Lot to Norway Point

Legend:

Paved road		F	County route
Unpaved road			Off-road parking
Primitive road			Parking (toilet)
Creek			Campsite (toilet)
Escarpment		W	Drinking water
Trail (approx. miles between points) 1.5		C	Shelter (no toilet)

© 1999 Jack P. Hailman

miles
0   1   2

N

Norway Point

Iron Creek

Sadler Rd.

Norway Point Rd.

Bang Rd.

1.2

2.7

River

Nelson Landing

2.2

St. Croix

Bugger Lake Rd.

Foxes Lang ing Rd.

Spaulding Rd.

Spaulding Rd.

Gile Rd.

Gile Rd.

2.9

Brandt Pines Parking Lot

45

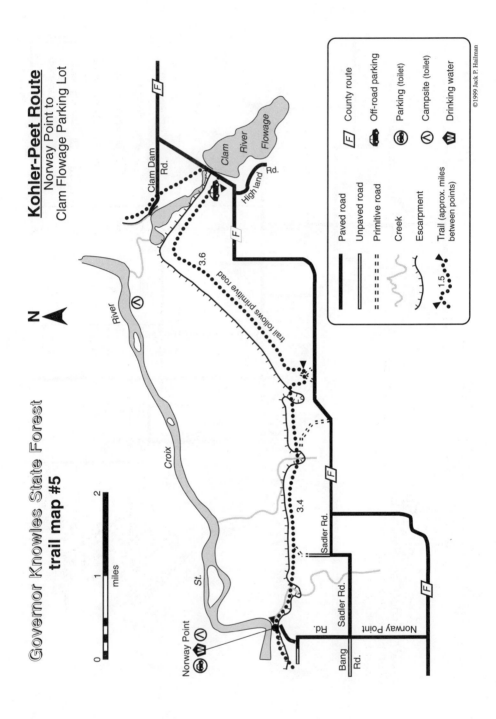

Kohler-Peet Route
Norway Point to
Clam Flowage Parking Lot

Governor Knowles State Forest
trail map #5

N

©1999 Jack P. Hailman

	Paved road		County route
	Unpaved road		Off-road parking
	Primitive road		Parking (toilet)
	Creek		Campsite (toilet)
	Escarpment		Drinking water
	Trail (approx. miles between points)		

Clam Dam Rd.

Clam River Flowage

Highland Rd.

3.6

trail follows primitive road

St. Croix River

Sadler Rd.

3.4

Sadler Rd.

Bang Rd.

Norway Point Rd.

Norway Point

0   1   2
miles

46

Governor Knowles State Forest
trail map #6

Sioux Portage Route
Clam Flowage Parking Lot to
Sioux Portage Parking Lot

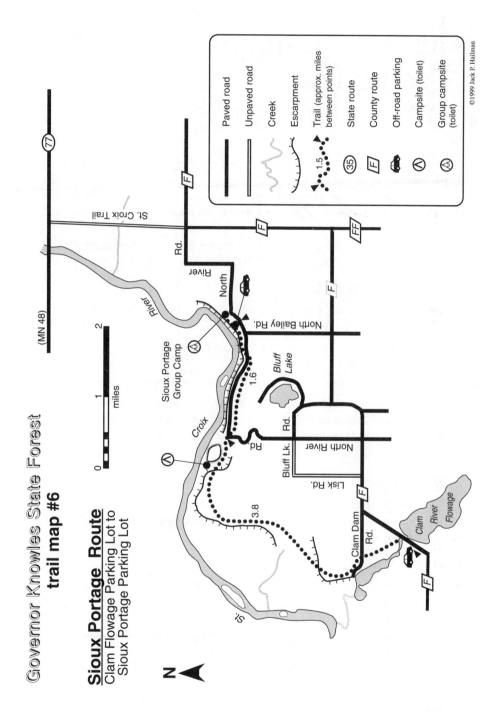

Legend:
- Paved road
- Unpaved road
- Creek
- Escarpment
- Trail (approx. miles between points)
- (35) State route
- F County route
- Off-road parking
- Campsite (toilet)
- Group campsite (toilet)

©1999 Jack P. Hailman

47

Ice Age National Scenic Trail

In the Northwest Region

The westernmost completed segment of the Ice Age Trail that is suitable for backpacking runs through lovely glacial topography in state and county lands near the middle of the Northwest region. Because these areas are little known except to hunters and fishermen, they offer the hiker virtually deserted trails.

LOCATION. Northwest region, coordinates B/C-4 on the official state highway map (Polk, Burnett, Washburn, and Barron Counties).

RATING. 🌲🌲🌲🌲

🌲 **Scenery:** the hills and lakes, especially of the McKenzie Creek area, are pleasant

🌲 **Quiet:** in all sections you can easily camp more than a mile from paved roads

🌲 **Trails:** at least 10 miles of trail accessible from camping places

🌲 **Solitude:** unlikely to meet parties on the trail except during hunting season, but fishermen will be encountered at lakes, and perhaps traffic and other people at road crossings

🌲 **Interest:** glacial topography, many birds

ENTRANCE FEE. None.

CAMPING. Trail camping (no campgrounds or established campsites). We could not find a public source of drinking water near any section of the trail.

PERMIT AND RESERVATIONS. None.

CONTACT INFORMATION. Ice Age Park & Trail Foundation of Wisconsin, Inc., 207 E. Buffalo St., Suite 515, Milwaukee, WI 53202-5712; phone: 800/227-0046; e-mail: cthisted@sbtsi.com. The office can put you in touch with the current coordinator of the Blue Hills Chapter, which has responsibility for this section of trail. *Also,* Ice Age National Scenic Trail, National Park Service, 700 Rayovac Dr., Suite 100, Madison, WI 53711; phone: 608/264-5610.

FINDING THE TRAIL. The southwestern end of the trail is on Polk County Highway O a little north of State Highway 48 (see trail map

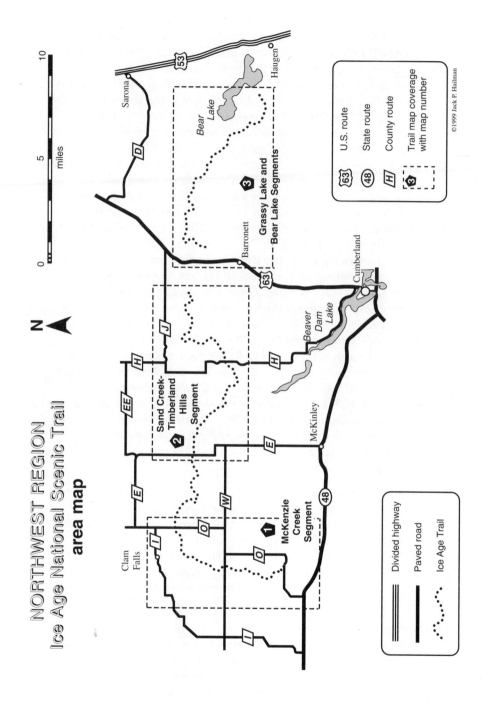

NORTHWEST REGION
Ice Age National Scenic Trail
area map

N

0   5   10
miles

53

Sarona

D

Haugen

Bear Lake

3

Barronett

Grassy Lake and Bear Lake Segments

63

H

J

H

EE

Sand Creek-Timberland Hills Segment

2

Beaver Dam Lake

Cumberland

E

McKinley

E

W

O

I

O

McKenzie Creek Segment

1

Clam Falls

I

48

I

63 U.S. route

48 State route

H County route

3 Trail map coverage with map number

Divided highway

Paved road

Ice Age Trail

© 1999 Jack P. Hailman

#1). There is a large parking lot and large sign at the trailhead. The **McKenzie Creek** segment (trail map #1) can also be accessed from a number of other paved and unpaved roads; all crossings have off-road parking areas. On Polk County Highway W the parking area is about 100 yards east of the trail rather than at the crossing itself.

The **Sand Creek-Timberland** segment (trail map #2) is considerably more difficult to access, and there are fewer parking areas at road crossings. We were unable to find the trail crossing on Polk County Highway E, the point where the trail comes in to 1 1/2 Ave. from the west, or the eastern terminus on Leech Lake Rd. The point where the trail meets the eastern end of 1 1/2 Ave., however, is obvious, as is the crossing of County Highway H on the Burnett-Barron county line, and the Timberland Hills ski area, which has an outhouse at the parking lot.

The **Grassy Lake** and **Bear Lake** segments (trail map #3) have long stretches without road access, and nowhere does the trail cross a paved road. *Warning:* The trail follows a primitive road running east to Leaman Lake from Leaman Lake Rd.; we deem this road suitable only for four-wheel drive vehicles, especially in wet weather. The best access is on 30th Ave., where the trail runs directly through the parking lot. At the southeastern end, the trail traverses property owned by the Boy Scouts of America. We were unable to find the terminus on Barron County Highway VV.

Trailheads are marked with yellow metal signs, usually about waist high, nailed to posts. In some places larger, fancier signs have been erected. If signs have been vandalized, look for rectangular yellow paint blazes on tree trunks to confirm that you are on the Ice Age Trail.

BACKGROUND NOTES.   The Ice Age Trail was the brainchild of Ray Zillmer of Milwaukee in the 1950s, but it was not until the fall of 1980 that Congress made it a national scenic trail. To be more than 1,000 miles when completed, the finished trail currently exists in bits and pieces totaling 400 miles or so. The two open sections in our Northwest region run mainly through county forest lands, with some trail on private property and one section in the McKenzie Creek State Wildlife Area.

OUR TRAIL NOTES.   It was Saturday in late May when we stepped from the car and were greeted by an adult and an immature Bald Eagle circling overhead. A good omen, we said, and the birds did indeed turn out to be as abundant and diverse as we hoped for. The down side was ticks—and rain, which backpackers anywhere east of the Rockies can expect to encounter. The trail north from County Highway O (trail map #1) was pleasant up-and-down hiking, but the sight of McKenzie Lake was especially lovely. Here we talked with a young fisherman who caught nothing large and reasoned, "Small lake, small fish." The peaceful lake sported a couple of aluminum rowboats, an inflatable Zodiac-type boat, and a canoe, the tranquility being due to the prohibition against motorboats. A middle-aged couple brought their canoe ashore and lifted it into the back of their truck, then, seeing our packs, asked us if we were actually backpacking. "But are there any campsites?" asked the woman. Jack answered with a shrug, and Liz explained that all we needed was a small flat area for our little tent. We found such a site, and after setting up camp, took a hike farther north along the trail in the failing light until rain chased us back. Bedtime was when we discovered that the few ticks pulled from our clothing during the day constituted merely the tip of this arachnid iceberg. It was a long night punctuated by expelling ticks from the tent, and we walked out in the surprisingly chilly morning to breakfast in our car—warm, dry, and tick-free.

Flora. At this latitude in eastern Wisconsin conifers of the north woods abound, but here in the western part of the state one finds mixed hardwood forests. We noted trees such as Sugar Maple, American Basswood, Quaking Aspen, and Paper Birch. The only conifer was Eastern White Pine: scattered and inconspicuous individuals south of McKenzie Lake, but some impressively large trees along the trail between the unpaved access road and the bridge over McKenzie Creek to the north. The woods contained small mushrooms with bicolored caps: orange-tan in the center with yellow-tan around the edge. Mosses clung to rocks, horsetails dotted an area near the wooden bridge over a stream a little north of County Highway O, Shining Clubmoss grew at a few places along the trail, and we found Bracken, Maidenhair, and other ferns. Some miscellaneous higher plants not (yet?) in flower were Stinging Nettle, Red Raspberry, and Cow-parsnip. Most of all, though, we enjoyed the spring wildflowers: Large-flowered (White, Large) Trillium, Large-flowered Bellwort, Wild Lily-of-the-valley (Canada Mayflower), Jump Seed, Columbine, Marsh-marigold (Cowslip), a yellow-flowered weed of the mustard family, Common Strawberry, a yellow vetch-like member of the pea family, Wild Geranium, Downy Yellow Violet, and Starflower.

Fauna. Let's face up to it immediately: little ticks and big ticks; red ticks, black ticks, and brown ticks; fast ticks and slow ticks; ticks where you see them and ticks where you don't. Neither of us seems yet to have come down with Lyme disease, Rocky Mountain spotted fever, or any other tick-borne malady, so we take it as a zoological rather than medical experience. We encountered virtually no mosquitoes, and indeed the insect of most interest was a very dark dragonfly hunting less than an inch off the ground along the trail. Also foraging on the trail was an impressively large bumblebee. A tiny "froglet" was probably a Wood Frog; one Northern Chorus Frog sang in a marsh the trail passed; voices of Gray Treefrogs filled the night air. We found deer tracks in the mud underfoot, and encountered one Least Chipmunk. The birds were incredible. Here is our surely incomplete list: Double-crested Cormorant, Great Blue Heron, Canada Goose, ducks that whizzed by overhead, Bald Eagle, Ruffed Grouse, Mourning Dove, Common Nighthawk, Belted Kingfisher, Yellow-bellied Sapsucker, Hairy Woodpecker, Pileated Woodpecker, Eastern Wood-Pewee, Great Crested Flycatcher, Red-eyed Vireo, Blue Jay, American Crow, Tree Swallow, Black-capped Chickadee, White-breasted Nuthatch, Veery, Yellow Warbler, Chestnut-sided Warbler, Black-throated Blue Warbler, American Redstart, Ovenbird, Common Yellowthroat, Chipping Sparrow, Song Sparrow, Rose-breasted Grosbeak, Indigo Bunting, Red-winged Blackbird, and American Goldfinch.

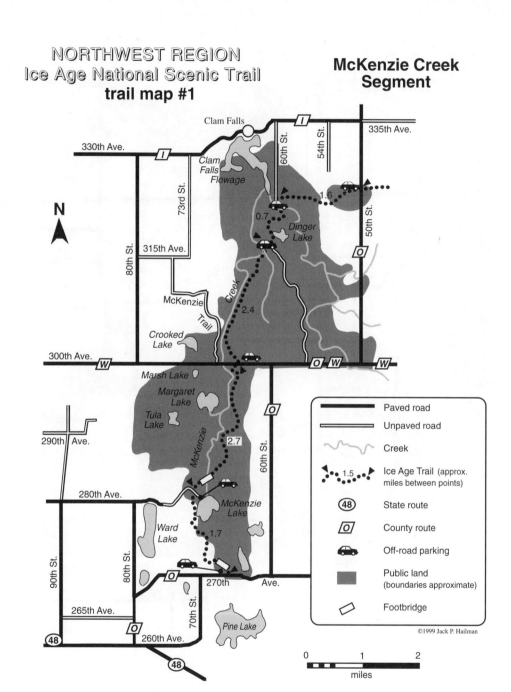

McKenzie Creek
Segment

Clam Falls

330th Ave.

I

I

335th Ave.

60th St.

54th St.

Clam
Falls
Flowage

73rd St.

N

1.6

0.7

315th Ave.

80th St.

Dinger
Lake

O

50th St.

McKenzie

Creek

2.4

Trail

Crooked
Lake

300th Ave.

W

O W

W

Marsh Lake

Margaret
Lake

Tula
Lake

McKenzie

O

2.7

290th Ave.

60th St.

280th Ave.

McKenzie
Lake

Ward
Lake

1.7

90th St.

80th St.

O

270th   Ave.

70th St.

265th Ave.

O

Pine Lake

48

260th Ave.

48

Paved road	
Unpaved road	
Creek	
1.5	Ice Age Trail (approx. miles between points)
48	State route
O	County route
🚗	Off-road parking
	Public land (boundaries approximate)
▱	Footbridge

©1999 Jack P. Hailman

0   1   2

miles

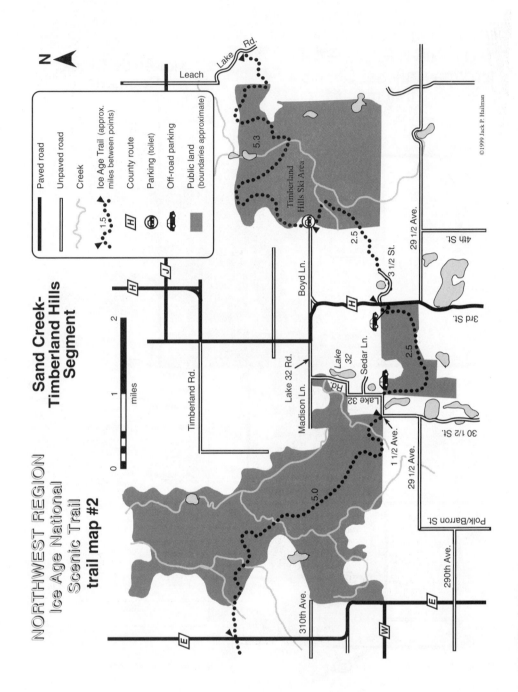

NORTHWEST REGION
Ice Age National
Scenic Trail
trail map #2

**Sand Creek-
Timberland Hills
Segment**

N

Legend:
- Paved road
- Unpaved road
- Creek
- Ice Age Trail (approx. miles between points)
- County route
- H — Parking (toilet)
- Off-road parking
- Public land (boundaries approximate)

miles
0   1   2

©1999 Jack P. Hailman

Leach
Lake Rd.

Timberland
Hills Ski Area
5.3
2.5

Boyd Ln.
3 1/2 St.
29 1/2 Ave.
4th St.
3rd St.

H
J
H

Timberland Rd.
Lake 32 Rd.
Madison Ln.
Lake 32
Sedar Ln.
Lake 32 Rd.
2.5
30 1/2 St.
1 1/2 Ave.
29 1/2 Ave.

5.0

310th Ave.
Polk/Barron St.
290th Ave.

E
W
E

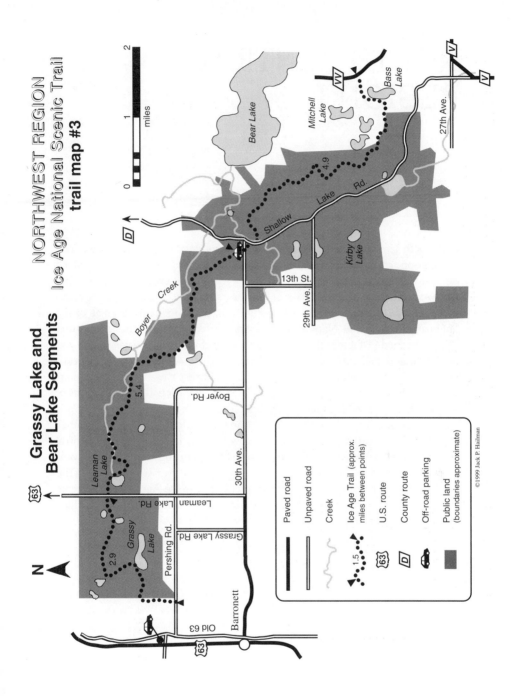

NORTHWEST REGION
Ice Age National Scenic Trail
trail map #3

Grassy Lake and
Bear Lake Segments

Legend:
- Paved road
- Unpaved road
- Creek
- Ice Age Trail (approx. miles between points)
- 1.5
- 63 U.S. route
- D County route
- Off-road parking
- Public land (boundaries approximate)

©1999 Jack P. Hailman

NORTH CENTRAL
REGION I

The North Central region gets the nod as offering the most numerous and diverse opportunities for backpacking of the six geographic regions into which we have divided Wisconsin. After all, with a national lakeshore, a national forest, two national scenic trails, two state forests, and a state park offering backpacking, what more could one ask for? Indeed, the Chequamegon side of the Chequamegon-Nicolet National Forest alone offers so many possibilities that we have accorded it a separate chapter following this one. In the very north you can find island backpacking on four of the islands in Apostle Islands National Lakeshore. In the northwest, Brule River State Forest has a ski-trail area suitable for backpacking when the white stuff is gone, and recently built sections of the North Country National Scenic Trail. East of the national forest land is beautiful Copper Falls State Park, where the backpacking sites are on another segment of the North Country Trail. Below the middle of the North Central region is Flambeau River State Forest, which has north and south ski-trail complexes connected by a linear trail along the lovely Flambeau River. Finally, in the southwestern part of the region are segments of the Ice Age National Scenic Trail that run through a county forest and other public lands where backpacking is off the beaten track.

NORTH CENTRAL REGION

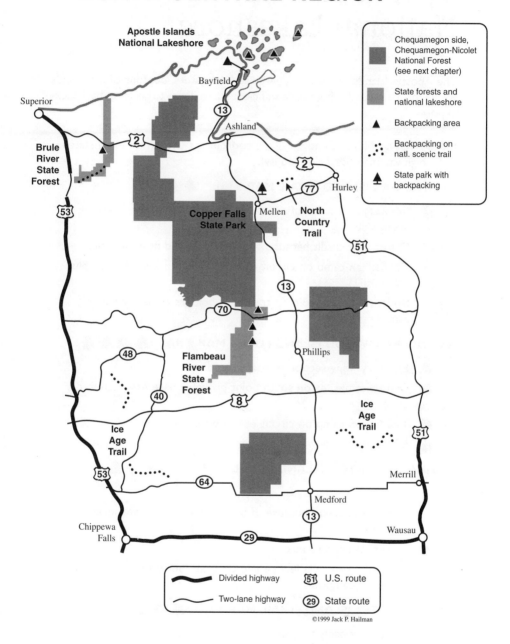

Apostle Islands National Lakeshore

Bayfield

Superior

13

Ashland

Brule River State Forest

53

2

2

77

Hurley

Mellen

North Country Trail

Copper Falls State Park

51

70

13

48

Flambeau River State Forest

40

Phillips

8

Ice Age Trail

51

Ice Age Trail

53

64

Merrill

Medford

13

Chippewa Falls

29

Wausau

Legend:

Chequamegon side, Chequamegon-Nicolet National Forest (see next chapter)

State forests and national lakeshore

▲ Backpacking area

Backpacking on natl. scenic trail

State park with backpacking

Divided highway 　　51 U.S. route

Two-lane highway 　　29 State route

©1999 Jack P. Hailman

Apostle Islands National Lakeshore

The Apostle Islands are mainly a paradise for boaters, but four of the islands within the national lakeshore have sufficient trail mileage to qualify as backpacking sites.

LOCATION. North Central region, coordinates D/E-1 on official state highway map (Bayfield County).

RATING: OAK ISLAND (TRAIL MAP #1a). 🌲 🌲 🌲

- **Scenery:** 1.5 miles of coastal trail (Sandspit) and an overlook on north side
- **Quiet:** half credit because of boats anchored near campsites
- **Trails:** can camp on circuit of more than 5 miles (Sandspit plus Loop trails)
- **Solitude:** few people on trails, but boaters come ashore at campsites

RATING: BASSWOOD ISLAND (TRAIL MAP #1b). 🌲 🌲 🌲 🌲

- **Scenery:** long section of coastal trail
- **Quiet:** campsites on south point probably have few anchored boats
- **Trails:** can camp on circuit of more than 5 miles
- **Solitude:** unlikely to encounter more than 2 parties per day

RATING: STOCKTON ISLAND (TRAIL MAP #2). 🌲 🌲 🌲

- **Scenery:** coastal trails
- **Quiet:** half credit because of probability of boats anchored near campsites
- **Trails:** at least 10 miles of trail
- **Solitude:** probably few people on trails, but boaters may come ashore at campsites

RATING: OUTER ISLAND (TRAIL MAP #3). 🌲 🌲 🌲

- **Quiet:** probably few boats anchor at Sand Point
- **Solitude:** unlikely to encounter more than 2 parties per day
- **Interest:** only backpacking island with a lighthouse

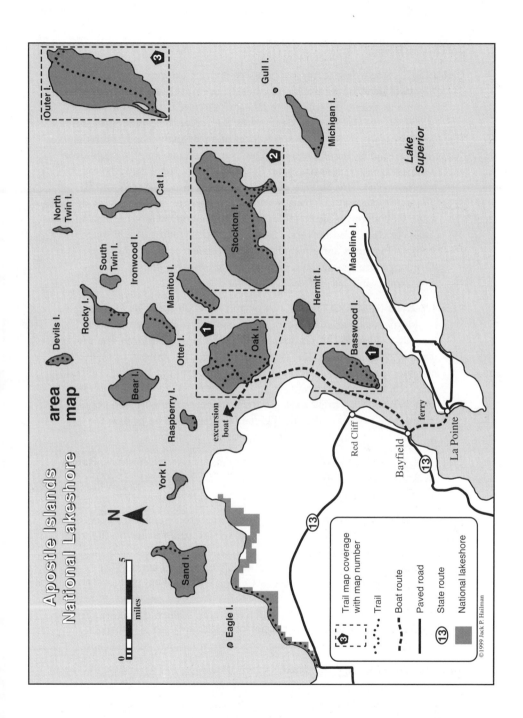

Apostle Islands
National Lakeshore

area map

N

0 miles 5

Sand I.

Eagle I.

York I.

Raspberry I.

Bear I.

Devils I.

Rocky I.

Otter I.

North Twin I.

South Twin I.

Ironwood I.

Manitou I.

Cat I.

Oak I.

excursion boat

Hermit I.

Stockton I.

Outer I.

Gull I.

Michigan I.

Basswood I.

Red Cliff

Bayfield

La Pointe

ferry

Madeline I.

Lake Superior

1

2

3

1

3

Trail map coverage with map number

Trail

Boat route

Paved road

State route

National lakeshore

13

©1999 Jack P. Hailman

59

ENTRANCE FEE. None.

CAMPING. According to the national lakeshore's camping brochure, "limited wilderness camping is available on most islands," but there are many restricted areas. The lakeshore's newspaper-like brochure notes that wilderness campers "must be prepared to pitch their tents among the trees where there is little open or flat ground and biting insects tend to be numerous." The four islands deemed suitable here have designated campsites, and Stockton Island has a campground in addition. The Park Service divides campsites into classes A and B. Class A campsites are usually within one-quarter mile of a boat dock, have well water, a picnic table, an outhouse and (where necessary) bear-resistant food lockers. Class B campsites tend to be in more remote locations and rarely have amenities other than a fire ring. Drinking water is available on Oak and Basswood Islands and on Stockton Island but not on Outer Island.

PERMIT AND RESERVATIONS. A permit is required for any camping (wilderness or designated campsite), and it is very expensive. The permit is good for 14 consecutive days, making it a bargain for the camper who stays put for an entire vacation, but outrageously costly for the weekend backpacker. Obtain your permit at the park office in Bayfield. Advance reservations for campsites are accepted in person and by phone up to 30 days before the trip; there is no additional charge for reservations, but the camping fee must be paid at the time of reservation (by credit card for phone reservations).

CONTACT INFORMATION. Apostle Islands National Lakeshore, Route 1, Box 4, Bayfield, WI 54814; phone: 715/779-3397; fax: 715/779-3049; e-mail: apis_webmaster@nps.gov.

SPECIAL INFORMATION. Only Oak and Stockton Islands are served by regularly scheduled commercial boat service, the former by the Inner Island Shuttle and the latter by the Islander. For current information on seasons of operations, daily schedules, and fees contact the Apostle Islands Cruise Service, P.O. Box 691, Bayfield, WI 54814 (phone: 800/323-7619 or 715/779-3925). Reservations are recommended, and are held until a half hour before departure. The cruise service also offers private, six-passenger charter shuttles to any island.

FINDING THE TRAIL. Bayfield is on State Highway 13, where the Inner Island Shuttle and the Islander leave from docks a block south of the dock for the Madeline Island ferry. Private charters of the cruise service can be arranged from Bayfield, Washburn, or Ashland. Stockton Island has two boat docks: in Quarry Bay and Presque Isle

Bay. The other three islands treated here have one boat dock each. The trail systems begin directly from the docks on all four islands.

BACKGROUND NOTES. The Apostle Islands National Lakeshore was created by Congress in 1970 to include 20 of the 22 islands. In 1986, Long Island (off Ashland) was added. The basin in which Lake Superior lies today has, off and on for eons, been the bottom of huge lakes and inland seas. Over those ages, sediments of sand have lithified into sandstones. Recently (within the last three million years or so), continental glaciers have come and gone several times, scouring passages through the sandstone bedrock and leaving mesa- and hill-like structures that are today's Apostle Islands. The surface of Lake Superior is about 600 feet above sea level, and some islands rise well above this (the high point on Oak Island is at 1,081 feet above sea level). Almost all of the islands are completely wooded with a mixture of boreal spruce-fir forest and northern hardwood forest. People are sometimes surprised to learn that large mammals such as Whitetail Deer and Black Bear inhabit many of the islands, but they can swim between islands, and it is no feat for deer, in particular, to cross the ice from the mainland in winter months.

OUR TRAIL NOTES. We were put ashore from the cruise boat at the dock of Oak Island in early afternoon on a Saturday in late June. We set out immediately for campsite #6 at the northern end of the island, climbing gently and then dipping into ravines, only to climb again, eventually passing near the island's high point and descending to the other side. After two hours of leisurely hiking we arrived at the campsite, which consisted of a fire ring and a metal box to keep bears out of campers' food. (The Park Service claims the site has a picnic table, but there was no table when we camped there.) Several yachts were anchored offshore, and while we cooked dinner, motorboats brought the owners and their canines to shore near us for "dog walks." A cheeky Whitetail doe strolled through camp. We turned in early, nicely tired from the day's hike, but more motorboats brought ashore men who stood drinking beer and talking loudly just a few feet from our tent. It rained very hard during the night, and on the hike out in the morning, we detoured to the overlook and took some snapshots of the lovely view. The cruise boat arrived ahead of its scheduled time, so we left the island not long after the noon hour.

    Flora. Perhaps the most interesting plants we found along the trail were not one but five kinds of parasitic or saprophytic flowering plants, which lack green leaves because such plants are nourished by the roots of a host plant or by decaying organic matter in the ground: Striped Coralroot, Spotted Coralroot, Indian-pipe, Pinesap,

Approaching Oak Island by boat, Apostle Islands National Lakeshore

and Squawroot. There were also various kinds of fungi, including a yellow mushroom, purple mushrooms, hoof fungus growing on tree trunks, and a remarkably curly, orange-yellow fungus growing out of the ground. Mosses covered the rocks; nonflowering vascular plants included horsetails, at least two kinds of clubmosses, and some interesting ferns. Wildflowers did not abound, but we did find Colicroot (Stargrass), Common (Tall) Buttercup, May-apple (Mandrake) in fruit, Thimbleberry in flower, and Orange Hawkweed. Paper Birch and Sugar Maple dominated much of the forest, but there were also Eastern Hemlock, Balsam Fir, Northern White-Cedar (Arborvitae), Quaking Aspen, Mountain Maple, and huge oaks whose trunks Jack could not encircle with his arms.

Fauna. Aside from the deer in our campsite, the only mammal we encountered was the noisy Red Squirrel. Bird life in the forest was sparse, but open areas near the shore augmented the avifauna: Common Loon, Double-crested Cormorant, Common Merganser (two females on the water), Spotted Sandpiper, Herring Gull, Belted Kingfisher, Pileated Woodpecker, Eastern Wood-Pewee, Least Flycatcher, Red-eyed Vireo, Blue Jay, Winter Wren (in beautiful full song), Swainson's Thrush, American Robin, Cedar Waxwing, Black-throated Green Warbler, Black-and-white Warbler, American Redstart, Ovenbird, Rose-breasted Grosbeak, Baltimore Oriole, House Finch, and others. The lone amphibian we found was a large American Toad.

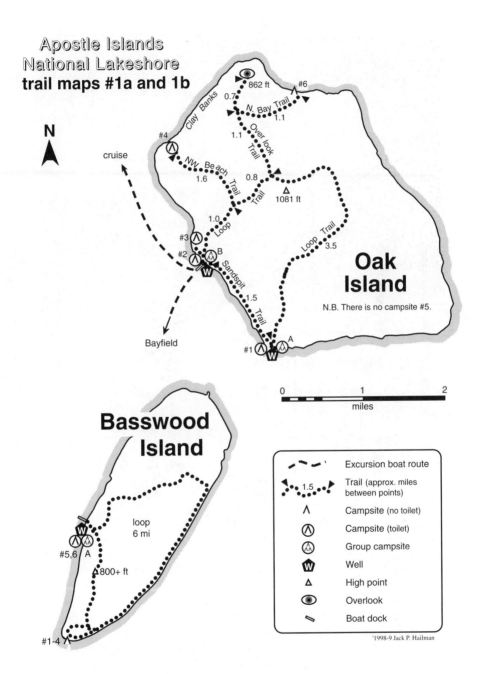

Apostle Islands
National Lakeshore
trail maps #1a and 1b

N

cruise

Bayfield

**Oak
Island**

Clay Banks

862 ft

0.7

N. Bay Trail

1.1

#6

#4

1.1

Overlook Trail

NW Beach Trail

1.6

0.8

△
1081 ft

1.0

Loop

Trail

#3

Loop Trail

3.5

#2

B

Sandspit

W

1.5

Trail

N.B. There is no campsite #5.

#1

A

W

**Basswood
Island**

W

#5,6 A

loop
6 mi

△ 800+ ft

#1-4

0			1		2

miles

- – – –   Excursion boat route
- •• 1.5 ••   Trail (approx. miles between points)
- ∧   Campsite (no toilet)
- ⊕   Campsite (toilet)
- ⊛   Group campsite
- W   Well
- △   High point
- ◉   Overlook
- ╱   Boat dock

'1998-9 Jack P. Hailman

63

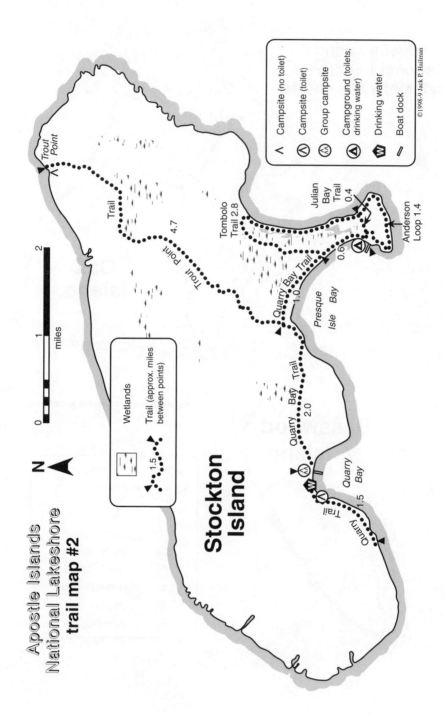

Apostle Islands National Lakeshore trail map #2

N

2 1 0
miles

Trout Point

Trail

4.7

Trout Point Trail

Tombolo Trail 2.8

Julian Bay Trail 0.4

Anderson Loop 1.4

Quarry Bay Trail 1.0

Presque Isle Bay

Quarry Bay Trail 2.0

Quarry Bay

Quarry Trail

1.5

Stockton Island

Wetlands

Trail (approx. miles between points)

1.5

∧ Campsite (no toilet)

⊗ Campsite (toilet)

Ⓦ Group campsite

Ⓐ Campground (toilets, drinking water)

Ⓦ Drinking water

— Boat dock

©1998-9 Jack P. Hailman

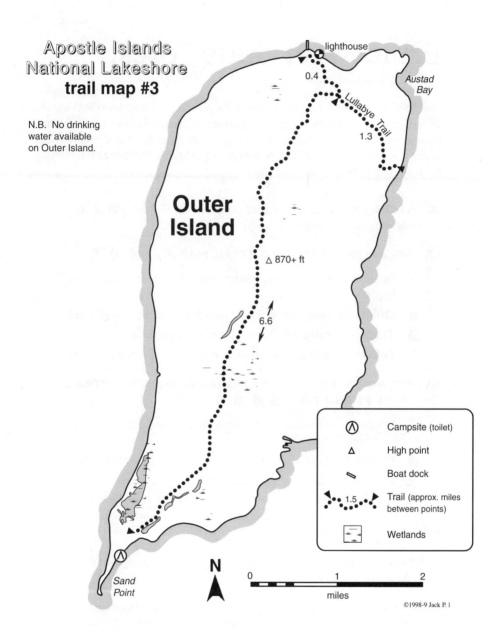

Apostle Islands National Lakeshore
trail map #3

N.B. No drinking water available on Outer Island.

lighthouse

Austad Bay

0.4

Lullabye Trail

1.3

Outer Island

△ 870+ ft

6.6

Ⓐ	Campsite (toilet)
△	High point
▬	Boat dock
◄••1.5••►	Trail (approx. miles between points)
🗺	Wetlands

N

0   1   2
miles

©1998-9 Jack P. I

Sand Point

Brule River State Forest

The Bois Brule River is known as one of the premier trout streams in the state as well as one of the best canoeing routes, but its backpacking possibilities should not be overlooked. A ski-trail complex offers solitude to the wilderness camper. Sections of the North Country National Scenic Trail are also attractive because of the scenery and wildlife.

LOCATION. North Central region, coordinates C-2 on official state highway map (Douglas County).

RATING: AFTER HOURS TRAIL (TRAIL MAP #1).

 Scenery: half credit for pleasant vista overlooking Little Joe Rapids

 Quiet: can camp more than a mile from nearest paved road

 Trails: can camp on circuit of more than 5 miles

 Solitude: unlikely to encounter more than 2 parties per day

RATING: NORTH COUNTRY NATIONAL SCENIC TRAIL (TRAIL MAPS #2 AND #3).

 Scenery: overlooks river from a high ground, features park-like pine area

 Quiet: can camp more than a mile from nearest paved road

 Solitude: unlikely to encounter more than 2 parties per day

 Interest: both wolves and coyotes heard at night by backpacker; also, southern end is historical portage path with monuments along the trail

ENTRANCE FEE. None; state sticker required for campgrounds and Bois picnic area only.

CAMPING. Wilderness camping for backpackers (no campsites). Tents must be set out of sight from rivers, trails, and roads. (Camping by hunters in deer season is subject to other restrictions. Canoeists must use designated campsites within campgrounds.) For the After Hours Trail, drinking water is available at a wayside where U.S. Highway 2 crosses the Bois Brule River. For the North Country Trail, water is available at the picnic area on Upper St. Croix Lake and at the Highland Town Hall near the trail on County Highway S (trail map #2).

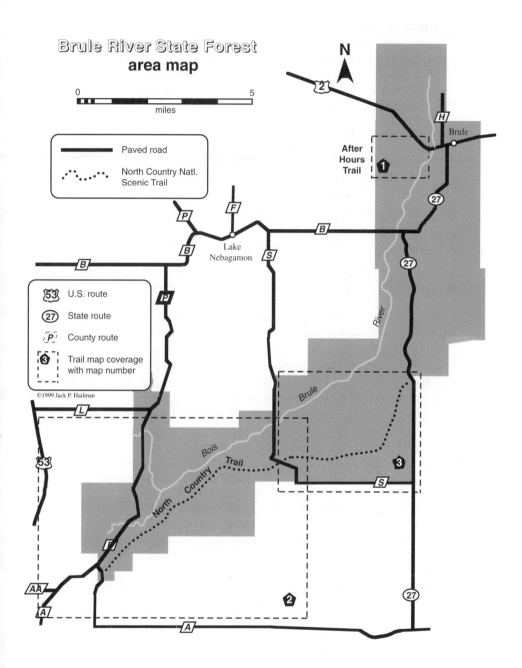

Brule River State Forest
area map

0   5

miles

Paved road

North Country Natl.
Scenic Trail

N

After
Hours
Trail **①**

Brule

H

2

27

27

P

F

B

Lake
Nebagamon

S

B

B

P

River

Brule

Bois

North Country Trail

53

L

53   U.S. route

27   State route

P   County route

3   Trail map coverage
     with map number

©1999 Jack P. Hailman

③

S

Γ

AA

A

②

A

27

PERMIT AND RESERVATIONS. Free camping permit required. Obtain permit at forest office, which is found by driving south from U.S. Highway 2 on Ranger Rd. The office is past the campground, about 1.5 miles south of the wayside on U.S. 2. The office is ordinarily open during business hours on weekdays, so writing or phoning ahead for a permit is wise.

CONTACT INFORMATION. Brule River State Forest, 6250 S. Ranger Rd., Brule, WI 54820; phone: 715/372-5678; fax: 715/372-4836.
North Country National Scenic Trail. North Country Trail Association, 49 Monroe Center NW, Suite 200B, Grand Rapids, MI 49503; phone: 616/454-5506; web site www.northcountrytrail.org. *Also,* National Park Service, North Country National Scenic Trail, 700 Rayovac Dr., Suite 100, Madison, WI 53711; phone: 608/264-5610; web site: www.nps.gov/noco.

FINDING THE TRAIL. The **After Hours Trail** system begins at the (signed) parking lot just off U.S. Highway 2 on After Hours Rd., less than a mile west of the highway bridge over the Bois Brule River.

The completed section of the **North Country Trail** can be accessed at several points. In the southwest, near Solon Springs, the trail begins on Douglas County Highway A across from the wayside at the north end of Upper St. Croix Lake (trail map #2). Farther northeast the trail can be found by driving north from Jersett Rd. on Rifle Range Rd. or on an unnamed primitive road (trail map #2). This latter road is passable by ordinary (two-wheel drive) cars. The next road crossing is at County Highway S, where cars may be parked and water obtained at the nearby town hall. Between this point and State Highway 27 the only access point is via Motts Ravine Rd. (trail map #3). A parking lot is planned for the trailhead on Highway 27.

BACKGROUND NOTES. The Bois Brule River, sometimes called simply the Brule, should not be confused with Wisconsin's other Brule River, which runs almost east-west through the Nicolet side of the Chequamegon-Nicolet National Forest and forms part of the boundary between Michigan and Wisconsin. Both Brules are favorites of canoeists and fishermen. Brule River State Forest began with a gift of more than 4,000 acres to the state from Frederick Weyerhaeuser in 1907, after all the towering White Pines had been lumbered during the previous decade. The state forest was officially established by the legislature in 1932 and reforested by the Civilian Conservation Corps beginning in 1934.

The valley in which the Bois Brule now flows northward was carved by a river flowing south from glacial Lake Duluth, the much higher predecessor of present-day Lake Superior. The area of the ski trails is on red clay that was deposited on the bottom of the large lake of Ice Age times. The river has cut a pleasant bluff into the clay below Little Joe Overlook on the River Loop of the After Hours Trail. Three forest types occur within the state forest boundaries: cedar-spruce bog (not encountered on the ski trails), oak-pine-aspen woods, and boreal conifer forest.

The southwestern 2 miles of this section of the North Country Trail follow a path known locally as the Old Portage Trail. At least as far back as 1680, Native Americans, voyageurs, and missionaries portaged this route after paddling up the Bois Brule from Lake Superior. By putting their canoes in at the Upper St. Croix Lake, they could go all the way to the Mississippi River on the St. Croix River. Four stone monuments were erected on the trail by the Solon Springs Historical Society to commemorate some of the famous people who used the Old Portage Trail.

OUR TRAIL NOTES. Our mid-September trip on the After Hours Trail turned into a mini-adventure when we took the wrong fork at an unmarked intersection with a trail not shown on maps available to us. We believed we had turned at a trail intersection shown on the map. It became clear that we were not on the After Hours Trail complex, and the afternoon was waning, so we decided to venture onto an unmarked trail heading in the direction needed to return us to the marked trail complex. We should have retraced our steps

The portage landing at Bois Brule River, Brule River State Forest

instead, but decided to chance the direct route rather than be overtaken by darkness. We recommend that readers do as we say, not as we do (see Introduction).

The trail gave out after a half mile, but the die had been cast; we continued dead reckoning cross-country without the aid of the sun's direction in the increasingly heavily overcast skies. (We had a compass but put our trust in Jack's uncommonly good sense of direction to hold a steady bearing.) We eventually hit a hunter's trail, amazingly enough right where a bow hunter was standing. He said we were headed in the right direction but it was still a long way, so we accepted his offer of a ride, walked to his truck, threw our packs in the back, and let him chauffeur us back to the trailhead. We set off once again, taking a surer route, and managed to erect the tent before the skies let loose. The next day, we hiked a pleasant circuit that included the overlook above the Little Joe Rapids.

Flora. Bracken Fern was everywhere, all dried up and a lovely deep brown in color—typical of "edge" habitat along ski trails and back roads. The three prevalent conifers were Eastern White Pine, Eastern Hemlock, and Balsam Fir, and we noted both Quaking and Bigtooth Aspen among the hardwoods. Our notes recorded no wildflowers in this, the second half of September.

Fauna. Grouse hunters must love this area, as we seemed to kick up a Ruffed Grouse from along the trail every 10 minutes or so. Canada Geese were frequently honking overhead, as they had been all through the night. We found that the best stretch of trail for forest birds was the River Loop (see trail map #1), especially the southern part where it is near the river. Among the birds we found were Belted Kingfisher, Downy Woodpecker, Northern Flicker, Black-capped Chickadee, both Red- and White-breasted Nuthatches, Golden-crowned Kinglet, Hermit Thrush, American Robin, Yellow-rumped and Palm Warblers, and Scarlet Tanager. The mammal in evidence was the noisy little Red Squirrel, and the amphibian ilk was represented by an American Toad and a ranid frog (probably a young Wood Frog) found on the trail.

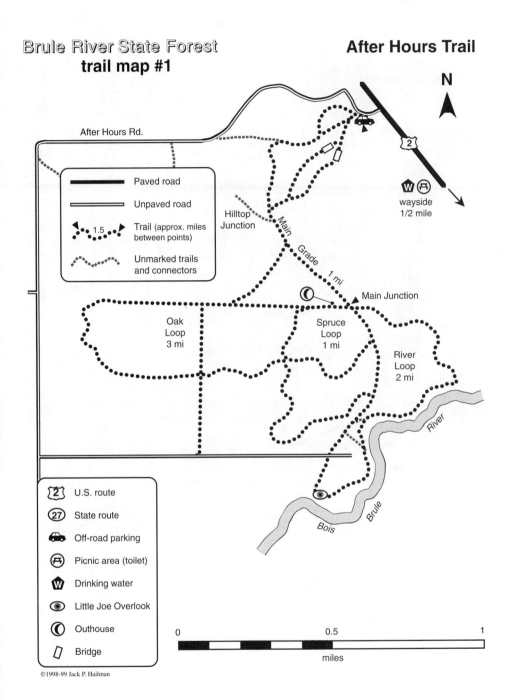

Brule River State Forest
trail map #1

After Hours Trail

N

After Hours Rd.

2

wayside
1/2 mile

Legend:
- Paved road
- Unpaved road
- 1.5 — Trail (approx. miles between points)
- Unmarked trails and connectors

Hilltop
Junction

Main Grade

1 mi

Main Junction

Oak
Loop
3 mi

Spruce
Loop
1 mi

River
Loop
2 mi

River

Brule

Bois

Symbol key:
- 2 — U.S. route
- 27 — State route
- Off-road parking
- Picnic area (toilet)
- W — Drinking water
- Little Joe Overlook
- Outhouse
- Bridge

©1998-99 Jack P. Hailman

0   0.5   1
miles

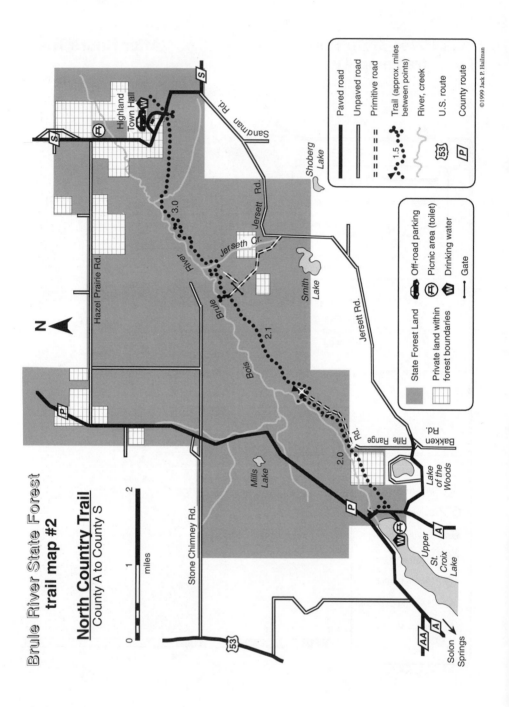

Brule River State Forest
trail map #2

North Country Trail
County A to County S

©1999 Jack P. Hailman

72

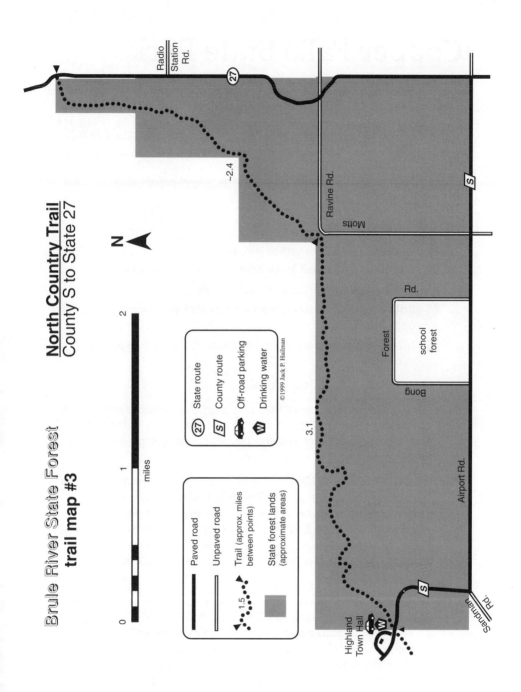

Brule River State Forest
trail map #3

North Country Trail
County S to State 27

N

miles
0   1   2

Paved road

Unpaved road

Trail (approx. miles
between points)

1.5

State forest lands
(approximate areas)

27 State route

S County route

Off-road parking

W Drinking water

©1999 Jack P. Hailman

Radio
Station
Rd.

27

~2.4

Ravine Rd.

Motts

3.1

Bong   Forest   Rd.

school
forest

Airport Rd.

S

Sandman
Rd.

Highland
Town Hall

W

S

73

Copper Falls State Park

If you enjoy waterfalls and river gorges, Copper Falls State Park is the place to go in Wisconsin. The two backpacking campsites—reached by hiking the North Country National Scenic Trail—are nicely situated on the Bad River, downstream from the various falls and across from scenic sandstone ledges.

LOCATION. North Central region, coordinates D/E-2/3 on official state highway map (Ashland County).

RATING. 🌲🌲🌲🌲

🌲 **Scenery:** spectacular waterfalls, gorge

🌲 **Quiet:** campsite well away from high use area in park

🌲 **Trails:** at least 5 miles of walkable trails

🌲 **Solitude:** unlikely to meet anyone on trail to campsite, but other trails heavily used

🌲 **Interest:** best display of bedrock geology of any backpacking area in the state

ENTRANCE FEE. State sticker required.

CAMPING. Only at designated sites (see map). An outhouse serves both campsites, which are located in the far northern part of the park. Each campsite has a fire ring (no tables). Drinking water is available at the picnic area and campgrounds.

PERMIT AND RESERVATIONS. Permit required for a specific campsite. Obtain a permit at the park office (HQ on the map). Advance reservations of campsites are accepted by the state's phone reservation service at 888/947-2757 (9 A.M. to 10 P.M. weekdays and 9 A.M. to 6 P.M. weekends) or on the web at www.wiparks.net; reservation fee charged. Reservations may be a good idea for this much visited park.

CONTACT INFORMATION. Copper Falls State Park, Rt. 1, Box 17AA, Mellen, WI 54546; phone: 715/274-5123; fax: 715/274-2325.

North Country National Scenic Trail. North Country Trail Association, 49 Monroe Center NW, Suite 200B, Grand Rapids, MI 49503; phone: 616/454-5506; web site: www.northcountrytrail.org. *Also,* National Park Service, North Country National Scenic Trail, 700 Rayovac Dr., Suite 100, Madison, WI 53711; phone: 608/264-5610; web site: www.nps.gov/noco.

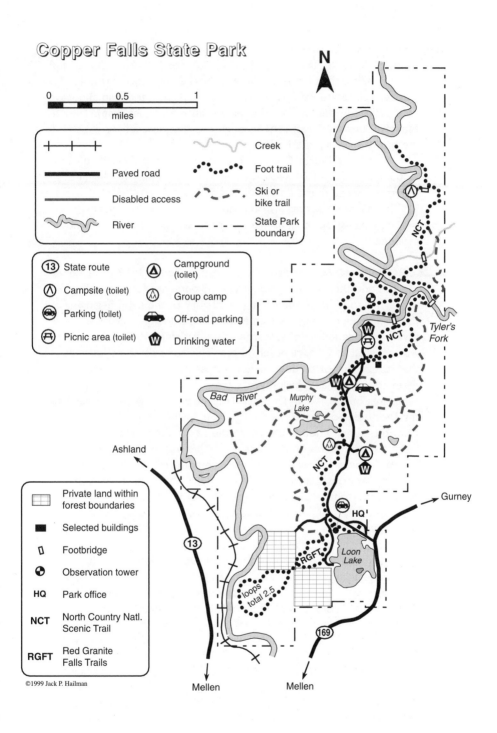

Copper Falls State Park

N

0   0.5   1
miles

┼┼┼┼		Creek
Paved road		Foot trail
Disabled access		Ski or bike trail
River		State Park boundary

(13) State route		Campground (toilet)	
Campsite (toilet)		Group camp	
Parking (toilet)		Off-road parking	
Picnic area (toilet)		Drinking water	

NCT

Tyler's Fork

Bad River

Murphy Lake

Ashland

Gurney

HQ

Loon Lake

RGFT

loops total 2.5

(13)

(169)

Mellen   Mellen

Private land within forest boundaries	
Selected buildings	
Footbridge	
Observation tower	
HQ	Park office
NCT	North Country Natl. Scenic Trail
RGFT	Red Granite Falls Trails

©1999 Jack P. Hailman

75

FINDING THE TRAIL. From State Highway 13 at Mellen (about 25 miles south of Ashland), take State Highway 169 north toward Gurney for about 2 miles, then left onto the well-marked entrance road of Copper Falls State Park. Drive to the end of the park road and leave your vehicle in the lot near the maintenance area (see map). The **North Country Trail** runs through the area; just follow the trail to the bridge over Tyler's Fork.

Note: The North Country Trail is complete and certified from Copper Falls State Park west through the community of Mellen to Kornstead Road in the Lower North part of Chequamegon (Chapter 3). That section runs mainly on roads and over private lands where explicit permission to camp has not been secured, so we have not included it.

BACKGROUND NOTES. The park was established in 1929 to preserve the falls and their unique geological environment. You can walk through a good bit of the geological history of the park, beginning at the backpacking campsites (see map), where, looking across the Bad River, you see ledges of sandstone that was deposited when this area was covered by an ancient inland sea. This sea existed so long ago that its age cannot be determined with accuracy, but it certainly dates to more than a billion years ago. Walking south from the campsites on the North Country Trail, at the fork go right (west) to the footbridge over the river gorge near Devil's Gate. Downstream from this constriction in the gorge the Bad River exposes shales that were also laid down on the bottom of that inland sea, whereas upriver at Devil's Gate you see conglomerate rock—lots of small stones of various sizes cemented together. These three kinds of rocks (sandstone, shale, and conglomerate) were lithified from the ancient lake-bottom sediments of sand, mud, and rocky sand, respectively.

Upstream of Devil's Gate the Bad River is relentlessly cutting back into lavas, some reddish ones near Devil's Gate and others black. These lavas (properly called basalts) were deposited a billion years ago over the yet older rocks you have seen exposed downstream. Fissures opened up in the earth and extruded unimaginably immense volumes of lava—so much lava that the earth sagged under the weight and created the huge basin in which Lake Superior lies today. If you turn around and walk back past the fork to the bridge over Tyler's Fork, you see Brownstone Falls, where the water plunges over the basalt into the gorge. Tyler's Fork, with less water than the main river, has not cut much of a gorge of its own, but a little upstream the Tyler's Fork Cascades are carving back a smaller drop in the black basalt. Continuing on toward the picnic grounds, you see Copper Falls, where the Bad River's gorge begins in the thick basalt. The north-flowing Bad River and Tyler's Fork apparently began cutting paths down through this solidified lava as much as 200 million years ago, so the relatively short gorge is a testament to the hardness of this black basalt.

Finally, in the bluffs near the concession stand you can see red clays. These and other materials such as boulders were deposited as recently as tens of thousands of years ago, on top of the billion-year-old lavas. These late additions were brought by the continental glaciers that bulldozed soil and rocks from Canada, leaving them here as the ice melted back. Perhaps nowhere else in Wisconsin can you view such a long history of the formation of rock layers of so many different types.

OUR TRAIL NOTES.   It was a beautiful day in early October when we arrived at Copper Falls State Park and set out with day packs on the Red Granite Falls Trail in the southern part of the park (see map). Yes, there actually is yet another, albeit undramatic, cascade here, far from the falls seen by the vast majority of visitors. After this pleasant diversion, we walked all the trails in the Copper Falls area, including the nature trail, and climbed the observation tower. Finally, we switched to full backpacks and made the easy walk to the campsite. The night was uneventful except for the fact that a mouse somehow managed to run over the outside of our tent (we heard it) and to find Liz's boots in the vestibule. Why any animal likes to chew through laces we do not know, but we have a cat that does so, and now a mouse engaged in the same annoying behavior. Besides that, we remember this trip mainly for the amount of film Jack exposed in the two cameras he brought along, and the golden hue of the woods in fall color.

Flora. The park trails boast a variety of deciduous hardwoods; we noted Quaking Aspen, Bigtooth Aspen, Eastern Hophornbeam (Ironwood), American Basswood, Sugar Maple, birches, and oaks. A dominant conifer was Eastern Hemlock, especially along the river in damp environments, with Eastern White Pine in drier areas. We also came across the woody but low-growing Common Juniper. Nonflowering plants included mosses, horsetails (along the river), ground pines, and ferns. This late in the year we found no wildflowers in bloom.

Fauna. The color missing in the wildflower category was made up partly by the birds: Pied-billed Grebe (on Loon Lake), a *Buteo* hawk (probably Broad-winged Hawk), Yellow-bellied Sapsucker, Blue

Jay, American Crow, Common Raven, Black-capped Chickadee, White-breasted Nuthatch, Brown Creeper, Golden- and Ruby-crowned Kinglets, American Robin, White-throated Sparrow, and Dark-eyed Junco. We also saw some mammals: Whitetail Deer (in several places), Red Squirrel, Gray Squirrel, and Eastern Chipmunk.

North Country National Scenic Trail

Want to be one of the first ever to backpack on a given piece of national scenic trail? Here is your chance, because at writing we think that no one, ourselves included, has yet backpacked on the fairly recently certified North Country Trail east of Weber Lake.

LOCATION. North Central region, coordinates E-2/3 on official state highway map (Iron County).

RATING. 🌲🌲🌲

  🌲 **Scenery:** lovely woods and rocks, great viewpoint just off trail

  🌲 **Solitude:** unlikely to encounter more than 2 parties per day

  🌲 **Interest:** geologically interesting iron-bearing rocks

ENTRANCE FEE. None.

CAMPING. Wilderness camping; shelters available at two places along trail. There is a family campground at the county park on Weber Lake with designated campsites (fee charged).

PERMIT AND RESERVATIONS. None needed for wilderness camping.

CONTACT INFORMATION. North Country Trail Association, 49 Monroe Center NW, Suite 200B, Grand Rapids, MI 49503; phone: 616/454-5506; web site www.northcountrytrail.org. The office can put you in touch with the Heritage Chapter, which has responsibility for this section of trail. *Also,* National Park Service, North Country National Scenic Trail, 700 Rayovac Dr., Suite 100, Madison, WI 53711; phone: 608/264-5610; web site: www.nps.gov/noco.

FINDING THE TRAIL. The three accesses to the **North Country Trail** can be reached from State Highway 77, which runs between Hurley in the northeast and Mellen in the southwest. Find the southwest terminus of the trail at Weber Lake by taking State Highway 122 north from State 77 at Upson to County Highway E or County E west from State 77. The county park at Weber Lake can be accessed on both the south and north sides; you should take the unpaved road leading to the parking lot on the north side. The road into the park immediately forks; the parking lot is on the left fork, and just to the right of the fork is the signed trailhead.

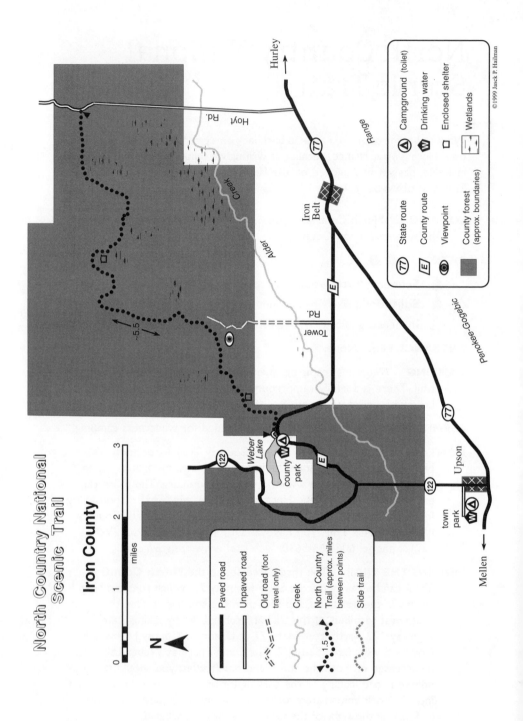

North Country National Scenic Trail

Iron County

©1999 Jack P. Hailman

Vista on North Country National Scenic Trail

Tower Road, going north from County Highway E, is passable by vehicle for only a short distance. There is room at the end to park one or two cars. You then walk the old causeway road across the valley of Alder Creek, but during wet summers, this old road may be under water. At the foot of the hills begin climbing until reaching the signed trail on the left. This side trail leads to the North Country Trail, but before going there, take the short side trail to the left, which climbs the hill to the viewpoint.

Finally, on Hoyt Road, the trail is 2 miles north of State Highway 77 and briefly follows Snowmobile Trail 6. Because other trails leave the road to the west, make certain you find North Country Trail markers before setting out on the trail.

Note: This is the only completed section of the North Country Trail between Hurley to the east and Copper Falls State Park to the west. Very likely the next section to be completed will be to the west of Upson Lake (southwest of Weber Lake).

BACKGROUND NOTES. State Highway 77 runs along the northern base of the Penokee-Gogebic range of ancient mountains, which bear the ore that gives Iron County its name. Across the valley of Alder Creek are other highlands, called ridges of Keweenawan trap rock, over which the North Country Trail runs. These ridges were formed by ancient lava flows, and the rock layers slant upward to the

81

southeast, breaking into parallel ridges (monoclines) with steep faces on the southeastern side and gentle slopes toward the northwest. The ridges are broken transversely by stream-eroded valleys. From the viewpoint (see map) you not only have a panoramic view of the Penokee-Gogebic Mountains to the southeast across the lovely Alder Creek valley, but can also see Lake Superior and the Bayfield County highlands by looking northwest along the stream valley.

OUR TRAIL NOTES. This is our only trail description based on helping to build a trail rather than backpacking along it. On a beautiful June day, we joined the Heritage Chapter of the Wisconsin North Country Trail Association for the National Trails Day hike. The chapter leaders spoiled us by dropping us off on Tower Road, from which we could access the trail and hike back to Weber Lake. The lovely woods we hiked through were shady and open underneath, giving a summery greenish tinge to everything. We took the side trail to the scenic view, where the wind was blowing so hard we had to remove our hats. This overlook was the site of many photos by hikers in our small group, including pictures of Lake Superior visible to the north. After a while, we passed a shelter—used mainly by winter skiers—which had recently been built after the old one was destroyed by vandals. The comic highlight of the day was finding a pair of cross-country skis sticking out of the bushes, as if someone

Vista on North Country National Scenic Trail

had issued his last breath at this point. The efficient organizers had a wonderful cookout waiting for us at the end of the morning hike.

The delicious meal gave us energy to start the afternoon's project of working on a new section of trail. We were assigned to help mark a projected route with flagging tape. Moving through the woods to stake out the new trail proved to be more strenuous than it looked because the terrain was very hummocky and irregular. The system worked like this: the leader scouted the route using a map and compass, two people followed close behind marking the route by tying flagging tape to trees in easily visible places, and a fourth person also with tape followed farther behind and inserted markers wherever the distance seemed to be too great for easy sighting. Two parties worked toward each other, one coming from the east and one from the west, and actually met up very close to the planned rendezvous point, thanks to outstanding map-and-compass work. Returning to our car was easy—we followed the trees we had just marked.

Building trail is harder work than routing, as we learned on a different work trip. Now we used picks, shovels, and rakes of special sorts while others wielded chain saws and other implements of destruction. The task involves more than clearing the way of vegetation. The tread must be flat, so when the trail runs along the side of a hill, you hack away at the uphill side and fill the downhill side to make the trail more level. Those rocks and roots the hiker could trip over must also be removed.

Maintenance of an already built trail requires yet another set of skills, which we acquired on a third work trip in the area. Lopping branches that have grown out to scrape the hiker is no different from trimming in a suburban yard, but then there is the brush hog. That sounds like the name of some kind of wild animal, but actually it is a machine something like a super power mower that cuts everything from grass to tree saplings. The brush hog is self-propelled, but pushing it across even the smallest stream or through mud is a physical challenge. We enjoy it all: ferreting out a route, building the trail, and maintaining the way.

Flora and fauna. We did not take natural history notes on these outings with the Heritage Chapter, but Weber Lake proved as interesting as anywhere else on the trail. On one of our trips a pair of Common Loons came rather near us, spending more time on dives than swimming on the surface. On another trip the focus was on an Osprey that continually circled above the lake searching for a fish to pounce upon.

Flambeau River State Forest

Well known to canoeists for its many miles of lovely river, Flambeau River State Forest also offers the backpacker fine opportunities for wilderness camping accessed by its multiple-use ski trails. This is a large forest, second in size among the state's properties (after Northern Highland–American Legion State Forest).

LOCATION. North Central region, coordinates D/E-4 on official state highway map (principally Sawyer County).

RATING: OXBO TRAILS (TRAIL MAP #1).

🌲 **Quiet:** can camp more than a mile from nearest paved road

🌲 **Trails:** can camp on circuit, and many miles of trail accessible from camping places

🌲 **Solitude:** unlikely to encounter more than 2 parties per day

RATING: SNUSS TRAIL (TRAIL MAP #2).

🌲 **Scenery:** half credit for occasional glimpses of Flambeau River

🌲 **Quiet:** can camp more than a mile from nearest paved road

🌲 **Trails:** at least 10 miles of trail accessible from camping places

RATING: FLAMBEAU HILLS TRAILS (TRAIL MAP #3).

🌲 **Scenery:** half credit for occasional glimpses of Flambeau River

🌲 **Quiet:** can camp more than a mile from nearest paved road

🌲 **Trails:** at least 10 miles of trail accessible from camping places

🌲 **Solitude:** unlikely to encounter more than 2 parties per day

ENTRANCE FEE. State sticker required for parking lots and other state forest facilities.

CAMPING. Wilderness camping virtually anywhere in the state forest out of sight of established trails and recreational areas. There are no established campsites available to backpackers; campsites along the Flambeau River are for use only by boaters. The state forest's information sheet "Backpack Camping" lists the Flambeau/Oxbo Hiking and Skiing Trails (treated in this account), two hunter's walking trails, and "many miles of snowmobile/ATV trails." We do not recommend hiking on routes used by motorized equipment. The only public source of drinking water we could find near the trails was at the canoe landing shown on trail map #1.

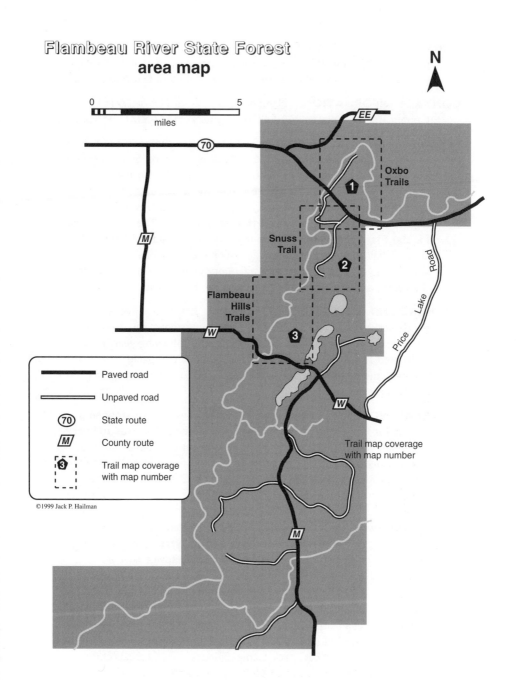

Flambeau River State Forest
area map

N

0   5
miles

70

EE

M

Oxbo
Trails

1

Snuss
Trail

2

Flambeau
Hills
Trails

Price   Lake   Road

W

3

W

Trail map coverage
with map number

Paved road

Unpaved road

70   State route

M   County route

3   Trail map coverage
with map number

©1999 Jack P. Hailman

M

PERMIT AND RESERVATIONS. Free camping permit required. Obtain a permit at the park office (HQ on trail map #3), open only during working hours on weekdays, or phone ahead to obtain one by mail.

CONTACT INFORMATION. Flambeau River State Forest, W1613 County Rd. W, Winter, WI 54896; phone: 715/332-5271 (no fax).

FINDING THE TRAIL. State Highway 70 traverses the northern part of the forest about 20 miles west of Fifield, which is on State Highway 13. The parking area for the **Oxbo Trails** and the **Snuss Trail** is on the north side of State 70, about a mile and a half east of the bridge over the Flambeau River. County Highway W also traverses the forest, about 25 miles north-northwest of Phillips. The parking area for the **Flambeau Hills Trails** is on the north side of County W, about a half mile east of the bridge over the Flambeau River. State 70 and County W are connected by County Highway M to the west of the forest and the unpaved Price Lake Rd. to the east.

BACKGROUND NOTES. In 1929, more than 3,000 acres were purchased by the state's Conservation Department; this land officially became the Flambeau River State Forest the following year. Land continued to be acquired, mainly from lumber companies that had cut over the original timber, until today the forest is more than 90,000 acres in size.

OUR TRAIL NOTES. The temperature was 84°F when we stopped in Phillips for fuel on an afternoon in early September. It was still very hot when we left the parking lot to set off on the Flambeau Hills Trails. Two and a half miles later we got the first glimpse of the Flambeau River where the trail crosses Rim Creek on a wooden bridge. Eventually we came to the short side trail leading to a three-sided shelter with a tent set up by it, where a friendly couple, their son, and two Dalmatians were camping. The man helpfully told us that decent campsites were rare, but to persevere to just beyond Mason Creek (where the Snuss Trail begins)—advice that we followed. Before night fell, the Barred Owls were calling up and down the river valley, and the next morning Red Squirrels chattered incessantly for an hour after dawn, beckoning us to emerge from the tent and begin our day. We hiked the return trip on the trails to the east, away from the river but through some pleasant glaciated terrain with dry kettle holes.

    Flora. The forest had a nice mix of trees; we passed through an area with lots of lovely Paper Birches and also noted Eastern Hemlock (by far the most predominant conifer), Balsam Fir, Blue Spruce (obviously planted, since it is native only to the Rocky Mountains), Eastern White Pine, Quaking and Bigtooth Aspen, and

Our campsite on the trail, Flambeau River State Forest

Sugar Maple. We saw several kinds of fungus, including the easily recognized Hoof Fungus growing on tree trunks, and also nonflowering plants, including at least two species of ground pines and some nice ferns. The flowers of summer were fading from view, but we found a chickweed, a (tall) Ox-eye Daisy-like composite that was new to us, and a species of goldenrod.

Fauna. Squirrel Trail is presumably named for the chattering Red Squirrels that pepper these woods in places; they were the only mammals we encountered. Ranid frogs leapt from the grass on the trail, and the slightly misnamed Spring Peepers peeped away after dark near our camp. Birds, as usual, were the most abundant and diverse vertebrate animals: Common Mergansers on the river, a Cooper's Hawk complaining of our incursion into his solitude, Ruffed Grouse sharing our trail, Hairy Woodpecker, Great Crested Flycatcher, Blue Jay, American Crow, Black-capped Chickadee, Red-breasted Nuthatch, Golden-crowned Kinglet, American Robin, Cedar Waxwing, and one of those "confusing fall warblers" of field-guide fame.

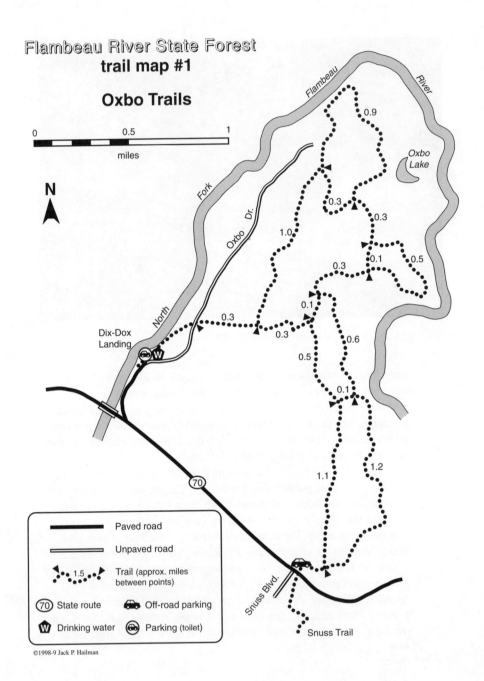

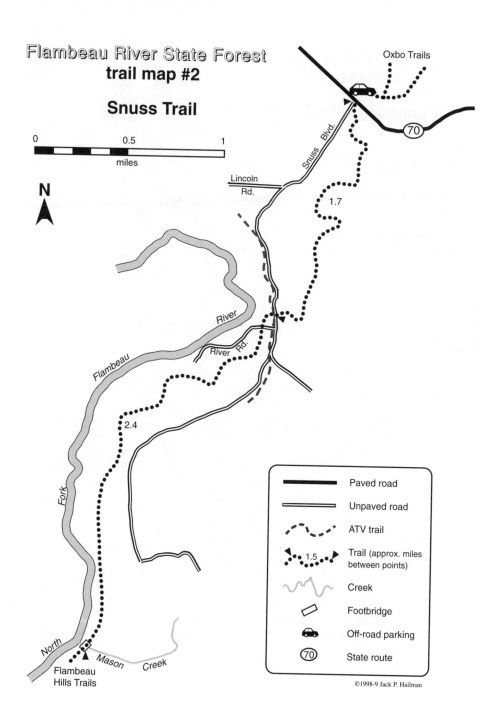

Flambeau River State Forest
trail map #2

Snuss Trail

Oxbo Trails

0   0.5   1
miles

N

Snuss Blvd.

70

Lincoln Rd.

1.7

River

River Rd.

Flambeau

2.4

Fork

North

Mason Creek

Flambeau Hills Trails

▬▬▬	Paved road
══	Unpaved road
◠◠◠	ATV trail
◄•••1.5•••►	Trail (approx. miles between points)
∿∿∿	Creek
▱	Footbridge
🚗	Off-road parking
70	State route

©1998-9 Jack P. Hailman

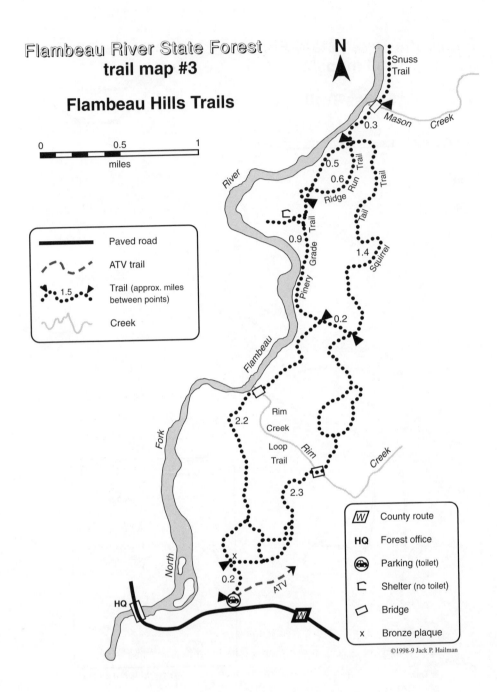

Flambeau River State Forest
trail map #3

Flambeau Hills Trails

N

0   0.5   1
miles

Snuss
Trail

Mason   Creek

0.3

River

0.5

0.6

Ridge   Run   Trail   Trail

1.4   Squirrel

Tail

0.9

Pinery   Grade   Trail

Paved road

ATV trail

1.5   Trail (approx. miles
between points)

Creek

0.2

Flambeau

2.2

Rim
Creek

Loop   Rim   Creek
Trail

2.3

Fork

North

x

0.2   ATV

HQ

W   County route

HQ   Forest office

Parking (toilet)

Shelter (no toilet)

Bridge

x   Bronze plaque

©1998-9 Jack P. Hailman

Ice Age National Scenic Trail

In the North Central Region

Completed sections of the Ice Age Trail include especially lovely glacial scenery of numerous kettle lakes within the Chippewa Moraine Ice Age National Scientific Reserve. Farther east are some of the remotest portions of completed trail.

LOCATION. North Central region, coordinates C-4 (northern section, Barron and Rusk Counties), C/D-5 (southern section, Chippewa County), and E/F-5 (Taylor and Lincoln Counties) on official state highway map.

RATING: CHIPPEWA MORAINE SEGMENT (TRAIL MAP #3). 🌲 🌲 🌲 🌲

🌲 **Scenery:** wonderful kettle-hole lakes

🌲 **Quiet:** can camp more than a mile from nearest paved road

🌲 **Trails:** at least 10 miles of trail accessible from camping places

🌲 **Interest:** glacial geology; interpretative display in visitor center

RATING: WOOD LAKE SEGMENT (TRAIL MAP #5). 🌲 🌲 🌲 🌲

🌲 **Scenery:** trail goes along scenic valley of Gus Johnson Creek

🌲 **Quiet:** can camp a mile or more from nearest paved road

🌲 **Trails:** at least 10 miles of trails accessible from camping place

🌲 **Solitude:** unlikely to encounter more than 2 parties per day

🌲 **Interest:** trail goes by old log cabin and campsites

RATING: OTHER SEGMENTS (TRAIL MAPS #1, #2, #4, AND #6). 🌲 🌲 🌲 🌲

🌲 **Scenery:** pleasant glacial scenery

🌲 **Quiet:** can camp more than a mile from nearest paved road

🌲 **Trails:** at least 10 miles of trail accessible from camping places

🌲 **Solitude:** unlikely to encounter more than 2 parties per day

ENTRANCE FEE. None.

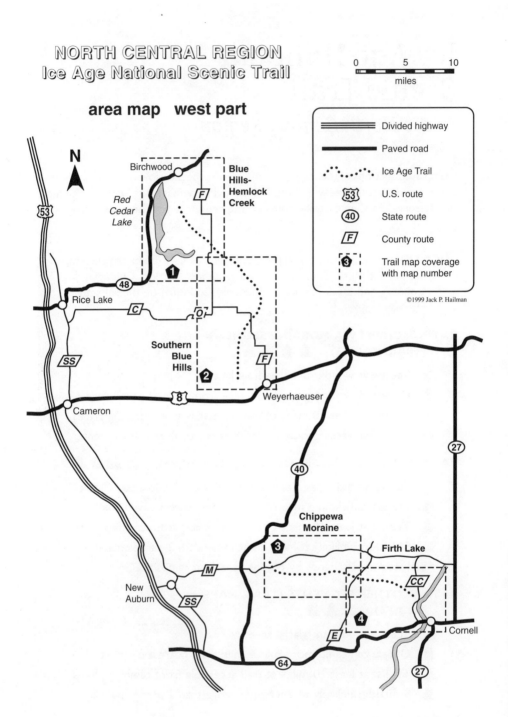

NORTH CENTRAL REGION
Ice Age National Scenic Trail

area map   west part

N

Legend:

Symbol	Description
	Divided highway
	Paved road
	Ice Age Trail
53	U.S. route
40	State route
F	County route
3	Trail map coverage with map number

©1999 Jack P. Hailman

Birchwood

Blue Hills-Hemlock Creek

Red Cedar Lake

F

53

48

1

Rice Lake

C

O

SS

Southern Blue Hills

F

2

8

Cameron

Weyerhaeuser

27

40

Chippewa Moraine

3

Firth Lake

M

CC

New Auburn

SS

4

E

Cornell

64

27

NORTH CENTRAL REGION
Ice Age National Scenic Trail

area map   east part

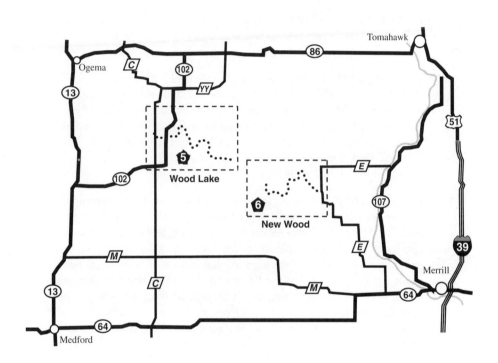

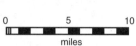

N

0	5	10

miles

Tomahawk

86

Ogema

C

102

13

YY

51

5

Wood Lake

102

E

6

New Wood

107

E

M

39

Merrill

C

13

M

64

64

Medford

39	Interstate route
51	U.S. route
64	State route
C	County route
3	Trail map coverage with map number

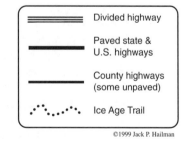

	Divided highway
	Paved state & U.S. highways
	County highways (some unpaved)
	Ice Age Trail

©1999 Jack P. Hailman

CAMPING. Wilderness camping on county forest lands. There is a family campground at Wood Lake County Park (trail map #5); fee charged. The state plans to build a backpacking campsite on its land within the Chippewa Moraine Ice Age National Scientific Reserve (trail map #3). The only public sources of drinking water we could find close to the trail were at the visitor center of the scientific reserve (trail map #3) and at Wood Lake campground (trail map #5).

PERMIT AND RESERVATIONS. None needed for wilderness camping. When the state's campsite at the scientific reserve is built, camping there will require a permit (fee).

CONTACT INFORMATION. Ice Age Park & Trail Foundation of Wisconsin, Inc., 207 E. Buffalo St., Suite 515, Milwaukee, WI 53202-5712; phone: 800/227-0046; e-mail: cthisted@sbtsi.com. The office can put you in touch with the current coordinators of the Blue Hills and Chippewa Moraine Chapters. *Also,* Ice Age National Scenic Trail, National Park Service, 700 Rayovac Dr., Suite 100, Madison, WI 53711; phone: 608/264-5610.

FINDING THE TRAIL. The northern end of the **Blue Hills–Hemlock Creek** segment in Barron County (trail map #1) is a little tricky to find. From State Highway 48 on the north side of Red Cedar Lake, take Loch Lomond Rd. (paved) south until it divides, and continue going south on either of the two parallel and intermittently paved roads until you can go no farther south. The southernmost east-west street is called Finohorn Rd., or 28 11/16th St. (No, we didn't make that up.) The Ice Age Trail leaves from this street, virtually right next to a private home. The trailhead is signed (but there is no off-road parking). The other road crossings on trail map #1 are best accessed from Rusk County Highway F running south from State Highway 48.

The **Southern Blue Hills** segment (trail map #2) can be accessed in only three places. From the north follow Rusk County Highway F south from State Highway 48. From the west take Barron County Highway C east from County SS just south of the community of Rice Lake. When County C crosses into Rusk County it assumes the new designation O, which runs into County F. From the south take County F north from Weyerhaeuser, on U.S. Highway 8. Where County Highways O and F run together for several miles (see trail map #2) you can go north on Stout Rd. to find a trailhead with parking at the end, or access the trail where it crosses Highways O/F. In the latter case, the off-road parking area is about 100 yards west of the trail crossing. The southern terminus is on a road called Railroad Way when it leaves Weyerhaeuser, Bass Lake Rd. or Old 14 Rd. west of Weyerhaeuser, and Old 14 Rd. west of Bass Lake. Find this road from Weyerhaeuser or by driving north from U.S. Highway 8 on either Rusk County Highway W (paved) or Cranberry Lake Rd. (unpaved). The trailhead has no off-road parking.

The **Chippewa Moraine** and **Firth Lake** segments (trail maps #3 and #4) are best accessed by driving east from New Auburn on Chippewa County Highway M. This highway crosses the north loop of the Ice Age Trail within the scientific reserve and provides further access via unpaved roads running south from it. From the south, State Highway 64 provides access via County Highways E and CC (both paved).

The **Wood Lake** segment (trail map #5) is located east of State Highway 102 in Taylor County north of Medford and south of U.S. Highway 8. Take State Highway 13 north from Medford and go east on State Highway 102. This road intersects Taylor County Highway C, where there is a parking lot at the western end of the trail. State 102 also leads to Wilderness Ave., from which the eastern parking area on Tower Rd. can be reached.

The **New Wood** segment (trail map #6) is in Lincoln County east of U.S. Highway 51 and State Highway 107. From State Highway 107 northwest of Merrill go to the intersection with Lincoln County Highway E, cross the Wisconsin River and follow County Highway E west, and then south to reach Conservation Ave. The parking place is west on Conservation Ave. *Note:* The trail is due to be extended in the year 2000 westward through county forest lands to Tower Rd.

BACKGROUND NOTES.   Chippewa Moraine is one of nine units of the Ice Age National Scientific Reserve, which total more than 40,000 acres, all in Wisconsin. The most recent of at least four major continental glaciations began about 70,000 years ago and ended only about 10,000 years ago, leaving a sweeping curve of hills made of glacial debris. This line of terminal moraines provides the route for the Ice Age National Scenic Trail, which will be more than 1,000 miles in length when completed. The units of the reserve protect the most scenic of the morainal areas, and the trail connects them. The Chippewa Moraine unit is notable for its many kettle-hole lakes, formed when large blocks of ice under the glacial debris melted, so that the land slumped down into a kettle-shaped depression that subsequently filled with water.

OUR TRAIL NOTES.   The Saturday in early October provided brisk air that seemed to intensify the fall colors bedecking the hilly terrain. We entered in our notes the comment that the area was "more kettle-morainy than Kettle Moraine State Forest," an inelegant way of praising the beauty of the glacial landscape. Having begun at the visitor center, we hiked east into the county forest, and eventually made camp at a scenic spot overlooking one of the numerous lakes. After dinner, we took a two-hour walk still farther east, and had to find our way back in pitch blackness (admittedly with the help of a flashlight). Two Barred Owls carried on a conversation across "our" lake, and Canada Geese honked their way across the night sky. The next morning after breakfast, it was with some reluctance that we began the hike back.

Flora. The trees provided most of the fall color, large Eastern White Pines punctuating the deciduous forest containing Red Maple, Quaking Aspen, Paper Birch, White Oak, Black Oak, and Northern Red Oak. Small plants included Running Pine (a type of lycopodium), lots of nice ferns, Maple-leaf Viburnum with jet-black berries, and late wildflowers that included an evening-primrose and two kinds of aster.

Fauna. A few Spring Peepers called from the trees. We were surprised to hear Common Ravens, which we had not realized came this far south in west central Wisconsin. Other birds included Pied-billed Grebe, Canada Goose, Wood Duck, Barred Owl, Red-bellied Woodpecker, Hairy Woodpecker, Blue Jay, American Crow, Black-capped Chickadee, White-breasted Nuthatch, Hermit Thrush, White-throated Sparrow, and Dark-eyed Junco, the last three undoubtedly migrating. The two mammals we saw were Gray Squirrels foraging in the leaf litter and Eastern Chipmunks loudly proclaiming their territories.

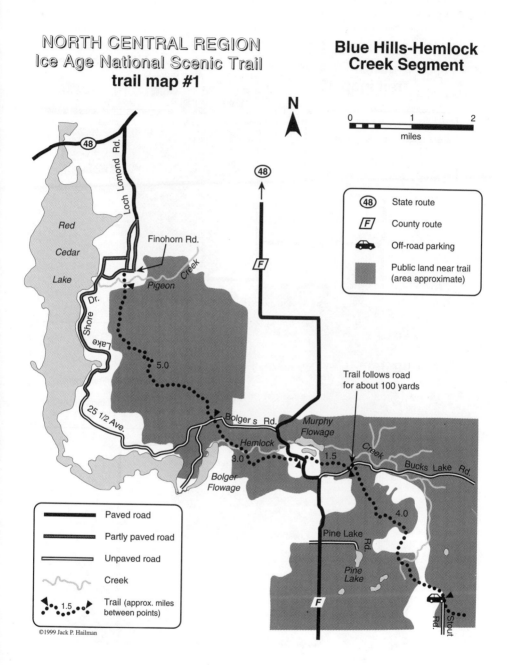

NORTH CENTRAL REGION
Ice Age National Scenic Trail
trail map #1

Blue Hills-Hemlock
Creek Segment

N

0   1   2
miles

48

Loch Lomond Rd.

48

F

Red

Cedar

Lake

Finohorn Rd.

Creek

Pigeon

Shore Dr.

Lake

5.0

25 1/2 Ave.

Bolgers Rd.

Hemlock

3.0

1.5

Bolger
Flowage

Murphy
Flowage

Creek

Bucks Lake Rd.

Trail follows road
for about 100 yards

4.0

Pine Lake Rd.

Pine
Lake

F

Stout Rd.

Legend:

48   State route

F   County route

🚗   Off-road parking

Public land near trail
(area approximate)

Paved road

Partly paved road

Unpaved road

Creek

1.5   Trail (approx. miles
between points)

©1999 Jack P. Hailman

97

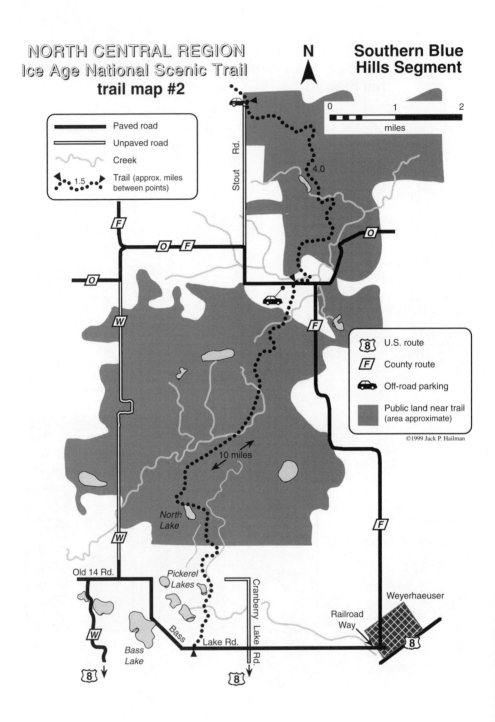

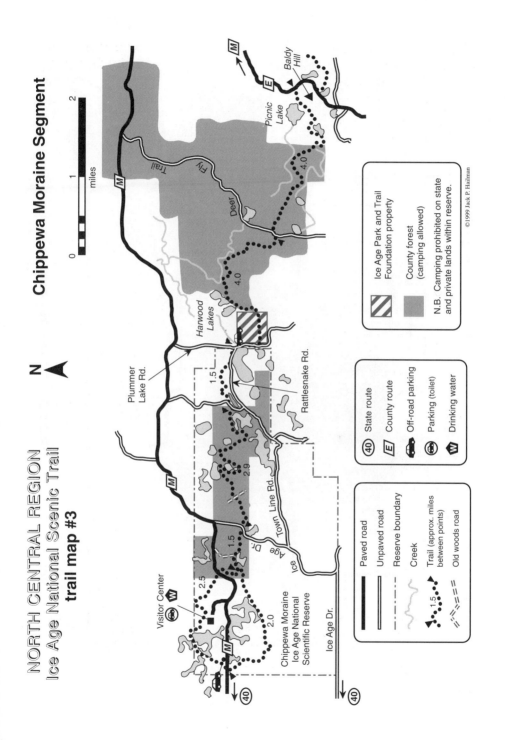

NORTH CENTRAL REGION
Ice Age National Scenic Trail
trail map #3

Chippewa Moraine Segment

N

miles

0   1   2

Visitor Center

2.5

1.5

2.0

Chippewa Moraine
Ice Age National
Scientific Reserve

Ice Age Dr.

Ice Age Dr.

Town Line Rd.

2.9

1.5

Rattlesnake Rd.

Plummer
Lake Rd.

Harwood
Lakes

4.0

Deer Fly Trail

4.0

Picnic
Lake

Baldy
Hill

	Paved road
	Unpaved road
	Reserve boundary
	Creek
1.5	Trail (approx. miles between points)
	Old woods road

40	State route
E	County route
	Off-road parking
	Parking (toilet)
W	Drinking water

Ice Age Park and Trail
Foundation property

County forest
(camping allowed)

N.B. Camping prohibited on state
and private lands within reserve.

© 1999 Jack P. Hailman

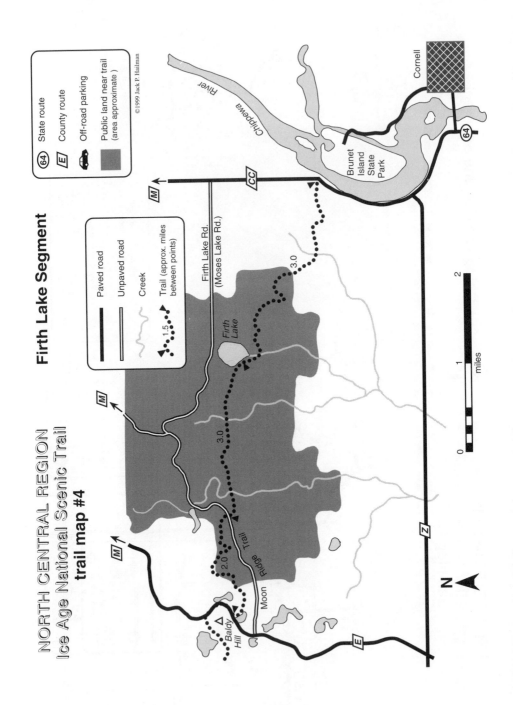

NORTH CENTRAL REGION
Ice Age National Scenic Trail
trail map #4

Firth Lake Segment

	Paved road
	Unpaved road
	Creek
●●●1.5	Trail (approx. miles between points)

Baldy Hill

Moon Ridge Trail

2.0

3.0

3.0

Firth Lake Rd. (Moses Lake Rd.)

Firth Lake

Chippewa River

Brunet Island State Park

Cornell

64	State route
E	County route
🚗	Off-road parking
	Public land near trail (area approximate)

©1999 Jack P. Hailman

N

0   1   2
miles

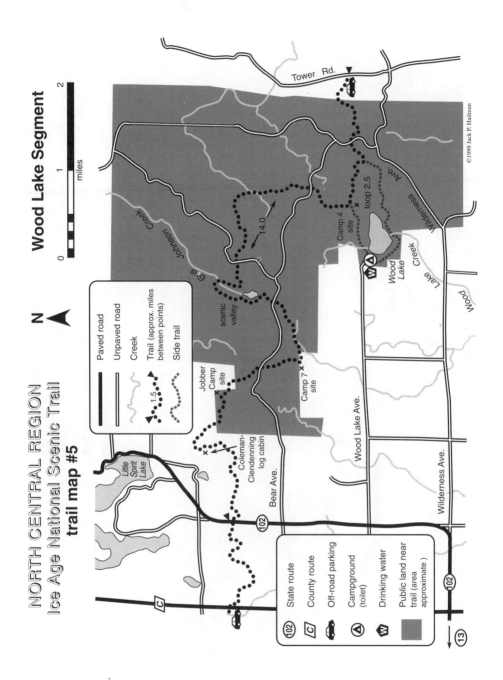

NORTH CENTRAL REGION
Ice Age National Scenic Trail
trail map #5

Wood Lake Segment

N

miles
0   1   2

Legend:
- Paved road
- Unpaved road
- Creek
- Trail (approx. miles between points)
- Side trail

1.5

- State route
- County route
- Off-road parking
- Campground (toilet)
- Drinking water
- Public land near trail (area approximate)

102 State route
C   County route

Little Spirit Lake

Johnson Creek

Big Johnson Creek

scenic valley

14.0

Jobber Camp site

Coleman-Clendenning log cabin

Bear Ave.

Camp 7 site

Camp 4 site

loop 2.5

Wood Lake

Wood Lake Ave.

Wilderness Ave.

Wilderness Ave.

Wood Lake Creek

Tower Rd.

©1999 Jack P. Hailman

13

101

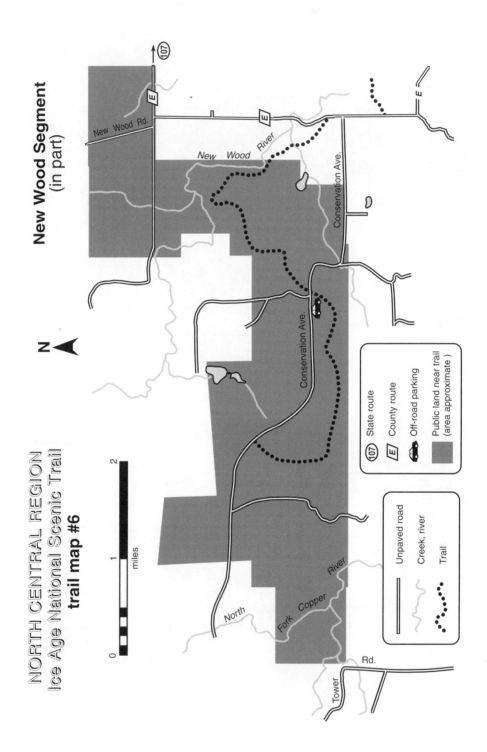

NORTH CENTRAL REGION II: CHEQUAMEGON

At more than 850,000 acres, the Chequamegon side of the Chequamegon-Nicolet National Forest is the largest unit of public land in Wisconsin. Different references tell us with uniform authority how to pronounce this "q-less" Ojibwa word: *She-wam-a-gon, Sho-wa-me-gon,* and *Sho-wah-ma-gon* are among the renditions found in published materials. One is allowed to camp almost anywhere in all national forests, but Chequamegon offers special inducements to the backpacker: wilderness and semi-primitive areas, ski-trail complexes that are virtually deserted when the ground is clear of snow, and two national scenic trails. In the northern part of the forest the North Country National Scenic Trail runs for 60 continuous miles, whereas in the southern part the Ice Age National Scenic Trail runs for 41 continuous miles. This chapter is divided for convenience into four parts (see map): the contiguous Upper and Lower North parts, the East part, and the South part. These parts correspond with the forest's ranger districts as follows: Washburn (Upper North), Great Divide (Lower North), Park Falls section of Medford/Park Falls (East), and Medford section of Medford/Park Falls (South).

Because you can backpack nearly anywhere in Chequamegon, our accounts in this chapter should be considered recommendations of the best and safest areas. If you do strike out on some back trail not covered in this book, be certain to have a compass and detailed maps of the area—and know how to use them. It is also wise to check with a forest ranger before embarking on a wilderness trip on unmarked trails.

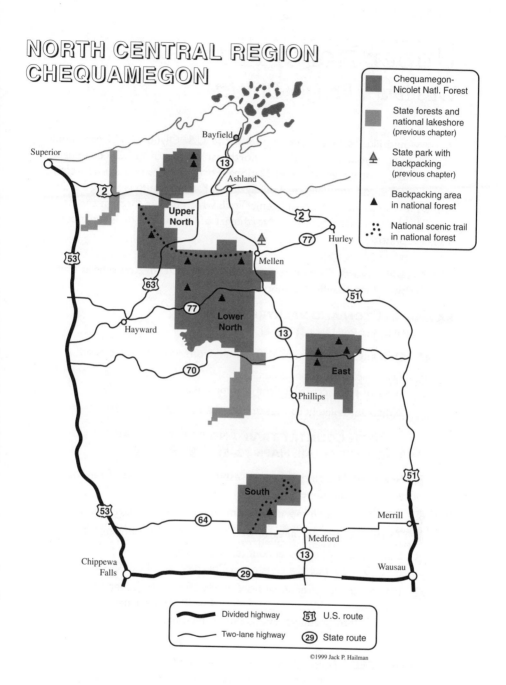

NORTH CENTRAL REGION
CHEQUAMEGON

■	Chequamegon-Nicolet Natl. Forest
▓	State forests and national lakeshore (previous chapter)
⛄	State park with backpacking (previous chapter)
▲	Backpacking area in national forest
⁝	National scenic trail in national forest

Superior

Bayfield

Ashland

Upper North

2

53

63

77

Hayward

Lower North

70

Hurley

77

Mellen

51

13

East

Phillips

South

64

53

Medford

13

Merrill

51

Wausau

Chippewa Falls

29

⬭ Divided highway	51	U.S. route
— Two-lane highway	29	State route

©1999 Jack P. Hailman

Upper North Part
Washburn Ranger District

If you would like to hike trails on which the U.S. Olympic Ski Team once trained, here is your chance: the far northeast corner of the Chequamegon side of the Chequamegon-Nicolet National Forest boasts two ski-trail complexes, the Teuton and Valkyrie Trail Systems. Farther south is a long section of the North Country National Scenic Trail, which passes through the Rainbow Lake Wilderness. The Upper North part of Chequamegon is great backpacking country.

LOCATION. North Central region, coordinates C/D-1/2 on official state highway map (Bayfield County).

RATING: TEUTON AND VALKYRIE TRAILS (TRAIL MAP #1). 🌲🌲🌲

🌲 **Quiet:** can camp more than a mile from nearest paved road

🌲 **Trails:** can camp on circuit of more than 5 miles, and at least 10 miles of trail accessible from camping places

🌲 **Solitude:** unlikely to meet more than 2 parties per day

RATING: NORTH COUNTRY TRAIL AND RAINBOW LAKE WILDERNESS (TRAIL MAPS #2–5). 🌲🌲🌲🌲

🌲 **Scenery:** fine glacial scenery, especially in wilderness (trail map #3) and Lake Owen areas (trail map #5)

🌲 **Quiet:** can camp more than a mile from nearest paved road

🌲 **Trails:** at least 10 miles of trail accessible from camping place

🌲 **Solitude:** unlikely to encounter more than 6 parties per day on most of trail, but higher use in wilderness and Lake Owen areas

🌲 **Interest:** special national history: glacial terrain (especially in Rainbow Lake Wilderness), centuries-old White Pines (Drummond Woods Interpretative Trail), and scenic beauty (especially Lake Owen)

ENTRANCE FEE. Forest Service vehicle sticker (or daily pass) required to park in some forest lots or to use other national forest facilities.

CAMPING. Wilderness camping only; no designated campsites. Tents must be set up at least 50 feet from trails. Along the North Country Trail, traditional camping places include Rainbow and Reynard Lakes

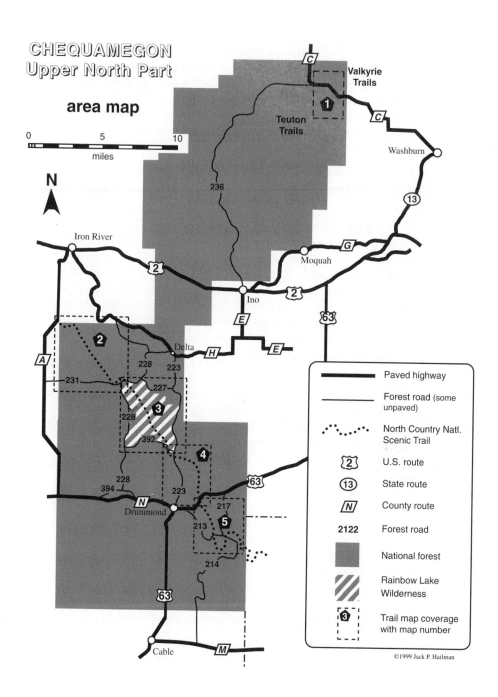

(trail map #3) and Esox Lake (trail map #4). There are also Forest Service campgrounds (fees charged) at Perch Lake (trail map #3) and Lake Owen (trail map #5). Drinking water is available from a pump in the southeast corner of the parking area for the Teuton and Valkyrie Trails. The only public sources of water that we have located on the North Country Trail are pumps at the campgrounds and at the Lake Owen Picnic Ground.

PERMIT AND RESERVATIONS. None needed for wilderness camping.

CONTACT INFORMATION. Washburn Ranger District, 113 Bayfield St., P.O. Box 578, Washburn, WI 54891; phone: 715/373-2667; fax: 715/373-2878; TTY: 715/373-2668; e-mail: tholmes/r9-cheni @fs.fed.us. *Also,* Forest Supervisor's Office, Chequamegon-Nicolet National Forest, 1170 4th Avenue S., Park Falls, WI 54552; phone: 715/762-2461; fax: 715/762-5179; TTY: 715/762-5701.

North Country National Scenic Trail. North Country Trail Association, 49 Monroe Center NW, Suite 200B, Grand Rapids, MI 49503; phone: 616/454-5506; web site: www.northcountrytrail.org. *Also,* National Park Service, North Country National Scenic Trail, 700 Rayovac Dr., Suite 100, Madison, WI 53711; phone: 608/264-5610; web site: www.nps.gov/noco.

FINDING THE TRAIL. From Washburn on State Highway 13, go 8.5 miles west on Bayfield County Highway C to the parking lot shown on trail map #1. **Teuton Trails** begin here and **Valkyrie Trails** leave from the other side of the road.

The western terminus of the **North Country Trail** is 4.5 miles south of the town of Iron River, on Bayfield County Highway A, across from the intersection with Gravel Pit Road (trail map #2). The **Rainbow Lake Wilderness** is reached either by driving south on Forest Road 223 from Delta or by driving north on 223 from Drummond (trail map #3). The North Country Trail crosses U.S. Highway 63 a little over a mile east of Drummond (trail maps #4 and #5). The southeast sections of the trail are best reached by driving southeast from Drummond on Forest Road 213 (trail map #5). Those road crossings of the North Country Trail that have small off-road parking places are shown on the trail maps.

BACKGROUND NOTES. The winter recreation area that includes the Valkyrie and Teuton ski trails, called Mt. Valhalla, is a popular place for snowmobiling as well. The North Country Trail began here in Chequamegon in the 1960s as a "long" (60-mile) trail through national forest lands. In March 1980, Congress created the North Country National Scenic Trail, which, when completed, will stretch more than 4,000 miles across seven states from North Dakota to the Vermont border of New York. The nearly 30 miles of trail in the Upper North part of Chequamegon traverse glaciated terrain with many lakes.

Rainbow Lake Wilderness. Named for the lake nearest the center, this wilderness area of 6,600 acres is a favorite place for fishermen and backpackers. The fire tower of Tower Lake is gone, and former forest roads through the area have been closed to vehicles. The woods consist of aspens, mixed hardwoods, and mixed conifers. In July 1999, two separate windstorms a couple of weeks apart caused extensive tree falls across roads and trails. The trails may not be fully cleared for years.

Drummond Woods Interpretative Trail. Most of the old-growth trees were gone by the time lumbering operations fizzled out in the early twentieth century. Just east of Drummond, however, stands a copse of Eastern White Pines that are 200–400 years old. The Forest Service has built a loop trail off the North Country Trail here with signs explaining and identifying many trees and shrubs.

Lake Owen. The largest lake on Chequamegon's North Country Trail provides the hiker with scenic views from the bluffs along which the trail runs. Here also are large Eastern Hemlocks, Eastern White Pines, and especially impressive Red Pines.

OUR TRAIL NOTES. It was dawn in early June when we looked at one another inside the tent and shrugged our shoulders in answer to the question that didn't need to be asked: what *was* that sound? It was a mechanical noise yet had the cadence of a woodpecker's drumming, with the notes first rapid and then more spaced out. We were in the Teuton Trail System, far from any possible mechanical contrivance. The noise ceased before we struggled out of the tent into a horde of waiting mosquitoes, but later, as we were packing up to leave, the mystery sound returned. And there was the source: a Yellow-bellied Sapsucker about 50 feet away, drumming on a small metal marker for the ski trail. We found the trails to be very well signed, with frequent trail markers and a metal map at every trail junction. The woodpeckers apparently appreciated the markers, too.

Flora. Although here in the far north of Wisconsin one might expect northern coniferous forest, the woods were instead composed of deciduous hardwoods: lots of Paper Birch, Black Oak, Sugar Maple, and Bigtooth Aspen. The only conifers we saw were scattered, large Eastern White Pines. What impressed us most about the plant life, though, was the endless blanket of Bracken: ferns 1–2 feet tall, covering every square yard of forest floor. Almost equally impressive was an enormous fungus growing on a tree trunk; bright orange in color, it was the size of a basketball. Besides mosses on the trails themselves, we found a few wildflowers: False Solomon's-seal (Solomon's Plume), Wild Lily-of-the-valley (Canada Mayflower), Common Strawberry, Fringed Polygala (Gaywings), Starflower, Common Dandelion, and Ox-eye Daisy.

Fauna. The area proved good for amphibians: a large American Toad hopping in the leaf litter, Gray Treefrogs calling here and there, and deafening choruses of Spring Peepers that helped keep Liz awake longer than she wanted to be. Among mammals, we saw Least Chipmunks, and (surprisingly) a Red Squirrel, usually found only in conifer woods. The birds were not overpowering in sight or song, but there were some pleasant species: Yellow-bellied Sapsucker, Northern Flicker, Eastern Wood-Pewee, Least Flycatcher, Eastern Phoebe, Blue Jay, Wood Thrush, American Robin, Black-throated Green Warbler, Ovenbird, Chipping Sparrow, Song Sparrow, Rose-breasted Grosbeak, and (at the edge of the clearing on Pitt Hill) Indigo Bunting.

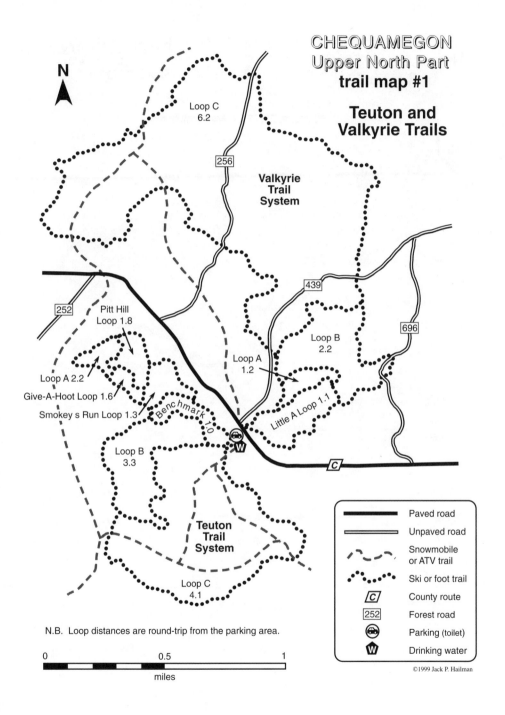

N

CHEQUAMEGON
Upper North Part
trail map #1

**Teuton and
Valkyrie Trails**

Loop C
6.2

256

**Valkyrie
Trail
System**

252

Pitt Hill
Loop 1.8

439

696

Loop B
2.2

Loop A
1.2

Loop A 2.2

Give-A-Hoot Loop 1.6

Smokey s Run Loop 1.3

Benchmark 1.0

Little A Loop 1.1

Loop B
3.3

W

C

**Teuton
Trail
System**

Loop C
4.1

N.B. Loop distances are round-trip from the parking area.

	Paved road
	Unpaved road
	Snowmobile or ATV trail
	Ski or foot trail
C	County route
252	Forest road
	Parking (toilet)
W	Drinking water

©1999 Jack P. Hailman

0   0.5   1
miles

111

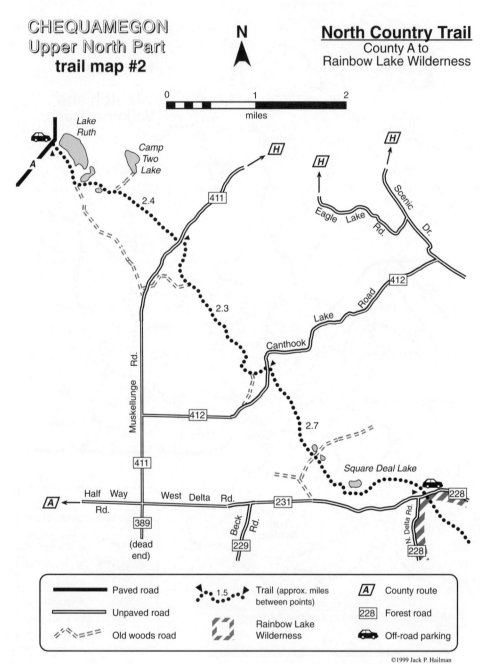

CHEQUAMEGON
Upper North Part
trail map #2

N

North Country Trail
County A to
Rainbow Lake Wilderness

0   1   2
miles

Lake
Ruth

Camp
Two
Lake

A

H

H

H

411

2.4

Eagle   Lake
Rd.

Scenic
Dr.

412

2.3

Lake   Road

412

Muskellunge   Rd.

Canthook

412

411

2.7

Square Deal Lake

228

Half   Way
Rd.

West   Delta   Rd.

231

N. Delta Rd.

A

389
(dead
end)

Beck
Rd.

229

228

▬▬▬▬ Paved road	●●1.5●● Trail (approx. miles between points)	**A** County route
▭▭▭ Unpaved road		228 Forest road
≈≈≈ Old woods road	Rainbow Lake Wilderness	🚗 Off-road parking

©1999 Jack P. Hailman

112

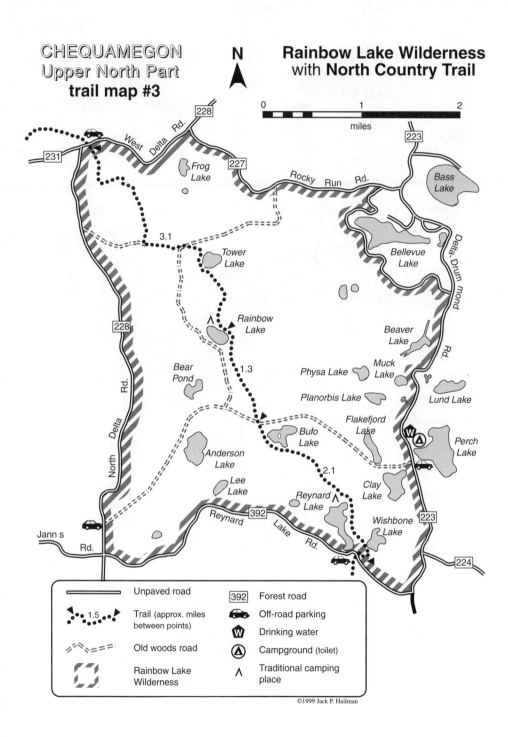

CHEQUAMEGON
Upper North Part
trail map #3

N

Rainbow Lake Wilderness
with North Country Trail

0   1   2
miles

228

223

West Delta Rd.

231

Frog Lake

227

Rocky Run Rd.

Bass Lake

3.1

Tower Lake

Bellevue Lake

Delta, Drummond Rd.

228

∧

►*Rainbow Lake*

Beaver Lake

North Delta Rd.

Bear Pond

1.3

Physa Lake

Muck Lake

Planorbis Lake

Lund Lake

Flakefjord Lake

W Ⓐ

Bufo Lake

Perch Lake

Anderson Lake

2.1

Lee Lake

Clay Lake

Reynard Lake ∧

Reynard Lake Rd.

392

Wishbone Lake

223

Jann s Rd.

224

——— Unpaved road	392 Forest road	
►•••1.5•••► Trail (approx. miles between points)	🚗 Off-road parking	
═══ Old woods road	W Drinking water	
⟋⟍ Rainbow Lake Wilderness	Ⓐ Campground (toilet)	
	∧ Traditional camping place	

©1999 Jack P. Hailman

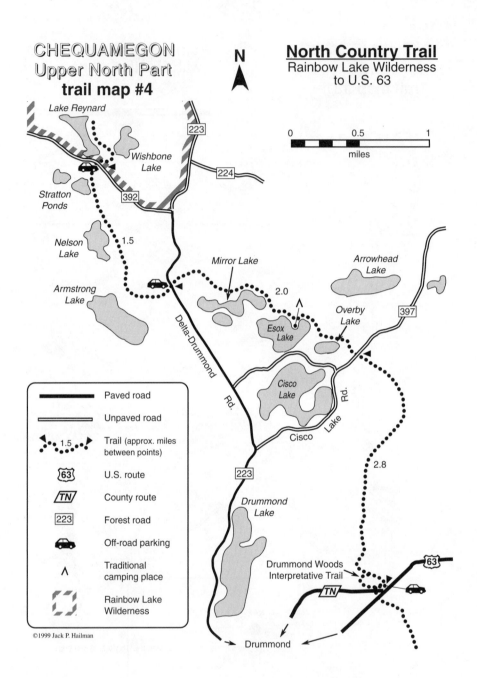

CHEQUAMEGON
Upper North Part
trail map #4

N

North Country Trail
Rainbow Lake Wilderness
to U.S. 63

0	0.5	1

miles

Lake Reynard

223

Wishbone
Lake

224

Stratton
Ponds

392

Nelson
Lake

1.5

Mirror Lake

Arrowhead
Lake

Armstrong
Lake

2.0

Overby
Lake

397

Esox
Lake

Delta-Drummond Rd.

Cisco
Lake

Cisco Lake Rd.

Paved road	
	Unpaved road
1.5	Trail (approx. miles between points)
63	U.S. route
TN	County route
223	Forest road
	Off-road parking
∧	Traditional camping place
	Rainbow Lake Wilderness

©1999 Jack P. Hailman

Cisco

223

2.8

Drummond
Lake

Drummond Woods
Interpretative Trail

63

TN

Drummond

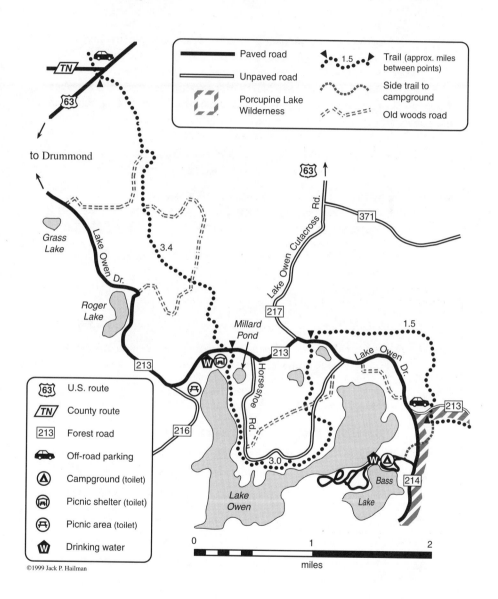

CHEQUAMEGON
Upper North Part
trail map #5

North Country Trail
U.S. 63 to
Porcupine Lake Wilderness

—— Paved road	Trail (approx. miles between points)
═══ Unpaved road	Side trail to campground
Porcupine Lake Wilderness	Old woods road

to Drummond

Grass Lake

Lake Owen Dr.

63

371

Lake Owen Cutacross Rd.

3.4

Roger Lake

Millard Pond

217

1.5

213

213

Lake Owen Dr.

213

Horseshoe Rd.

213

216

3.0

W

W

A

Bass Lake

214

Lake Owen

63	U.S. route
TN	County route
213	Forest road
🚗	Off-road parking
Ⓐ	Campground (toilet)
🏠	Picnic shelter (toilet)
🛆	Picnic area (toilet)
W	Drinking water

0   1   2

miles

©1999 Jack P. Hailman

Lower North Part
Great Divide Ranger District

The Lower North part of Chequamegon is like the Upper North "only more so." Like the Upper North part, it has 30 miles of North Country National Scenic Trail, which traverses a wilderness area, and a ski-trail complex elsewhere within the area. The Lower North part also has, however, the Penokee Mountain Ski Trail complex, through which the North Country Trail runs, and the popular Rock Lake Trail, a designated national recreation trail.

LOCATION. North Central region, coordinates D-2/3 on official state highway map (Bayfield, Ashland, and Sawyer Counties).

RATING: NORTH COUNTRY NATIONAL SCENIC TRAIL, INCLUDING PORCUPINE LAKE WILDERNESS AND PENOKEE MOUNTAIN SKI TRAILS (TRAIL MAPS #1–6).

Scenery: vistas of some nice areas, with considerable relief (for Wisconsin)

Quiet: can camp more than a mile from nearest paved road

Trails: at least 10 miles of trail from camping places

Solitude: unlikely to encounter more than 2 parties per day

Interest: half credit for national history of Porcupine Lake Wilderness, plus homestead site

RATING: ROCK LAKE NATIONAL RECREATION TRAIL (TRAIL MAP #7).

Scenery: nice glacial landscape with scenic lakes

Quiet: can camp more than a mile from nearest paved road

Trails: can camp on circuit of more than 5 miles

RATING: WEST TORCH SKI TRAIL (TRAIL MAP #8).

Quiet: can camp nearly a mile from nearest paved road

Trails: can camp on circuit less than 5 miles in length

Solitude: unlikely to encounter more than 2 parties (or anyone at all)

ENTRANCE FEE. Forest Service vehicle sticker (or daily pass) required to park in some forest lots or to use other national forest facilities.

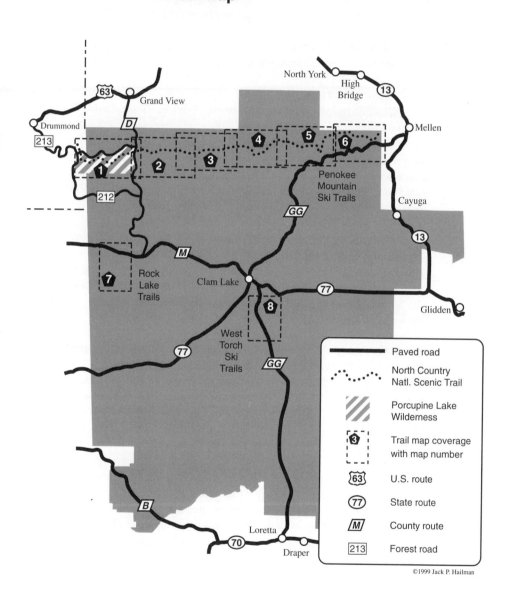

CAMPING. Mostly wilderness camping. Tents must be pitched at least 50 feet from the trail. On the North Country Trail, two Adirondack-type (three-sided) shelters are available to backpackers (trail maps #4 and #6). Forest Service campgrounds (fees charged) are located near the North Country Trail in three places (trail maps #1 and #4).

PERMIT AND RESERVATIONS. None needed for wilderness camping or use of the Adirondack shelters.

CONTACT INFORMATION.
    Chequamegon-Nicolet National Forest. Great Divide Ranger District, Hayward Office, P.O. Box 896, Hayward, WI 54843; phone and TTY: 715/634-4821; fax: 715/634-3769; or, Great Divide Ranger District, Glidden Office, P.O. Box 126, Glidden, WI 54527; phone and TTY: 715/264-2511; fax: 715/264-3307. *Also*, Forest Supervisor's Office, Chequamegon-Nicolet National Forest, 1170 4th Ave. S., Park Falls, WI 54552; phone: 715/762-2461; fax: 715/762-5179; TTY: 715/762-5701.
    North Country National Scenic Trail. North Country Trail Association, 49 Monroe Center NW, Suite 200B, Grand Rapids, MI 49503; phone: 616/454-5506; web site: www.northcountrytrail.org. *Also*, National Park Service, North Country National Scenic Trail, 700 Rayovac Dr., Suite 100, Madison, WI 53711; phone: 608/264-5610; web site: www.nps.gov/noco.

FINDING THE TRAIL. The western portions of the **North Country Trail** within the Lower North part of Chequamegon, including the Porcupine Lake Wilderness (trail maps #1 and #2), can be accessed from U.S. Highway 63 by going south on Forest Road 213 (paved) from Drummond or on Bayfield County Highway D from Grand View. From County Highway M to the south, go north on County D.
    The eastern portions of the North Country Trail (trail map #6) are most easily accessed from the Penokee Overlook, 3 miles west of Mellen on Ashland County Highway GG. The eastern terminus of the North Country Trail within the national forest is 2 miles west of Mellen on unpaved Forest Road 390 (Kornstead Rd.). Central sections of the North Country Trail (trail maps #2–5) can be approached only by driving on unpaved forest roads and finding trail crossings.
    The **Rock Lake Trail** system is easily found on Bayfield County Highway M, 12 miles west of Clam Lake. There are two off-road parking places where the trail crosses Forest Road 207 2.6 and 3.4 miles south of County M. The **West Torch Trail** system is also readily found, 2.5 miles south of Clam Lake on Ashland County

Highway GG. This trail system has two road crossings on Forest Road 339.

    Note: The North Country Trail is complete and certified from Kornstead Rd. east through the community of Mellen to Copper Falls State Park (previous chapter). Since that section runs mainly on roads and over private lands where explicit permission to camp has not been secured, it is not included in this book.

BACKGROUND NOTES. The North Country Trail here in the Lower North part of Chequamegon has more relief, and hence more scenic views, than does the western section in the Upper North part because of the Penokee Range. These volcanic mountains, formed perhaps two billion years ago, are so eroded as to be merely remnants of their once-magnificent selves. Nevertheless, they still provide noticeable relief by Wisconsin standards, and they played an important part in early mining history because of their copper and iron ore.

OUR TRAIL NOTES. We have been backpacking on the North Country Trail in Lower North Chequamegon a number of times, but choose to recall here a short trip to the rolling terrain of Rock Lake. We had spent a Saturday afternoon in mid-May east of Mellen building trail with other members of the North Country Trail Association. Then we were off to the area west of Mellen to make field checks of

Liz putting on her boots, Rock Lake National Recreation Trail

maps, pausing on the drive south to cook dinner in a Forest Service picnic area. So the hour was late when we arrived in the Rock Lake area, and we decided to take the path of least resistance in finding a suitable campsite before dark. We parked on Rock Lake Rd. and walked a short distance west, where we quickly found a room with a view overlooking Rock Lake. A campfire flickering in the woods on the other side of the lake told us that others had sought the same quiet of the wilds. Dawn, however, was anything but quiet because a loon was proclaiming this lake for his own, his voice drowning out all the other birds save the Hairy Woodpeckers, which were giving their kingfisher-like spring calls all around our campsite. The intermittent light rain could not dampen our spirits during breakfast. On our walk out that morning, we met some mountain bikers and Liz chided two of the four girls for not wearing helmets as their four male companions were doing.

Flora. The forest here is mainly mixed hardwoods: Paper Birch, Sugar Maple, oaks, and aspens. The deeper glens are darkened by stands of Eastern Hemlock, and Eastern White Pines occupy highland areas near Rock Lake. We found nonflowering plants such as mosses and lichens on rocks, and lycopodium on the woodland floor. Spring peppered the forest with wildflowers including Large-flowered (White, Large) Trillium, Large-flowered Bellwort, Wood Anemone, and Downy Yellow Violet.

Fauna. The damp evening provoked a bedtime chorus of Spring Peepers, Northern Cricket Frogs, and American Toads. A Wood Thrush had been singing as night fell, and a Barred Owl gave the last avian utterance of the day. The Common Loon and Hairy Woodpeckers dominated the morning's sounds, but many other birds vied to be heard: a duck quacking as it flew by overhead, a hawk of unknown persuasion calling noisily from the woods across the lake, Blue Jay, American Robin, Northern Parula, Black-throated Green Warbler, Ovenbird, and Song Sparrow. And chipping persistently around our campsite were diminutive Red Squirrels.

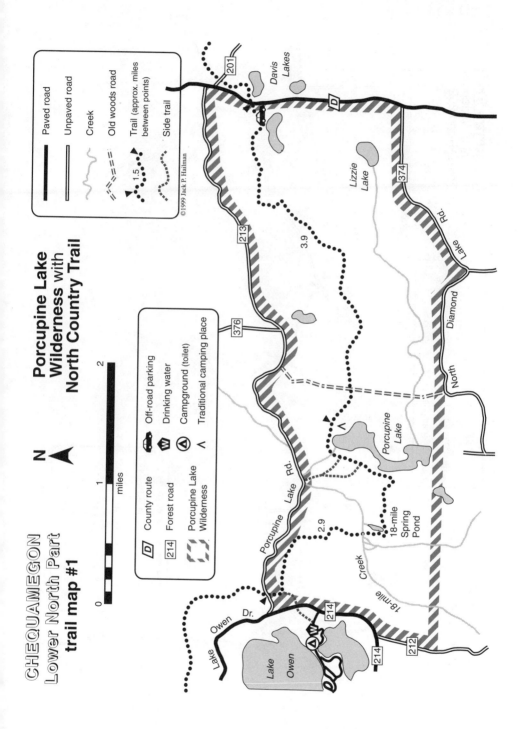

CHEQUAMEGON
Lower North Part
trail map #1

N

Porcupine Lake Wilderness with North Country Trail

miles

0   1   2

Legend:

- Paved road
- Unpaved road
- Creek
- Old woods road
- 1.5 ▸ Trail (approx. miles between points)
- Side trail

©1999 Jack P. Hailman

- D County route
- 214 Forest road
- Porcupine Lake Wilderness
- 🚗 Off-road parking
- 💧 Drinking water
- 🅐 Campground (toilet)
- ⋀ Traditional camping place

Davis Lakes

201

D

Lizzie Lake

374

Diamond Lake Rd.

North

213

3.9

376

Porcupine Lake

⋀

Porcupine Lake Rd.

2.9

18-mile Spring Pond

18-mile Creek

214

212

Lake Owen Dr.

Lake Owen

214

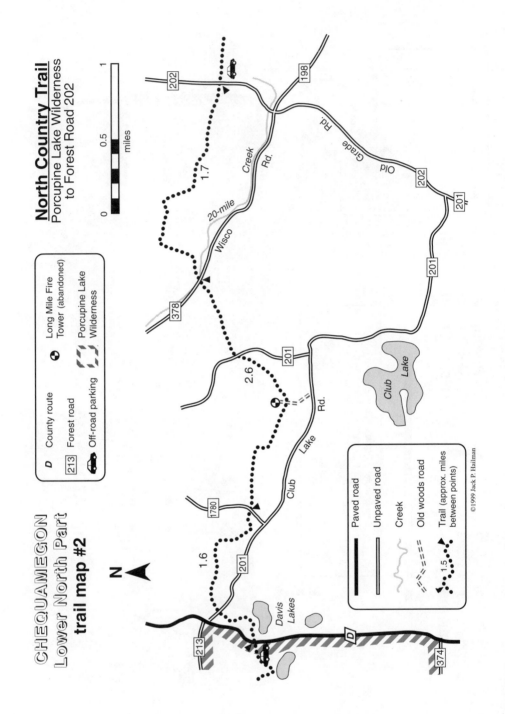

North Country Trail
Porcupine Lake Wilderness
to Forest Road 202

miles
0   0.5   1

CHEQUAMEGON
Lower North Part
trail map #2

N

County route *D*
Forest road [213]
Off-road parking

Long Mile Fire
Tower (abandoned)

Porcupine Lake
Wilderness

Paved road
Unpaved road
Creek
Old woods road
Trail (approx. miles
between points)   1.5

©1999 Jack P. Hailman

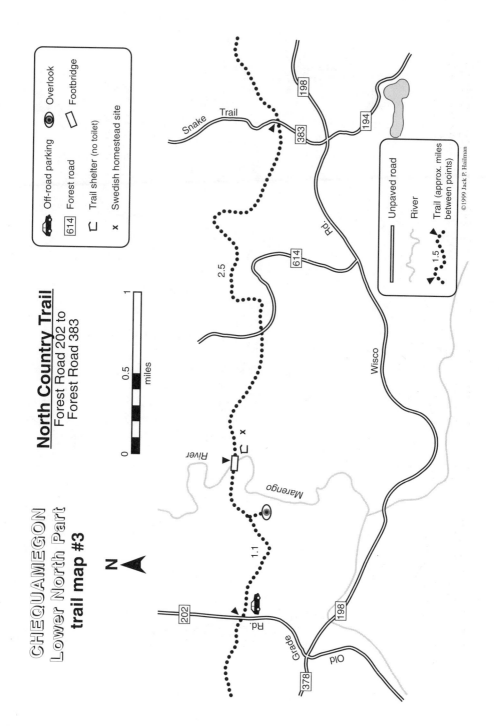

North Country Trail
Forest Road 202 to
Forest Road 383

CHEQUAMEGON
Lower North Part
trail map #3

N

Off-road parking ◉ Overlook

614 Forest road   ☐ Footbridge

⊏ Trail shelter (no toilet)

× Swedish homestead site

miles
0   0.5   1

Snake Trail

2.5

1.5

198

194

383

614

Rd.

Wisco

River

Marengo

×
⊏

1.1

202

Rd.

Grade

Old

378

198

Unpaved road

River

Trail (approx. miles
between points)

©1999 Jack P. Hailman

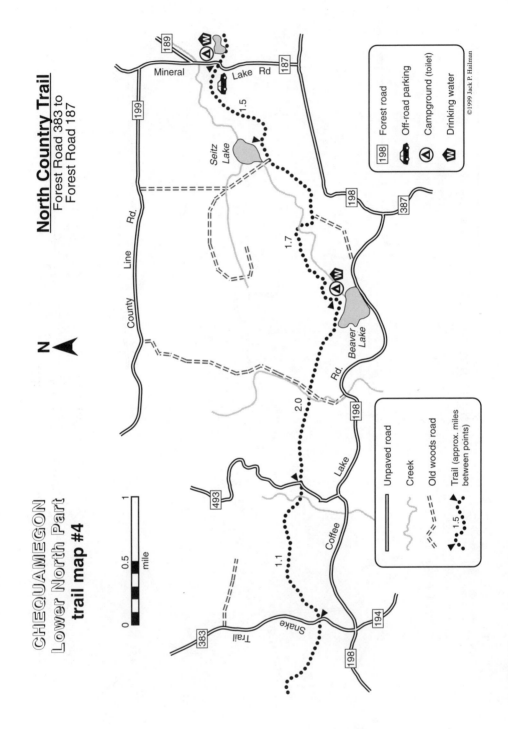

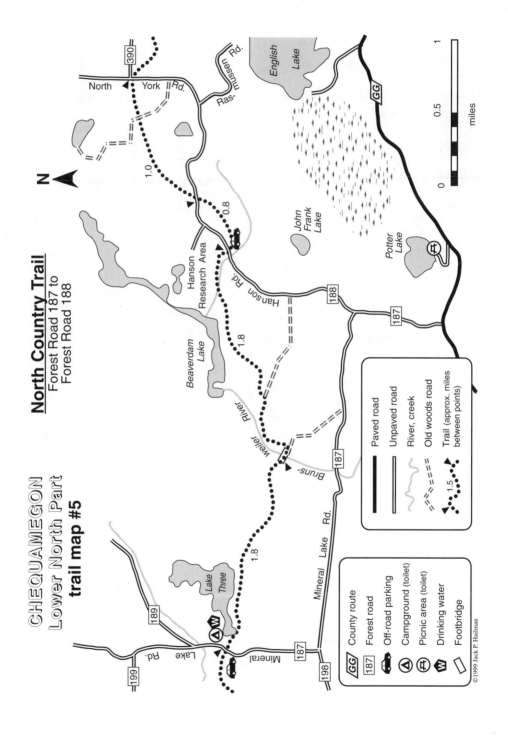

CHEQUAMEGON
Lower North Part
trail map #5

North Country Trail
Forest Road 187 to
Forest Road 188

N

North York Rd.

Ras-mussen Rd.

390

English Lake

GG

1.0

0.8

Hanson Research Area

Hanson Rd.

John Frank Lake

Potter Lake

Beaverdam Lake

1.8

188

187

Weller River

Bruns-

1.8

187

Lake Three

189

199

Lake Rd.

Mineral

Mineral Lake Rd.

187

198

1.5

Paved road

Unpaved road

River, creek

Old woods road

Trail (approx. miles between points)

GG   County route

187   Forest road

Off-road parking

Campground (toilet)

Picnic area (toilet)

Drinking water

Footbridge

0   0.5   1
miles

© 1999 Jack P. Hailman

125

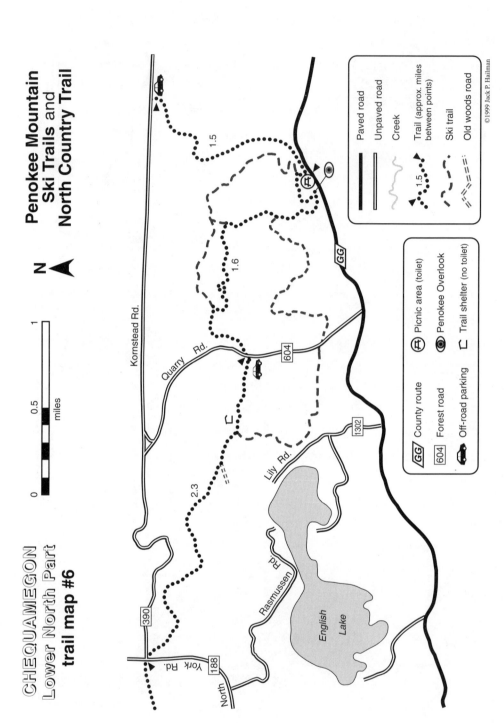

CHEQUAMEGON
Lower North Part
trail map #6

0   0.5   1
miles

N

Penokee Mountain
Ski Trails and
North Country Trail

Kornstead Rd.

Quarry   Rd.

604

1.5

1.6

2.3

GG

Lily Rd.

1302

Rasmussen   Rd.

English
Lake

390

York Rd.

North

188

Paved road
Unpaved road
Creek
Trail (approx. miles
between points)
Ski trail
Old woods road

1.5

GG   County route
604   Forest road
      Off-road parking

Picnic area (toilet)
Penokee Overlook
Trail shelter (no toilet)

©1999 Jack P. Hailman

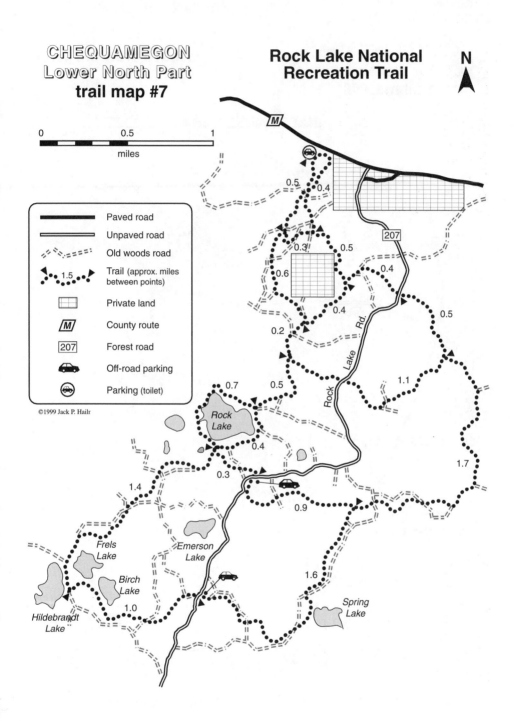

CHEQUAMEGON
Lower North Part
trail map #7

Rock Lake National
Recreation Trail

N

0   0.5   1
miles

Paved road

Unpaved road

Old woods road

1.5   Trail (approx. miles between points)

Private land

M   County route

207   Forest road

Off-road parking

Parking (toilet)

©1999 Jack P. Hailr

0.5
0.4
M
207
0.3   0.5
0.6
0.4
0.4
0.2
0.5
1.1
1.7

Rock Lake Rd.

0.7   0.5
Rock Lake
0.4
0.3
0.9
1.4
Frels Lake
Emerson Lake
Birch Lake
1.6
1.0
Spring Lake
Hildebrandt Lake

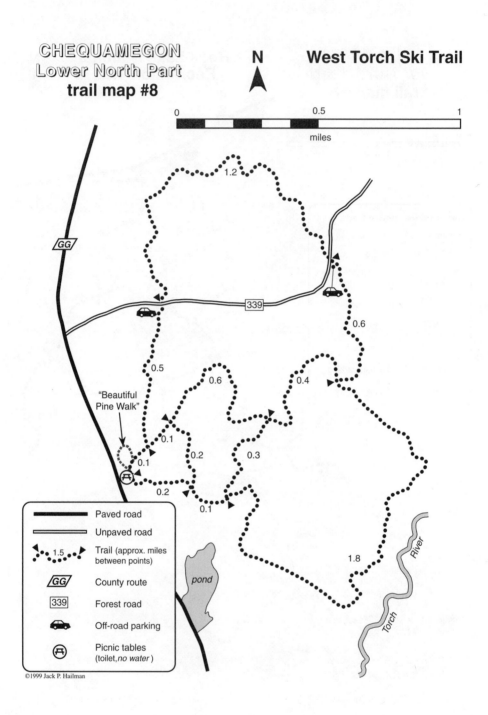

East Part

Park Falls Section of Medford/Park Falls Ranger District

The East part of Chequamegon offers fine backpacking possibilities: two ski complexes, a linear foot trail, and a semi-primitive area where no motorized transportation is allowed.

LOCATION. North Central region, coordinates E-3/4 on official state highway map (mainly Price County).

RATING: NEWMAN SPRINGS TRAILS (TRAIL MAP #1). 🌲🌲🌲🌲

🌲 **Scenery:** extensive wet areas often provide pleasant open scenery

🌲 **Quiet:** can camp almost a mile from nearest paved road

🌲 **Trails:** can camp on loop longer than 5 miles

🌲 **Solitude:** unlikely to encounter more than 2 parties per day

🌲 **Interest:** wet areas probably attract more wildlife than usual

RATING: WINTERGREEN TRAILS (TRAIL MAP #2). 🌲🌲🌲🌲

🌲 **Scenery:** better than average glacial scenery, including some vistas

🌲 **Quiet:** can camp more than a mile from nearest paved road

🌲 **Trails:** can camp on loop longer than 5 miles

🌲 **Solitude:** unlikely to encounter more than 2 parties per day

🌲 **Interest:** one of the few places in Wisconsin where we have seen Gray Jays, a boreal species

RATING: HOGSBACK TRAIL (TRAIL MAP #3). 🌲🌲

🌲 **Quiet:** can camp more than a mile from nearest paved road

🌲 **Solitude:** unlikely to encounter more than 2 parties on entire trail

RATING: ROUND LAKE SEMI-PRIMITIVE AREA (TRAIL MAP #4). 🌲🌲🌲🌲

🌲 **Scenery:** views of Round Lake from some trails, also trails to other lakes

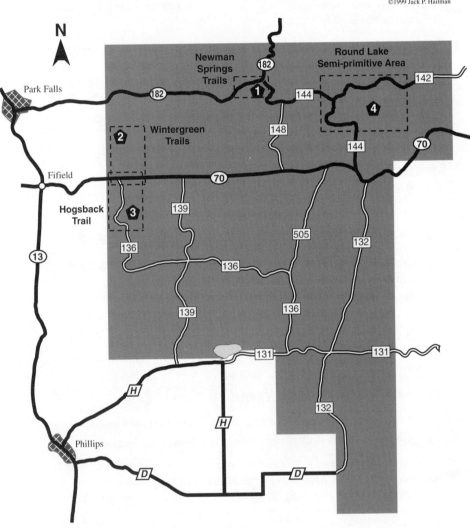

CHEQUAMEGON
East Part

area map

0   5   10

miles

	Paved road
	Unpaved road
70	State route
H	County route
144	Forest road
3	Trail map coverage with map number

©1999 Jack P. Hailman

N

Park Falls

Newman Springs Trails

Round Lake Semi-primitive Area

182

142

182

1

144

148

144

70

2

Wintergreen Trails

Fifield

70

Hogsback Trail

3

139

136

505

132

136

136

13

139

136

131

131

H

H

Phillips

132

D

D

🌲 **Quiet:** can camp more than a mile from nearest paved road, but Round Lake allows powerboats

🌲 **Trails:** can camp on loop longer than 5 miles

🌲 **Solitude:** likely to meet only 3 to 6 parties per day

🌲 **Interest:** reconstructed logging dam

ENTRANCE FEE. Forest Service vehicle sticker (or daily pass) required to park in some forest lots or to use other national forest facilities.

CAMPING. Wilderness camping. Campsites on Round Lake are for boaters and cannot be accessed by established trail system. There is a campground (camping fees charged) just north of the primitive area. The only public source of drinking water we could locate is at this campground.

PERMIT AND RESERVATIONS. None needed for wilderness camping.

CONTACT INFORMATION. Medford/Park Falls Ranger District, 1170 S. 4th Ave. S., Park Falls, WI 54552; phone: 715/762-2461; fax: 715/762-5179; TTY: 715/762-5701.

FINDING THE TRAIL. All four backpacking areas are easily accessed from state highways. **Newman Springs Trails** are 13 miles east of Park Falls on State Highway 182. Both the **Wintergreen** and **Hogsback Trails** begin at the parking lot 5 miles east of Fifield on State Highway 70. Farther east, 20 miles from Fifield (and about 18 miles west of Minocqua), take Forest Road 144 northbound 2 miles from State Highway 70 to **Round Lake Semi-primitive Area.** From the entrance road, one fork leads to the dam site and trail parking, the other to a boat ramp with toilet facilities. It is also possible to reach the Round Lake area from State Highway 182 by driving south on Forest Road 144 for about 4.5 miles.

BACKGROUND NOTES. The logging dam was faithfully reconstructed from old photographs. In spring, water would be held back until all the logs were ready to be floated to the mill, and then the sluice gates opened to raise the level of the South Fork of the Flambeau River to carry the large burden.

OUR TRAIL NOTES. It was the last day of September, and we were well behind schedule when we pulled into the Wintergreen parking lot as daylight was fading. Our destination was the "picnic area" on the Forest Service's ski map, just a little over 3 miles in by our chosen route. Before we arrived, however, lightning began to flash in the rapidly darkening sky. Surprise! The picnic area turned out to be a three-sided shelter with a picnic table inside. We have generally used our tent rather than shelters after we spent a night many years ago in a shelter on the Appalachian Trail. We got little sleep that night, having been confronted by an army of mice. We were happy to have the shelter here on the Wintergreen Trails, though, for stashing our packs and cooking breakfast in the rain. The spectacular electrical storm had brought rain that lasted all night but conveniently abated by morning for the walk out. As we left, we noticed that the Forest Service was already preparing for winter: the handle had been removed form the pump at the trailhead.

Flora. The forest here is mainly hardwood, such as Paper Birch and Quaking Aspen, with some spruces and plantations of Red Pine. There is also a nice Tamarack bog along the westernmost trail (shown on trail map #2), and the trail between the two small lakes runs above them on a ridge. There are also unexpected "balds" devoid of trees, perhaps clearings made to promote wildlife.

Fauna. The only mammal we saw was the Red Squirrel. The few species of birds were all pretty representative of northern woods: Ruffed Grouse, Downy Woodpecker, Blue Jay, Black-capped Chickadee, and Ruby-crowned Kinglet. The best bird of the trip, though, was a pair of Gray Jays—this is one of the few places in Wisconsin where we have seen this boreal species.

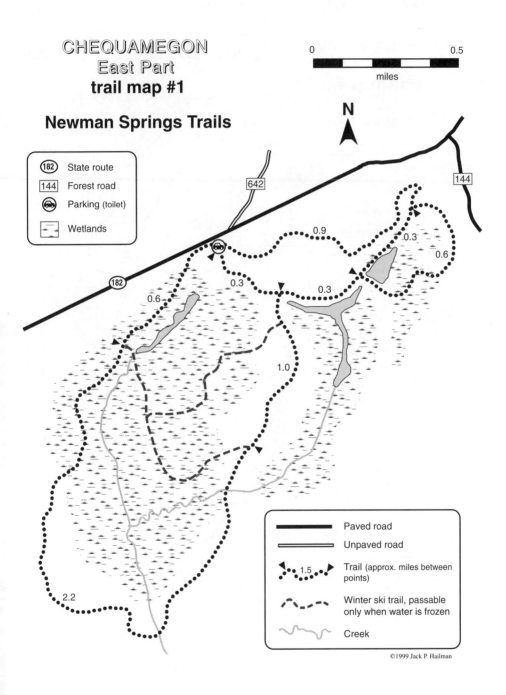

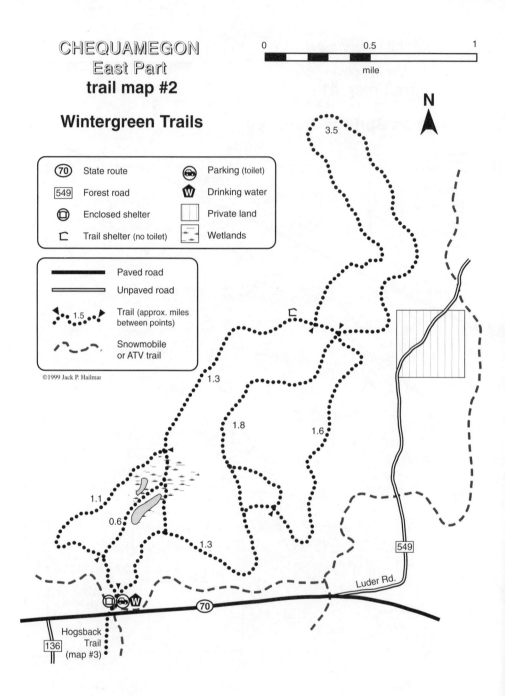

CHEQUAMEGON
East Part
trail map #2

Wintergreen Trails

0   0.5   1
mile

N

Legend:

(70)	State route	(car)	Parking (toilet)
549	Forest road	W	Drinking water
(shelter)	Enclosed shelter		Private land
C	Trail shelter (no toilet)		Wetlands

Paved road

Unpaved road

1.5 — Trail (approx. miles between points)

Snowmobile or ATV trail

©1999 Jack P. Hailmar

3.5

C

1.3

1.8

1.6

1.1

0.6

1.3

549

Luder Rd.

W

70

136

Hogsback Trail (map #3)

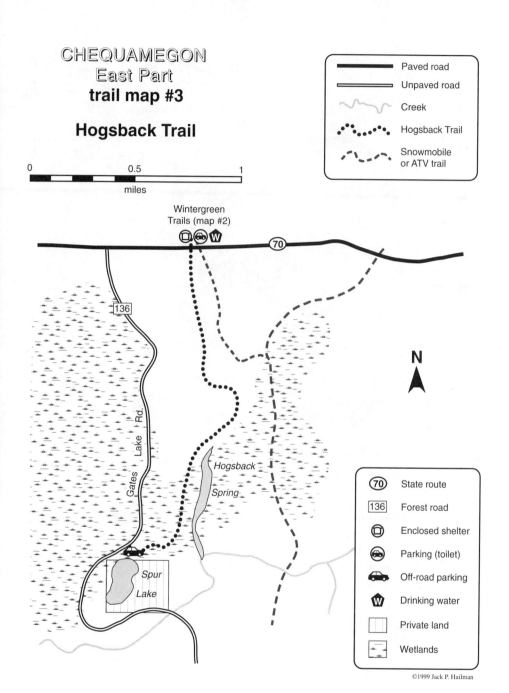

CHEQUAMEGON
East Part
trail map #3

Hogsback Trail

0   0.5   1
miles

Paved road	
Unpaved road	
Creek	
Hogsback Trail	
Snowmobile or ATV trail	

Wintergreen
Trails (map #2)

70

N

136

Gates Lake Rd.

Hogsback

Spring

Spur
Lake

70	State route
136	Forest road
	Enclosed shelter
	Parking (toilet)
	Off-road parking
W	Drinking water
	Private land
	Wetlands

©1999 Jack P. Hailman

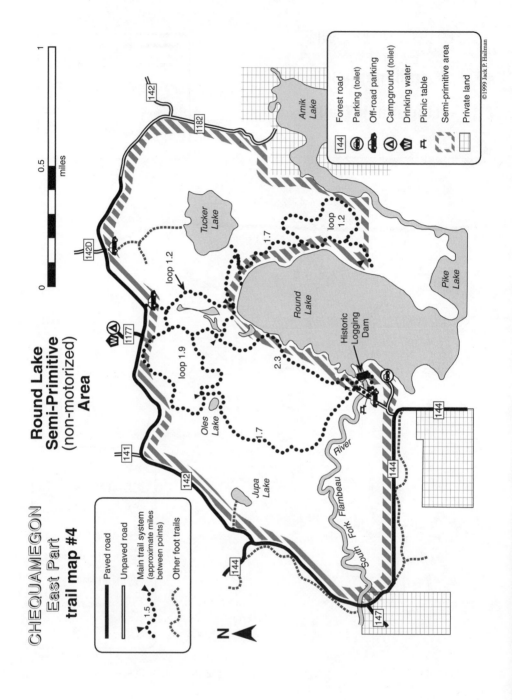

CHEQUAMEGON
East Part
trail map #4

**Round Lake
Semi-Primitive**
(non-motorized)
Area

©1999 Jack P. Hailman

miles
0   0.5   1

Legend:
— Paved road
— Unpaved road
••• Main trail system (approximate miles between points)
1.5
····· Other foot trails

N

Forest road   144
Parking (toilet)   6
Off-road parking   ◭
Campground (toilet)   ⚠
Drinking water   W
Picnic table   🏕
Semi-primitive area   ⌐⌐
Private land   ▦

142
1182
142D
177
141
142
144
144
147

Tucker Lake
loop 1.2
loop 1.2
1.7
loop 1.2
Round Lake
Pike Lake
Amik Lake
Historic Logging Dam
2.3
loop 1.9
Oles Lake
1.7
1.7
South Fork Flambeau River
Jupa Lake

South Part

Medford Section of Medford/Park Falls Ranger District

The southernmost part of Chequamegon offers a long section of the Ice Age National Scenic Trail with campsites. A looped side trail has a campsite nicely situated on a small lake.

LOCATION. North Central region, coordinates E-5 on official state highway map (Taylor County).

RATING: ICE AGE NATIONAL SCENIC TRAIL (TRAIL MAPS #1–4). 🌲🌲🌲

  🌲 **Scenery:** generally wooded, but passes some scenic lakes including Mondeaux Flowage

  🌲 **Quiet:** can camp more than a mile from paved roads on all sections of trail

  🌲 **Trails:** at least 10 miles of trail accessible from camping places

  🌲 **Solitude:** variable; most parts of trail are little used, but many people visit Mondeaux Flowage area

RATING: CHIPPEWA LOBE LOOP (TRAIL MAP #3). 🌲🌲🌲🌲

  🌲 **Scenery:** half credit for scenic campsite

  🌲 **Quiet:** can camp more than a mile from nearest paved road

  🌲 **Trails:** can camp on circuit of more than 5 miles, and at least 10 miles of trail accessible from this loop

  🌲 **Solitude:** unlikely to encounter more than 2 parties per day

ENTRANCE FEE. Forest Service vehicle sticker (or daily pass) required to park in some forest lots or use other national forest facilities.

CAMPING. Wilderness camping or at campsites provided by the national forest. Each campsite has an open throne toilet but no other amenities. Potable water is available at the campgrounds (trail maps #2 and #4).

PERMIT AND RESERVATIONS. None needed for wilderness camping or use of the trail campsites.

CONTACT INFORMATION. Medford/Park Falls Ranger District, Medford Office, 850 N. 8th St., Hwy. 13, Medford, WI 54451; phone

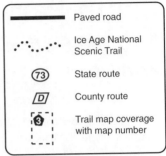

N

0   5   10
miles

Paved road

Ice Age National
Scenic Trail

(73) State route

D County route

3 Trail map coverage
with map number

©1999 Jack P. Hailman

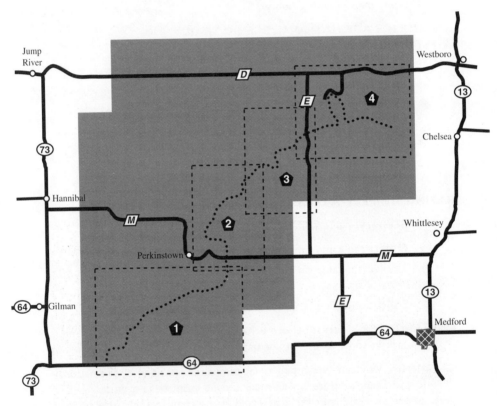

Jump
River

Westboro

D

E

4

13

Chelsea

73

3

Hannibal

M

2

Whittlesey

Perkinstown

M

64 Gilman

E

13

1

Medford

64

64

73

and TTY: 715/748-4875; fax: 715/748-5675. *Also,* Forest Supervisor, Chequamegon-Nicolet National Forest, 1170 S. 4th Ave., Park Falls, WI 54552; phone: 715/762-2461; fax: 715/762-5179; TTY: 715/762-5701.

Ice Age National Scenic Trail. Ice Age Park & Trail Foundation of Wisconsin, Inc., 207 E. Buffalo St., Suite 515, Milwaukee, WI 53202-5712; phone: 800/227-0046; e-mail: cthisted@sbtsi.com. The office can put you in touch with the current coordinator of the chapter responsible for this section of trail. *Also,* Ice Age National Scenic Trail, National Park Service, 700 Rayovac Dr., Suite 100, Madison, WI 53711; phone: 608/264-5610.

FINDING THE TRAIL. The Chequamegon-South section of the **Ice Age Trail** begins on State Highway 64 about 18 miles west of Medford. The trail crosses Taylor County Highways M and E and can also be accessed via forest roads leading from these three highways and from County Highway D in the north (see trail maps). The **Chippewa Lobe Loop** (trail map #3) is best found by walking the Ice Age Trail east from Forest Road 108, but can also be accessed by walking the Birch Hunter Trail south from Forest Road 102.

BACKGROUND NOTES. This was one of the first sections of certified Ice Age Trail.

Beaver dam at campsite, Chippewa Loop, Chequamegon National Forest

On an old beaver dam, Ice Age Trail, Chequamegon National Forest

OUR TRAIL NOTES.   Although we have taken multi-night backpacking trips on the Ice Age Trail in southern Chequamegon, we choose to recount here an overnight on the Chippewa Lobe Loop. It was a pleasant Saturday in late May 1998 when we arrived at the crossing of the Ice Age Trail on Forest Road 108, and we parked on the roadside in preference to the low, rutted parking area. We decided to walk the loop counter-clockwise, which turned out to be an unfortunate decision that caused us to backtrack the next day. A Barred Owl's call punctuated the afternoon air as we walked the trail, and many other birds, as well as some frogs, added to the noise as we cooked dinner at the lovely campsite situated on a small lake. The din continued during the night, with a Barred Owl calling from the campsite, Bullfrogs croaking in the little lake, Beavers slapping their tails on the water's surface, and a pack of Coyotes yipping not far away. The next day, we began having problems with the trail less than a half hour out of camp. Tree falls grew increasingly worse, and we had to take off our packs to get under some that could not be circumnavigated. Finally, in a swamp, there were so many trees down that we could no longer find trail markers, and we reluctantly turned back after having invested an hour and a half in very tough walking. If we had tried to come down the western loop the day before, we soon would have discovered the trail was impassable and thereby saved three hours that could have been spent in more pleasant

Lake on Ice Age Trail, Chequamegon National Forest

pursuits. This blowdown section has now been cleared and should no longer pose a problem. Retracing our steps on the way back along the eastern side of the loop, we met a handsome young couple with backpacks on their way to the campsite. We warned them about the impassable western side of the loop, but they didn't seem to believe us. We wished them well anyway as we headed for the Ice Age Trail and the pleasant walk back to our car.

Flora. The woods here are mixed conifers and hardwoods. We noted Balsam Fir, Black Spruce in boggy areas, White Spruce, dark, low areas of virtually pure Eastern Hemlock, and hardwoods such as American Elm, Sugar Maple, Paper Birch, and Yellow Birch. Mosses covered tree trunks and rocks, Rusty Hoof Fungus also grew on tree trunks, Running Ground Pine and its close relative Shiny Clubmoss grew on the ground, and ferns of various varieties were often thick in the damper areas of the forest. Although it was already late in the spring for woodland wildflowers, we found quite a few: Wild Calla (Water-arum), Clintonia (Corn-lily, Yellow Beadlily), Nodding Trillium, Large-flowered (White, Large) Trillium, Wild Lily-of-the-valley (Canada Mayflower), Showy (Pink) Lady's-slipper, Common (Tall) Buttercup, Common Strawberry, Red Raspberry, Wild Sarsaparilla, Bunchberry (Dwarf Correl), Starflower, and Field Pussytoes.

Fauna. Animals also knew it was spring. Aside from flies and mosquitoes, noticeable insects were mainly butterflies, including a black-and-white species, a small white butterfly, and a Tiger Swallowtail. Amphibians were also common: an American Toad on the trail, Gray Treefrogs singing from the swamps, and Bullfrogs singing from the lake. The birds were spectacular, with most of the songbird species in full song, and our list is doubtless incomplete: Great Blue Heron, Canada Goose honking overhead, Cooper's Hawk noisily chattering as it flew by, Red-tailed Hawk, Barred Owl, Belted Kingfisher, Yellow-bellied Sapsucker, Great Crested Flycatcher, Red-eyed Vireo, Blue Jay, Common Raven, Black-capped Chickadee, White-breasted Nuthatch, House Wren, Winter Wren, American Robin, Northern Parula, Black-throated Green Warbler, Ovenbird, Common Yellowthroat, Song Sparrow, White-throated Sparrow, and Red-winged Blackbird. Even the mammals were unusually well represented: Coyote, Red Squirrel, Beaver, and plenty of signs of Whitetail Deer.

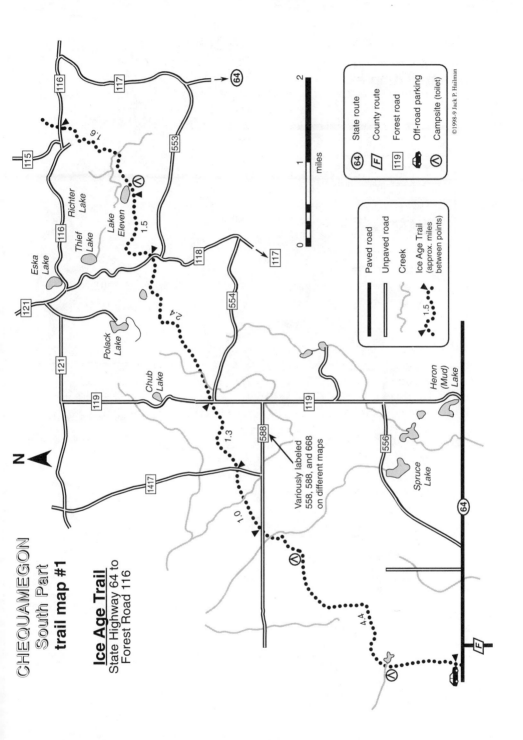

CHEQUAMEGON
South Part
trail map #1

Ice Age Trail
State Highway 64 to
Forest Road 116

N

State route
County route
Forest road
Off-road parking
Campsite (toilet)

©1998-9 Jack P. Hailman

Paved road
Unpaved road
Creek
Ice Age Trail
(approx. miles
between points)

1.5

0   1   2
miles

64
Ⓕ
119
⊗

116
117
→ 64
115
553
Richter
Lake
⊗
Lake
Eleven
Thief
Lake
1.5
116
Eska
Lake
121
118
→ 117
2.4
554
Polack
Lake
121
Chub
Lake
119
1.3
119
Heron
(Mud)
Lake
1417
588
Variously labeled
558, 588, and 668
on different maps
556
Spruce
Lake
1.0
⊗
64
4.4
⊗
Ⓕ

143

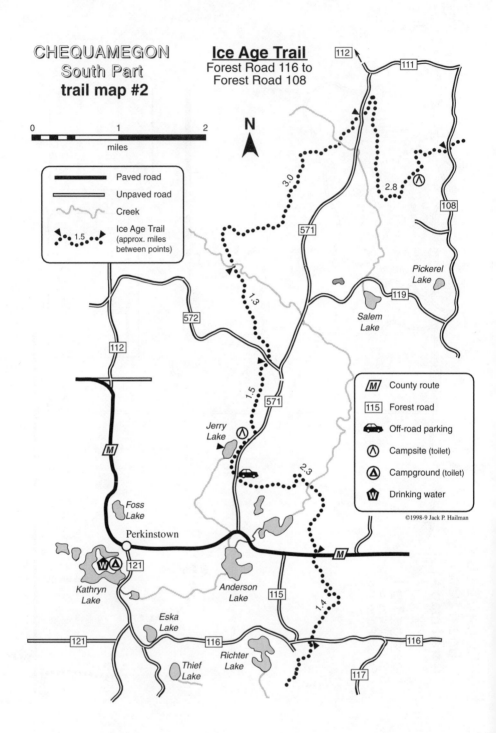

CHEQUAMEGON
South Part
trail map #2

Ice Age Trail
Forest Road 116 to
Forest Road 108

N

0   1   2
miles

▬▬▬▬▬	Paved road
▭▭▭▭▭	Unpaved road
〰〰〰	Creek
◄•••1.5•••►	Ice Age Trail (approx. miles between points)

112
111
108
571
Pickerel Lake
119
Salem Lake
572
112
M
Jerry Lake
571
Foss Lake
Perkinstown
W Δ 121
Kathryn Lake
Anderson Lake
115
Eska Lake
121
116
Richter Lake
Thief Lake
117
116
M

3.0
2.8
1.3
1.5
2.3
1.4

M	County route
115	Forest road
🚗	Off-road parking
Ⓐ	Campsite (toilet)
Ⓐ	Campground (toilet)
W	Drinking water

©1998-9 Jack P. Hailman

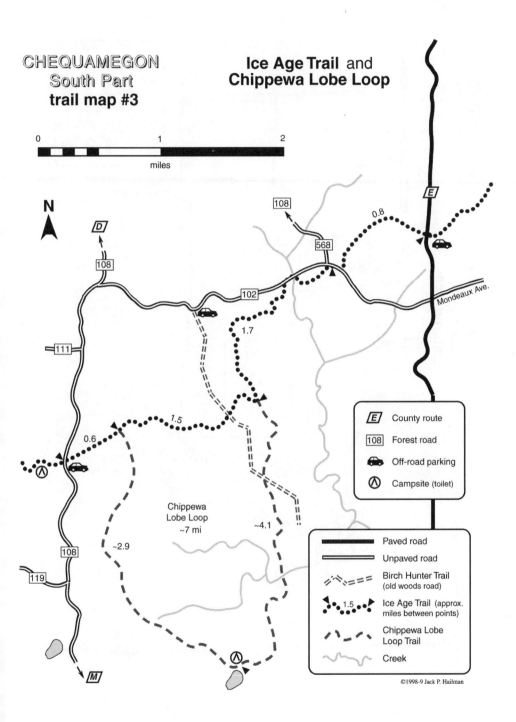

CHEQUAMEGON
South Part
trail map #3

Ice Age Trail and
Chippewa Lobe Loop

0   1   2
miles

N

[D]

[108]

[108]

[111]

[102]

[108]

[119]

[M]

[108]

568

[E]

0.8

Mondeaux Ave.

1.7

1.5

0.6

Chippewa
Lobe Loop
~7 mi

~4.1

~2.9

[E]	County route
[108]	Forest road
🚗	Off-road parking
Ⓐ	Campsite (toilet)

| Paved road |
| Unpaved road |
| Birch Hunter Trail (old woods road) |
| Ice Age Trail (approx. 1.5 miles between points) |
| Chippewa Lobe Loop Trail |
| Creek |

©1998-9 Jack P. Hailman

Ice Age Trail
Mondeaux Flowage area

CHEQUAMEGON
South Part
trail map #4

N

0   1   2
miles

Legend:
— Paved road
— Unpaved road
Creek
Ice Age Trail
(approx. miles
between points)

1.5

Map symbols:
E — County route
102 — Forest road
— Off-road parking
▲ — Campground (toilet)
♨ — Drinking water

© 1998-9 Jack P. Hailman

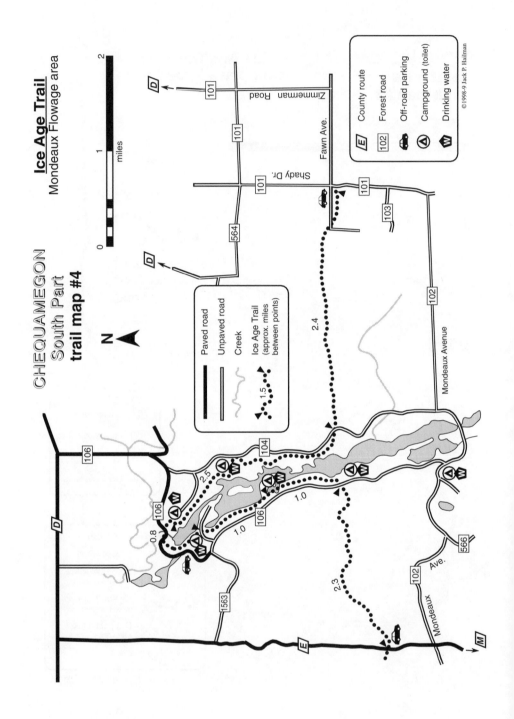

NORTHEAST REGION

Like the other northern regions, the Northeast offers many and varied backpacking possibilities. The state's largest single holding, the Northern Highland–American Legion State Forest, unfortunately allows backpacking on only one trail that fits our criteria, despite having numerous ski-trail complexes that are virtually deserted when the snow cover is gone. The Nicolet side of the Chequamegon-Nicolet National Forest is so large that the northern and southern parts are accorded separate accounts in this chapter, and both provide many trails and trail systems. Also beckoning are sections of the Ice Age National Scenic Trail running through county forest lands, along with at least one connecting ski-trail complex.

NORTHEAST REGION

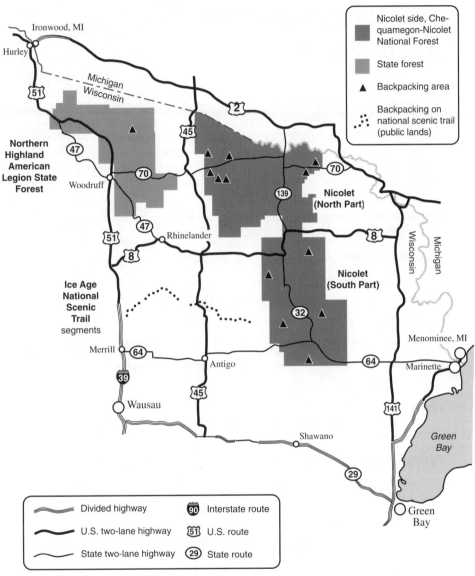

Nicolet side, Chequamegon-Nicolet National Forest

State forest

▲ Backpacking area

Backpacking on national scenic trail (public lands)

Ironwood, MI

Hurley

51

Michigan
Wisconsin

2

45

Northern Highland American Legion State Forest

47

70

Woodruff

139

Nicolet (North Part)

70

47

51

Rhinelander

8

8

Nicolet (South Part)

Ice Age National Scenic Trail segments

32

Menominee, MI

Merrill

64

Antigo

64

Marinette

39

45

141

Wausau

Shawano

Green Bay

29

Green Bay

Wisconsin

Michigan

Divided highway

90 Interstate route

U.S. two-lane highway

51 U.S. route

State two-lane highway

29 State route

© 1999 Jack P. Hailman

Northern Highland– American Legion State Forest

The Northern Highland–American Legion State Forest has the greatest number of marked trails potentially suitable for backpacking in the state, but allows backpacking on only one trail (in addition to unsuitable snowmobile trails) while the others remain essentially deserted the entire summer. The reason for this policy, which differs so strikingly from all the other northern state forests, is unclear.

LOCATION.   Northeast region, coordinates F-3/4 on official state highway map (Vilas, Iron, and Oneida Counties).

RATING: LUMBERJACK TRAIL.

 Scenery: trail passes scenic watercourses and lake

Quiet: can camp a mile or more from paved roads

Trails: at least 10 miles of trail accessible for hiking and camping

Solitude: unlikely to encounter more than 2 parties per day

ENTRANCE FEE.   State vehicle sticker required for parking lots and other state forest facilities.

CAMPING.   Wilderness camping (no designated campsites) anywhere along the trail, at least 50 feet away from the trail and 200 feet from water.

PERMIT AND RESERVATIONS.   Required for the Lumberjack Trail. Free permits may be obtained at the Woodruff and Boulder Junction offices listed below. Also in summer months you may obtain a permit at the contact stations at Crystal Lake or Clear Lake campgrounds. The Clear Lake contact station is in Oneida County, 4 miles east of Minocqua on County Highway J and then south on Woodruff Rd. Crystal Lake Campground is in Vilas County. Take U.S. Highway 51 north from Woodruff for 6.2 miles, then go northeast on County Highway M for 2.7 miles, then 2 miles east on County N.

CONTACT INFORMATION.   Northern Highland–American Legion State Forest, 8770 Hwy. J, Woodruff, WI 54568; phone: 715/356-5211; fax: 715/358-2352. *Also,* Trout Lake Forestry Headquarters, 4125

Northern Highland — American Legion State Forest

area map

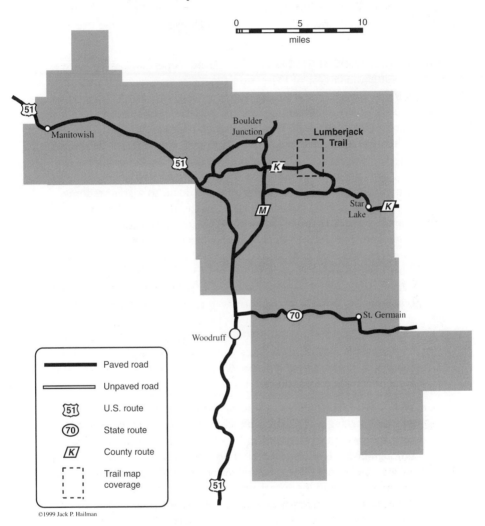

N

0 5 10
miles

Manitowish
51

Boulder Junction
51

Lumberjack Trail

K

M

Star Lake

K

70 St. Germain

Woodruff

51

Paved road

Unpaved road

51 U.S. route

70 State route

K County route

Trail map coverage

©1999 Jack P. Hailman

151

Cty. Hwy. M, Boulder Junction, WI 54512; phone: 715/385-2727; fax: 715/385-2752.

FINDING THE TRAIL. The western parking area for **Lumberjack Trail** is on "Old K" road, which intersects County Highway M in Boulder Junction. To reach the eastern parking area, take County M south from Boulder Junction or north from U.S. Highway 51, then go east on County K.

BACKGROUND NOTES. Northern Highland–American Legion State Forest is the largest of Wisconsin's state forests, with 220,000 acres in Vilas, Oneida, and Iron Counties. It was created in 1925 to preserve the headwaters of the Wisconsin, Flambeau, and Manitowish Rivers. The area is a vacation spot for many people from Wisconsin and elsewhere, and the forest is interspersed with much private land and many commercial ventures. A billion or more years ago, this part of Wisconsin was the site of lofty mountains. Erosion over so long a time wore the mountains down to a granite dome, but apparently it was never so low that the huge inland seas of North America covered this area. At least no sandstones and limestones remain here as they do farther to the west in Wisconsin, so if they were once deposited on top of the granite dome, they must have been taken away by water erosion and the continental glaciers of comparatively modern times. Today that granite dome crops out in only a few small places; it is mostly covered by the clay, gravel, rocks, and boulders brought here by the glaciers, the last of which retreated only about 10,000 years ago. Thus, the hills, lakes, bogs, and marshes of today's scenic topography were almost completely created by the glaciation, resulting in a beautiful area for vacationers and backpackers.

OUR TRAIL NOTES. We were told by the forest staff over the phone that backpacking was allowed on all the ski trails and we needed a permit only for Lumberjack Trail. We have since discovered that although hiking is allowed on all trails, backpacking is permitted only on the Lumberjack Trail (and snowmobile trails). So our short backpacking trip in the forest was on Statehouse Lake Trail, in retrospect apparently somewhere we were not supposed to be (not that it mattered much, as we did not meet another living soul). The long days near the summer solstice provided an opportunity to set up camp late in the evening: at 8:45 P.M. on a Friday in late June, having left our jobs in Madison at 3 P.M. to start the drive north. The evening's warmth (70°F at bedtime) was alleviated by a driving rainstorm in the second half of the night, which dropped temperatures to 62°F. After breaking camp in the morning, we hiked the short distance to our car and had breakfast in a small park on a lake in Manitowish Waters.

Flora. Along the trail we found evergreens such as Balsam Fir, Red Pine, and Eastern White Pine. The deciduous trees were Paper Birch and Sugar Maple, and on the forest floor were ferns.

Fauna. Even before going to sleep on Friday, we had heard a number of birds: Osprey, Whip-poor-will, Belted Kingfisher, Great Crested Flycatcher, American Crow, Black-capped Chickadee, Veery, Hermit Thrush, Ovenbird, Eastern Towhee, and Song Sparrow, as well as three members of the amphibian class: American Toad, Bullfrog, and Northern Cricket Frog. And we were fortunate enough to catch a glimpse of a Gray Fox. There was a host of new birds around in the morning: an immature Bald Eagle, Red-eyed Vireo, Blue Jay, Red-breasted Nuthatch, Wood Thrush, American Robin, Pine Warbler, American Redstart, and Common Yellowthroat. An Eastern Chipmunk added its chipping to the chorus.

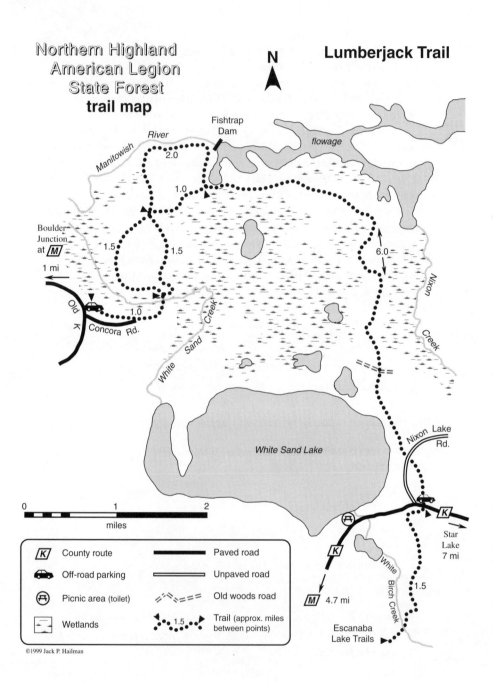

Northern Highland American Legion State Forest
trail map

N

Lumberjack Trail

Fishtrap Dam

Manitowish River

flowage

2.0

1.0

Boulder Junction at [M]

1 mi

1.5

1.5

1.0

Old K Concora Rd.

White Sand Creek

6.0

Nixon Creek

White Sand Lake

Nixon Lake Rd.

[K]

Star Lake 7 mi

[K]

[M] 4.7 mi

White Birch Creek

1.5

Escanaba Lake Trails

0	1	2
miles		

[K]	County route	▬▬▬	Paved road
🚗	Off-road parking	═══	Unpaved road
Ⓟ	Picnic area (toilet)	≋≋≋	Old woods road
〜	Wetlands	•••1.5•••	Trail (approx. miles between points)

©1999 Jack P. Hailman

Nicolet, North Part
Eagle River/Florence Ranger District

Away from the crowded tourist regions in northern Wisconsin, the North part of the Nicolet side of Chequamegon-Nicolet National Forest offers a great variety of outdoor recreation in scenic and secluded settings. The backpacking opportunities are numerous.

LOCATION. Northeast region, coordinates G/H-3/4 on official state highway map (Vilas, Oneida, Forest, and Florence Counties). The area we have called the North part corresponds approximately with the Eagle River/Florence Ranger District of the national forest.

RATING: BLACKJACK SPRINGS WILDERNESS (TRAIL MAP #1). 🌲🌲🌲🌲

🌲 **Scenery:** trail goes near Whispering Lake and Blackjack Springs

🌲 **Quiet:** can camp a mile or more from nearest paved road

🌲 **Solitude:** unlikely to encounter more than 2 other parties per day

🌲 **Interest:** wilderness area with four large, crystal-clear springs

RATING: ANVIL NATIONAL RECREATIONAL TRAIL (TRAIL MAP #2). 🌲🌲🌲

🌲 **Trails:** at least 10 miles of trail, because of connection with Nicolet North Trails

🌲 **Solitude:** unlikely to encounter more than 6 other parties per day

🌲 **Interest:** a "designated watchable wildlife area"

RATING: NICOLET NORTH TRAILS (TRAIL MAP #3). 🌲🌲🌲

🌲 **Scenery:** trail goes near Echo Lake and Pat Shay Lake

🌲 **Trails:** at least 10 miles of trail, because of connection with Anvil and Hidden Lakes Trails

🌲 **Solitude:** unlikely to encounter more than 2 other parties per day

RATING: HIDDEN LAKES TRAIL (TRAIL MAP #4). 🌲🌲🌲

🌲 **Scenery:** many lakes by trail

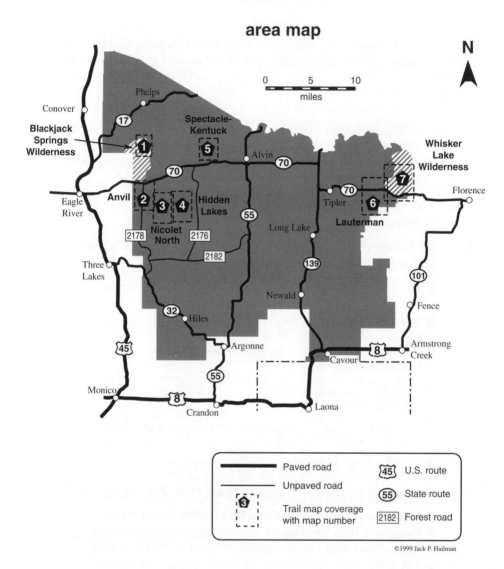

NICOLET SIDE
Chequamegon — Nicolet National Forest
North Part

area map

N

0   5   10
miles

Conover

Phelps

17

**Blackjack
Springs
Wilderness**

Spectacle-
Kentuck

1

5

Alvin

70   **70**

**Whisker
Lake
Wilderness**

7

Florence

Eagle
River

Anvil

70

2   **3**   **4**   **Hidden
Lakes**

Tipler   **70**

6

Lauterman

55

2178   **Nicolet
North**   2176

2182

Long Lake

Three
Lakes

139

101

Newald

Fence

32   Hiles

45

Argonne

55

Monico

Cavour

Armstrong
Creek

8

8

Crandon

Laona

▬▬▬ Paved road	🛡**45** U.S. route
─── Unpaved road	**55** State route
⬚**3** Trail map coverage with map number	2182 Forest road

©1999 Jack P. Hailman

🌲 **Trails:** at least 10 miles of trail, because of connection with Nicolet North Trails

🌲 **Interest:** Franklin Nature Trail at north parking area has northern hardwoods, pines, and hemlocks, with some trees over 400 years old, and boardwalk over bog

RATING: SPECTACLE LAKE–KENTUCK LAKE TRAIL (TRAIL MAP #5). 🌲🌲

🌲 **Scenery:** trail goes by Kentuck Lake and through wetlands

🌲 **Interest:** trail crosses river on railroad bridge of old Thunder Lake Railroad, used in early 1900s to transport logs to sawmill

RATING: LAUTERMAN NATIONAL RECREATION TRAIL (TRAIL MAP #6). 🌲🌲🌲🌲

🌲 **Scenery:** Perch and Lauterman Lakes; Ridge Trail has scenic view of Pine River

🌲 **Quiet:** can camp a mile or more from nearest paved road

🌲 **Trails:** at least 10 miles of trail accessible from camping place

🌲 **Interest:** Assessor's Loop Trail has interpretive signs and goes through large hemlock and hardwood forest; Ridge Trail passes through many forest types

RATING: WHISKER LAKE WILDERNESS (TRAIL MAP #7). 🌲🌲🌲🌲

🌲 **Scenery:** trail goes near many lakes and wetlands

🌲 **Quiet:** can camp a mile or more from nearest paved road

🌲 **Solitude:** unlikely to encounter more than 2 parties per day

🌲 **Interest:** wilderness area: no activity such as logging and use of recreational vehicles

ENTRANCE FEE. Forest Service vehicle sticker (or daily pass) required to park in some forest lots or use other national forest facilities.

CAMPING. Wilderness camping only on most of the trails covered here; designated campsites on Lauterman and Perch Lakes on the Lauterman Trail; trail shelters available on Anvil and Lauterman Trails. Wilderness camps must be set up at least 50 feet from trails. The campsites on Lauterman and Perch Lakes are comparatively luxurious, with table, tent pad, fire ring, and open throne toilet. There are also Forest Service campgrounds (fees charged) at Anvil Lake (trail map #2), Franklin Lake (trail map #4), Luna–White Deer Lakes (trail map #4), Spectacle Lake (trail map #5), Kentuck Lake (trail map #5), Chipmunk Rapids (trail map #6), and Lost Lake (trail

157

map #6). The only public sources of drinking water we found are at these campgrounds.

PERMIT AND RESERVATIONS.   None needed for wilderness camping, use of the campsites at Lauterman and Perch Lakes, or use of the shelters on Anvil and Lauterman Trails.

CONTACT INFORMATION.   Eagle River/Florence Ranger Station, Eagle River Office, P.O. Box 1809, 4364 Wall St., Eagle River, WI 54521; phone: 715/479-2827; fax: 715/479-6407; TTY: 715/479-1308; or, Eagle River/Florence Ranger Station, Florence Office, HC1, Box 83, Florence, WI 54121; phone: 715/528-4464; fax: 715/528-5172; TTY: 715/528-5298. *Also,* Forest Supervisor's Office, Chequamegon-Nicolet National Forest, 68 S. Stevens St., Rhinelander, WI 54501; phone 715/362-1300; fax: 715/362-1359; TTY: 715/362-1383.

FINDING THE TRAIL.   The trails are all accessed from forest roads that intersect State Highway 70 between Eagle River and Florence. **Blackjack Springs Wilderness** is about 5 miles north of State 70 on Forest Road 2178. There is a parking lot for the **Anvil Trail** on State 70; **Nicolet North** and **Hidden Lakes Trails** are best accessed from the west by going south on Forest Road 2178 (Military Rd.) to Forest Road 2181 (Butternut Lake Rd.). **Spectacle Lake–Kentuck Lake Trail** is half a mile north of State 70 on Forest Road 2176. Although connected by a trail, the Lauterman Lake and Perch Lake areas on the **Lauterman Trail** have separate parking lots off State 70; the Lauterman lot less than one tenth mile south on Forest Road 2154, and the Perch lot about half a mile north on Forest Road 2150. The trails in the **Whisker Lake Wilderness** can be accessed from three parking areas north of State 70 on Forest Road 2150.

BACKGROUND NOTES.   The former Nicolet National Forest was named for the French explorer Jean Nicolet, who visited the area in 1634. It is a land of beautiful forests and numerous lakes and provides a wealth of recreational opportunities. The Nicolet side of what is now the Chequamegon-Nicolet National Forest covers 661,000 acres, which have been divided into two ranger districts; the Eagle River/Florence district comprises what we have called the North part. The Anvil National Recreational Trail was built by the Civilian Conservation Corps in the 1930s. The original shelter was replaced in the summer of 1978 by the Young Adult Conservation Corps. The Blackjack Springs and Whisker Lake Wilderness Areas, which were logged in the early 1900s, were created by Congress in 1978. The Tipler fire in 1931 left only a few large trees along the shores of wetlands in the Whisker Lake Wilderness Area. These

Liz by a lake, Jones Springs, Nicolet National Forest

gave rise to the name Whisker Lake because the burnt trees reminded old timers of chin whiskers. Most of the hiking trails are old logging roads and railroad grades.

OUR TRAIL NOTES. We chose the Lauterman Lake area for a backpacking trip in early October when the Sugar Maple woods were decked out in breathtaking orange. We passed by lovely lakeside campsites that were already occupied, so decided to try the trail shelter, which was free. We left our packs in the shelter and took an unencumbered hike along the Little Porky loop, where we met a Whitetail Deer and saw some nice stands of White Spruce. We should have known better than to leave packs in a shelter, but we plain forgot about the little rodents that occupy most such structures. Luck was on our side, though, because the hungry mouse was able to get to the food without chewing through the pack itself. For the night, of course, we strung up our food high between two trees, as we always do. The spot was so lovely that just months later we used our photo of it for our Christmas card.

    Flora. We encountered a mixed deciduous forest with Sugar Maples as well as Quaking and Bigtooth Aspen, Eastern Hemlocks and White Spruce, ferns underneath, and two species of club moss on the ground. No wildflowers were in bloom so late in the year.

    Fauna. Besides the deer and pesky mouse, nonavian species were represented by Spring Peepers, peeping in the fall. There were

159

Trail by Ed's Lake, Nicolet National Forest

few species of birds: Downy Woodpecker, Blue Jay, Black-capped Chickadee, White-breasted Nuthatch, Brown Creeper, American Robin, White-throated Sparrow, and Dark-eyed Junco, the last three probably already in migration to spend the winter in more southerly climes.

Northeast Region

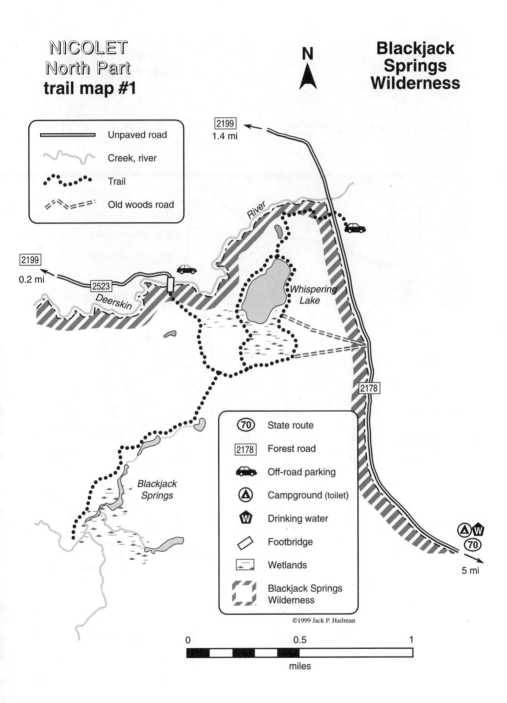

NICOLET
North Part
trail map #1

N

Blackjack
Springs
Wilderness

▬▬▬▬▬	Unpaved road
～～～	Creek, river
••••	Trail
⋍=⋍=⋍	Old woods road

2199
1.4 mi

River

2199
0.2 mi

2523

Deerskin

Whispering
Lake

2178

Blackjack
Springs

(70)	State route
2178	Forest road
🚗	Off-road parking
Ⓐ	Campground (toilet)
Ⓦ	Drinking water
◇	Footbridge
▱	Wetlands
▨	Blackjack Springs Wilderness

ⒶⓌ
(70)
5 mi

©1999 Jack P. Hailman

0   0.5   1

miles

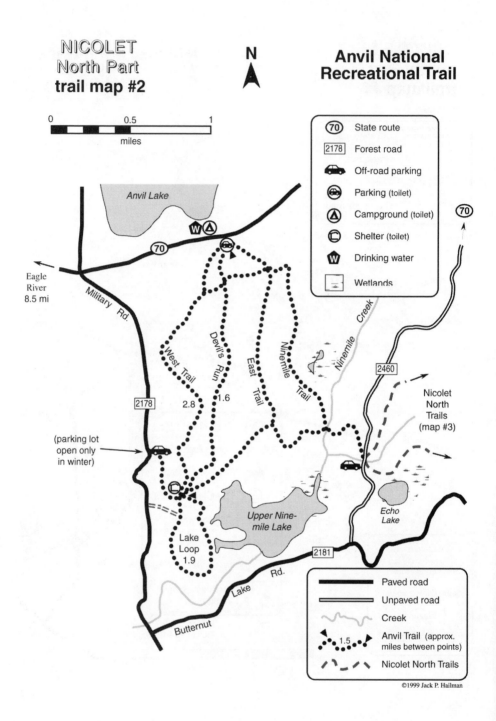

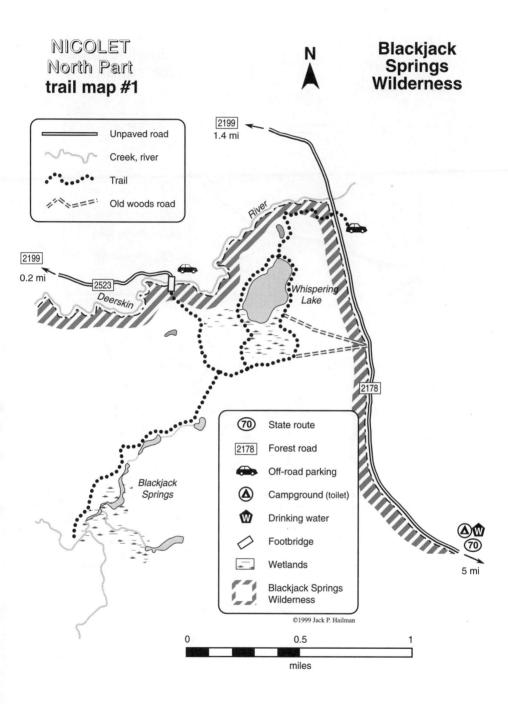

NICOLET
North Part
trail map #1

N

Blackjack
Springs
Wilderness

━━━━━━━	Unpaved road
〰〰〰	Creek, river
••••••	Trail
=‡==‡=	Old woods road

2199
1.4 mi

River

2199
0.2 mi

2523

Deerskin

Whispering
Lake

2178

Blackjack
Springs

(70)	State route
2178	Forest road
🚗	Off-road parking
Ⓐ	Campground (toilet)
Ⓦ	Drinking water
▱	Footbridge
⬚	Wetlands
⬚	Blackjack Springs Wilderness

©1999 Jack P. Hailman

ⒶⓌ
(70)
5 mi

0   0.5   1

miles

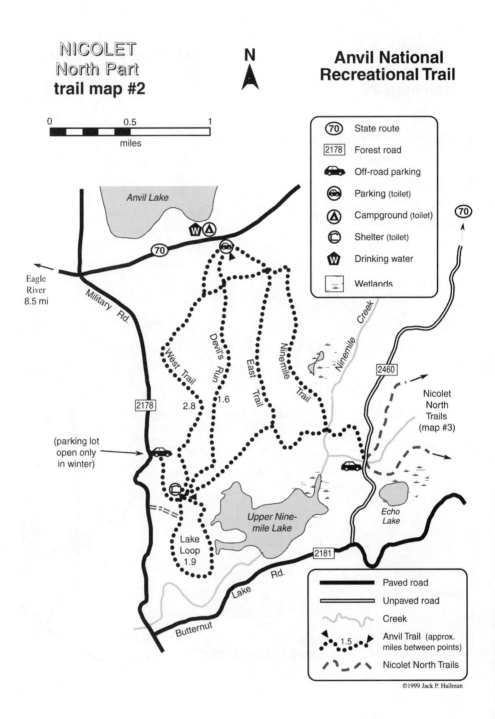

NICOLET
North Part
trail map #2

N

Anvil National
Recreational Trail

0   0.5   1
miles

⑦⓪	State route
2178	Forest road
🚗	Off-road parking
🚗	Parking (toilet)
Ⓐ	Campground (toilet)
Ⓒ	Shelter (toilet)
Ⓦ	Drinking water
	Wetlands

Anvil Lake

Ⓦ Ⓐ

70

Eagle
River
8.5 mi

Military Rd.

West Trail

Devil's Run

East Trail

Ninemile Trail

Ninemile Creek

70

2460

Nicolet
North
Trails
(map #3)

2178

2.8   1.6

(parking lot
open only
in winter)

🚗

Ⓒ

Upper Nine-
mile Lake

Echo
Lake

Lake
Loop
1.9

2181

Lake   Rd.

Butternut

▬▬▬	Paved road
═══	Unpaved road
∿∿∿	Creek
•••1.5•••	Anvil Trail (approx. miles between points)
╌╌╌	Nicolet North Trails

©1999 Jack P. Hailman

162

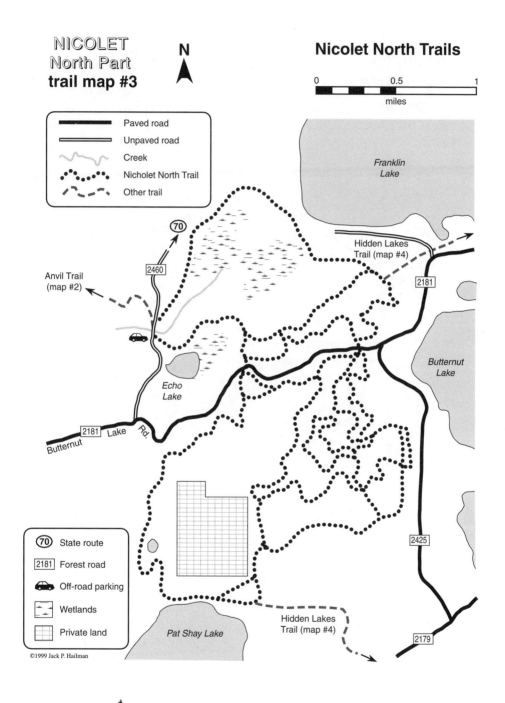

NICOLET
North Part
trail map #3

N

Nicolet North Trails

0   0.5   1
miles

Paved road
Unpaved road
Creek
Nicholet North Trail
Other trail

Franklin Lake

(70)

2460

Hidden Lakes
Trail (map #4)

2181

Anvil Trail
(map #2)

Echo Lake

Butternut Lake

2181   Lake   Rd.

Butternut

2425

(70) State route
2181 Forest road
Off-road parking
Wetlands
Private land

©1999 Jack P. Hailman

Hidden Lakes
Trail (map #4)

2179

Pat Shay Lake

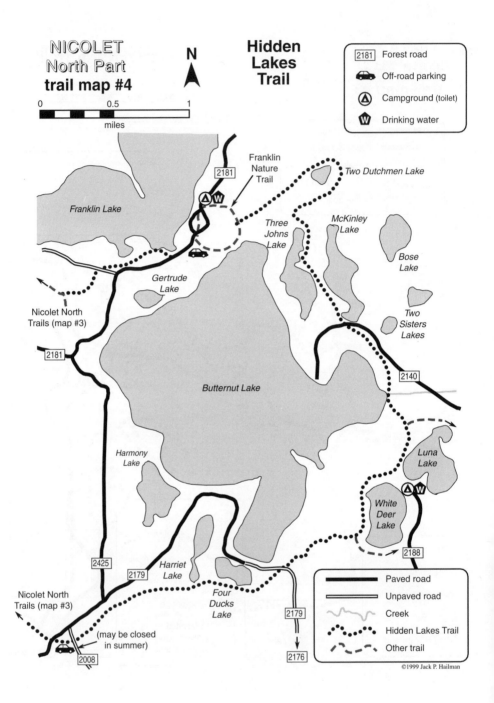

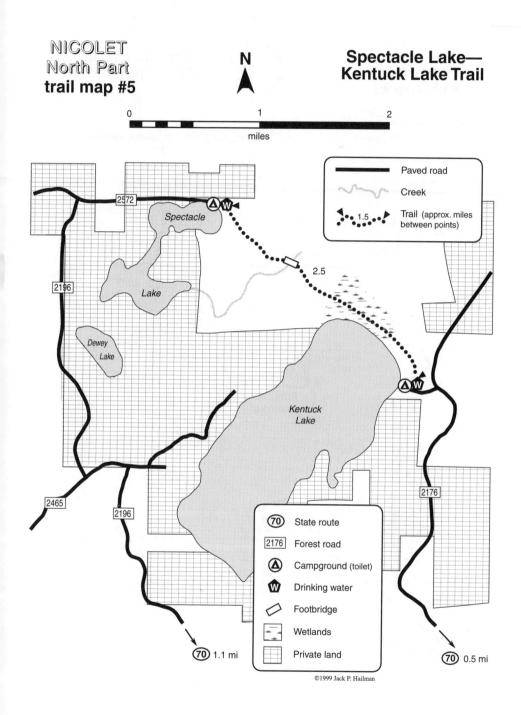

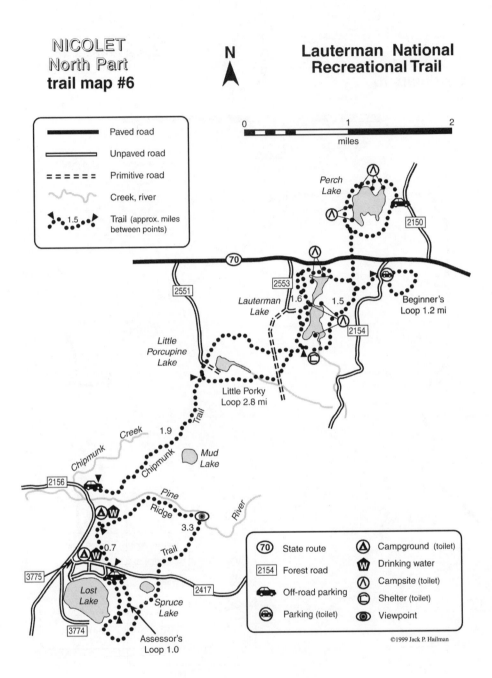

NICOLET
North Part
trail map #6

N

Lauterman National
Recreational Trail

━━━━━━	Paved road
═══════	Unpaved road
=======	Primitive road
～～～～	Creek, river
•••1.5•••	Trail (approx. miles between points)

0   1   2
miles

Perch Lake

2150

⑦⓪

2551

2553

Lauterman Lake

1.6   1.5

Beginner's
Loop 1.2 mi

2154

*Little
Porcupine
Lake*

Little Porky
Loop 2.8 mi

Chipmunk   *Creek*   1.9   Chipmunk   Trail

*Mud
Lake*

2156

Pine   Ridge

River

3.3

Trail

0.7

3775

*Lost
Lake*

2417

*Spruce
Lake*

3774

Assessor's
Loop 1.0

⑦⓪ State route		ⒶCampground (toilet)
2154 Forest road		🅆 Drinking water
🚗 Off-road parking		ⒶCampsite (toilet)
		ⒸShelter (toilet)
🚗 Parking (toilet)		◎ Viewpoint

©1999 Jack P. Hailman

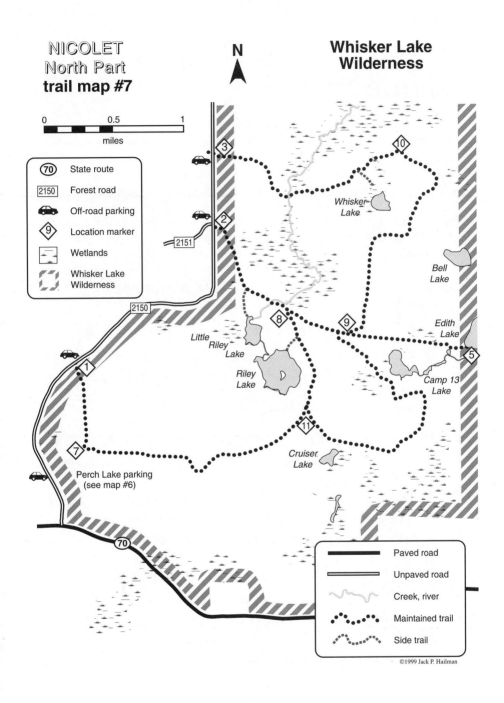

NICOLET
North Part
trail map #7

**Whisker Lake
Wilderness**

N

70	State route
2150	Forest road
🚗	Off-road parking
◇9	Location marker
	Wetlands
	Whisker Lake Wilderness

0   0.5   1
miles

2151

3

10

Whisker Lake

Bell Lake

2150

8

9

Edith Lake

Little Riley Lake

5

Riley Lake

Camp 13 Lake

1

11

7

Cruiser Lake

Perch Lake parking
(see map #6)

70

	Paved road
	Unpaved road
	Creek, river
•••••	Maintained trail
-----	Side trail

©1999 Jack P. Hailman

Ice Age National Scenic Trail
In the Northeast Region

Imagine a 1,000-mile trail all within a state that is only 400 miles on the longest diagonal! The Ice Age National Scenic Trail follows the moraines left by the continental glaciers and hence does a lot of wandering. From west to east the Ice Age Trail stays at about the same latitude from Minnesota to our Northeast backpacking region, where it turns a virtual right-angled corner and plunges southward.

LOCATION. Northeast region, coordinates F/G-5 on official state highway map (Langlade and Lincoln Counties).

RATING: UNDERDOWN SEGMENT (TRAIL MAP #1).

Quiet: can camp a mile or more from nearest paved road

Trails: at least 10 miles of trail accessible from camping place

Solitude: unlikely to encounter more than 2 other parties per day

RATING: HARRISON HILLS SEGMENT (TRAIL MAP #2).

Scenery: excellent views from tower at Lookout Mountain (1,920 feet)

Quiet: can camp a mile or more from nearest paved road

Trails: at least 10 miles of trail accessible from camping place

Solitude: unlikely to encounter more than 2 other parties per day; very remote segment

Interest: trail passes by old settlement sites, logging camp, and bottling plant

RATING: PARRISH HILLS SEGMENT (TRAIL MAP #3).

Quiet: can camp a mile or more from nearest paved road

Trails: at least 10 miles of trail accessible from camping place

Solitude: unlikely to encounter more than 2 other parties per day

Interest: one of most remote parts of Ice Age Trail; no road crossings for about 10 miles

NORTHEAST REGION
Ice Age National Scenic Trail

N

area map

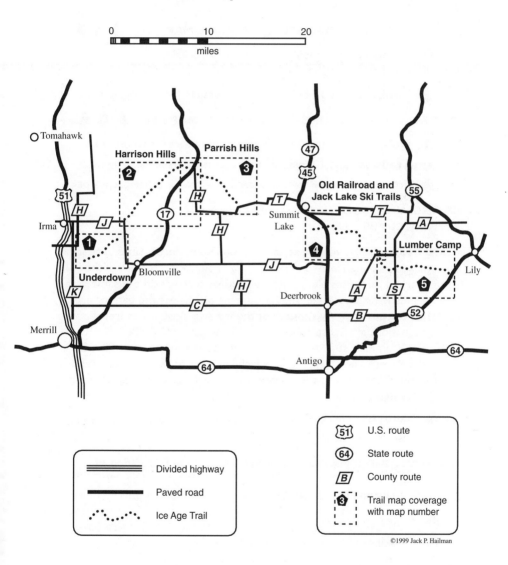

Divided highway
Paved road
Ice Age Trail

51 U.S. route
64 State route
B County route
3 Trail map coverage
with map number

©1999 Jack P. Hailman

RATING: JACK LAKE CROSS COUNTRY SKI TRAILS (TRAIL MAP #4). 🌲🌲

🌲 **Quiet:** can camp a mile or more from nearest paved road

🌲 **Solitude:** unlikely to encounter more than 2 other parties per day

RATING: OLD RAILROAD SEGMENT (TRAIL MAP #4). 🌲🌲🌲

🌲 **Scenery:** very pretty trail around Game Lake

🌲 **Quiet:** can camp a mile or more from nearest paved road

🌲 **Trails:** at least 10 miles of trail accessible from camping place

RATING: LUMBER CAMP SEGMENT (TRAIL MAP #5). 🌲🌲🌲

🌲 **Quiet:** can camp a mile or more from nearest paved road

🌲 **Trails:** at least 10 miles of trail accessible from camping place

🌲 **Solitude:** unlikely to encounter more than 2 other parties per day

ENTRANCE FEE. None.

CAMPING. Mainly wilderness camping on county forest lands. The local chapter of the Ice Age Park and Trail Foundation has established and marked campsites along the Underdown segment. In the same area, equestrians have established a camping place near the parking area on Copper Lake Ave., north of the Ice Age Trail; use is free (donations are accepted). There is a campsite off Turtle Lake Rd. in Harrison Hills segment and a shelter about a mile east of Pine Dr. in the Parrish Hills segment. The Jack Lake Ski trails have a centrally located shelter, and the county park at Jack Lake has a campground (fees charged).

PERMIT AND RESERVATIONS. None needed for wilderness camping or use of the shelter on the ski trail.

CONTACT INFORMATION. Ice Age Park & Trail Foundation of Wisconsin, Inc., 207 E. Buffalo St., Suite 515, Milwaukee, WI 53202-5712; phone 800/227-0046; e-mail: cthisted@sbtsi.com. The office can put you in touch with the current coordinator of the Langlade County and Northwoods Chapters (Lincoln County), which have responsibility for these segments of trail.

FINDING THE TRAIL. The **Underdown** segment is located in Lincoln County a short distance east of U.S. Highway 51. From Merrill go north on U.S. 51 to Irma, then east on County Highway J to County Highway H. Take County H south to Copper Lake Ave., from which you can access the parking places (most of which are tiny) indicated on trail map #1.

The **Harrison Hills** segment is east of U.S. Highway 51 in Lincoln County. The southern parking places are on or near Lincoln County Highway J, which goes east from U.S. Highway 51 at the little community of Irma. County Highway B, which leads to two more parking places, is reached from Tomahawk (on U.S. Highway 51) by going east on County Highway D and then south on County Highway B. State Highway 17, near the easternmost accesses, goes through the city of Rhinelander; go south about 15 miles to First Lake Rd., where a parking area is located.

The **Parrish Hills** segment is in Langlade County east of State Highway 17 and west of State Highway 47. The western parking lot is the same as the one on First Lake Rd. described above. The eastern parking place is on Langlade County Highway T, which can be reached from State Highway 17 by going south on County Highway H near Parrish, or from State Highway 47, which T intersects north of Antigo at Summit Lake.

The **Old Railroad** and **Lumber Camp** segments are in Langlade County and most easily accessed from the vicinity of Antigo. One parking area for the **Old Railroad** segment is on U.S. Highway 45 about 9 miles north of Antigo, a little north of County Highway J; the other, which also provides access to the **Jack Lake**

Liz on a bridge, ice Age Trail, Langlade County Forest

171

Ski Trails, is east on County Highway J. You could also leave your vehicle in the county park, at the far southern end past the campground in the lot where people park to walk the trail through the small arboretum, which connects with the Ice Age Trail. To reach the **Lumber Camp** segment, go northeast from Antigo on State Highway 52 (full of right-angle zig-zags), from which you can access County Highway S and its parking lot or continue on State 52. The parking lot shown off State 52 is up a gated road, which is usually closed. Park so as not to block the closed gate; the road is used year-round by forestry personnel.

BACKGROUND NOTES. Lincoln and Langlade Counties have extensive county forests with glacial scenery rivaling that of the national forest and other unspoiled areas. There are completed segments of the Ice Age Trail in both counties, and also cross-country ski trails suitable for backpacking.

OUR TRAIL NOTES. Summer was already here in early June when we hiked in the Jack Lake Ski Trails area of Landglade County Forest. Our destination was the shelter shown on the map on the bulletin board at the trailhead. Getting to that shelter proved to be a problem because of numerous old logging roads intersecting the main trail. Interpretive signs along the otherwise unmarked trail reassured us that we were still on an official route, but we did go down one

Liz fixing breakfast in the shelter, Jack Lake Ski Trail, Langlade County Forest

side trail thinking it was the correct way and had to turn around. The shelter seemed like a mecca after a hot and mosquito-ridden hike through a woods with many evergreens—Tamarack (Larch), White Spruce, Eastern White Pine, and Eastern Hemlock—as well as deciduous trees such as Sugar and Red Maple, Paper Birch, a hickory, and a grove of Quaking Aspen, and a disturbed and clear-cut region with some lumbering equipment. The shelter was enclosed on all four sides with windows and had outhouses nearby. A nesting pair of Eastern Phoebes kept going in and out through the space of several inches under the door; they were doubtless relieved when we departed after breakfast in the morning.

Flora. The understory of the woods was largely open, with lots of ferns. Among the early summer flowers we found Clintonia (Corn-lily, Yellow Beadlily), some Large-flowered (White, Large) Trillium (now deep pink with age), Wild Lily-of-the-valley (Canada Mayflower), Common (Tall) Buttercup, Winter Cress, Common Strawberry, Bunchberry (Dwarf Correl), Common Dandelion, and pussytoes. As the sandy ground was noticeably wet underfoot, we were not surprised to find a moss and a flat-topped mushroom. We identified the club moss *Lycopodium obscurum* and on some trees we found Hoof Fungus.

Fauna. We recorded many species of birds on the way in that evening: Canada Geese flying overhead, Hairy Woodpecker, Eastern Wood-Pewee, Red-eyed Vireo, Black-capped Chickadee, Eastern Bluebird, American Robin, Ovenbird, and Common Yellowthroat. The next morning we were lucky to hear Sandhill Cranes calling, and also encountered Black-throated Green Warbler, American Redstart, and Rose-breasted Grosbeak. A small bat had flown around in the opening outside the shelter at dusk after our hike in, and on the hike out we noticed footprints of Whitetail Deer in the damp trail.

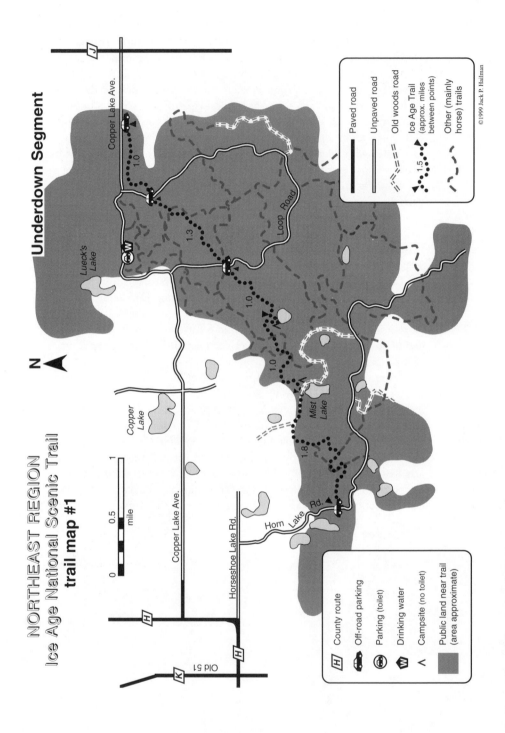

NORTHEAST REGION
Ice Age National Scenic Trail
trail map #1

Underdown Segment

Legend:
- Paved road
- Unpaved road
- Old woods road
- Ice Age Trail (approx. miles between points) 1.5
- Other (mainly horse) trails

- H County route
- Off-road parking
- Parking (toilet)
- Drinking water W
- Campsite (no toilet)
- Public land near trail (area approximate)

©1999 Jack P. Hailman

N

0   0.5   1
mile

Lueck's Lake
Copper Lake
Copper Lake Ave.
Loop Road
Mist Lake
Horn Lake Rd.
Horseshoe Lake Rd.
Old 51

1.0
1.3
1.0
1.0
1.8

J
H
K

174

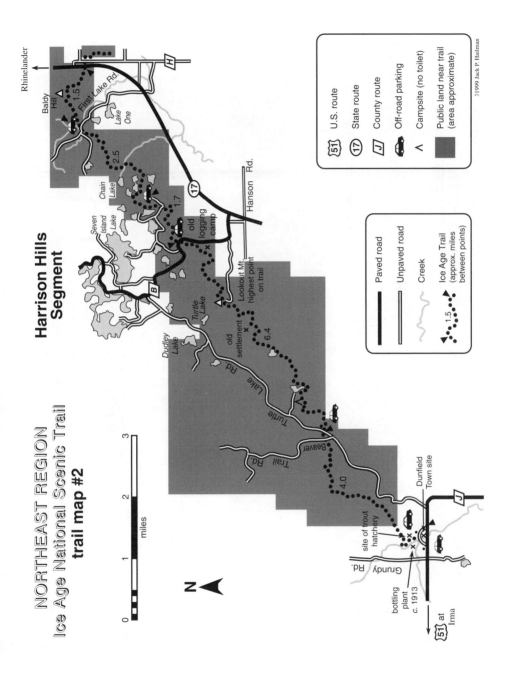

NORTHEAST REGION
Ice Age National Scenic Trail
trail map #2

Harrison Hills
Segment

©1999 Jack P. Hailman

Legend (route symbols)
- U.S. route
- State route
- County route
- Off-road parking
- Campsite (no toilet)
- Public land near trail (area approximate)

Legend (line symbols)
- Paved road
- Unpaved road
- Creek
- Ice Age Trail (approx. miles between points) — 1.5

miles
0   1   2   3

N

Rhinelander

Baldy Hill
First Lake Rd.
1.5
Lake One
2.5
Chain Lake
1.7
Seven Island Lake
old logging camp
Hanson Rd.
Lookout Mt. highest point on trail
Turtle Lake
Dudley Lake
Turtle Lake Rd.
old settlement
6.4
Beaver
Trail Rd.
4.0
Dunfield Town site
site of trout hatchery
bottling plant c. 1913
Grundy Rd.
51 at Irma

175

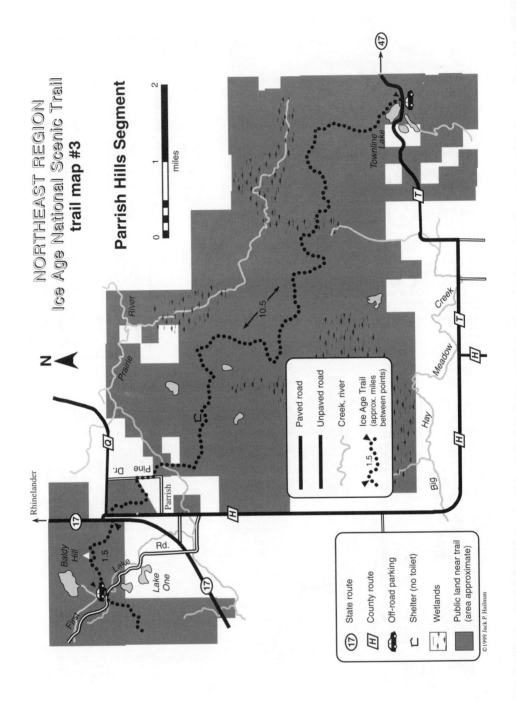

NORTHEAST REGION
Ice Age National Scenic Trail
trail map #3

Parrish Hills Segment

miles

0   1   2

N

Rhinelander

Prairie River

Baldy Hill

1.5

First Lake

Lake One

Rd.

Parrish

Pine Dr.

10.5

Hay   Meadow   Creek

Big

Townline Lake

Paved road

Unpaved road

Creek, river

Ice Age Trail
(approx. miles between points)

1.5

17 State route

H County route

Off-road parking

Shelter (no toilet)

Wetlands

Public land near trail
(area approximate)

©1999 Jack P. Hailman

176

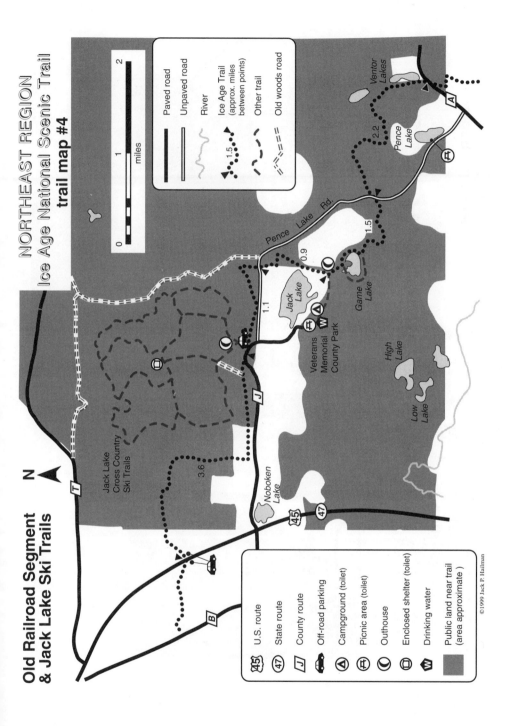

Old Railroad Segment & Jack Lake Ski Trails

NORTHEAST REGION
Ice Age National Scenic Trail
trail map #4

N

Legend (trail types):
- Paved road
- Unpaved road
- River
- Ice Age Trail (approx. miles between points) 1.5
- Other trail
- Old woods road

miles
0 1 2

Legend (symbols):
- 45 U.S. route
- 47 State route
- County route
- Off-road parking
- Campground (toilet)
- Picnic area (toilet)
- Outhouse
- Enclosed shelter (toilet)
- Drinking water
- Public land near trail (area approximate)

Jack Lake Cross Country Ski Trails

Veterans Memorial County Park

Jack Lake

Game Lake

High Lake

Low Lake

Noboken Lake

Pence Lake

Ventor Lakes

Pence Lake Rd.

3.6
1.1
0.9
1.5
2.2
1.5

T
J
B
A
45
47

©1999 Jack P. Hailman

177

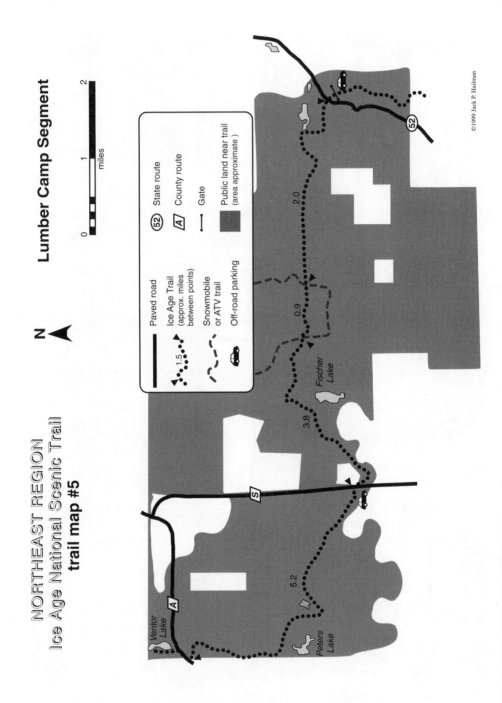

NORTHEAST REGION
Ice Age National Scenic Trail
trail map #5

N

Lumber Camp Segment

0   1   2
miles

Paved road

Ice Age Trail
(approx. miles
between points)

Snowmobile
or ATV trail

Off-road parking

52   State route

A   County route

Gate

Public land near trail
(area approximate)

Ventor
Lake

Fischer
Lake

Peters
Lake

©1999 Jack P. Hailman

Nicolet, South Part
Lakewood/Laona Ranger District

Though it does not have as many recreational opportunities and wild areas as the North part, the South part of Nicolet offers nice trails that are closer to the large metropolitan areas of eastern and southern Wisconsin.

LOCATION. Northeast region, coordinates G/H-4/5 on official state highway map (Forest, Langlade, and Oconto Counties). This South part corresponds approximately with the Lakewood/Laona Ranger District.

RATING: ED'S LAKE NATIONAL RECREATION TRAIL (TRAIL MAP #1).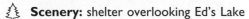

🌲 **Scenery:** shelter overlooking Ed's Lake

🌲 **Solitude:** unlikely to encounter more than 2 other parties per day

RATING: MICHIGAN RAPIDS TRAIL (TRAIL MAP #2).

🌲 **Scenery:** lovely views of Peshtigo River and Michigan Rapids

🌲 **Quiet:** can camp about 1 mile from nearest road

🌲 **Solitude:** likely to encounter fewer than 6 other parties per day, mostly day hikers

RATING: JONES SPRING AREA (TRAIL MAP #3).

🌲 **Scenery:** many lakes and wetlands, overlook above Jones Springs impoundment

🌲 **Quiet:** can camp a mile or more from nearest paved road

🌲 **Trails:** can camp on circuit of over 5 miles

🌲 **Interest:** variety of landscapes and wetlands

RATING: LAKEWOOD TRAILS (TRAIL MAP #4).

🌲 **Scenery:** beautiful wooded setting with rolling hills.

🌲 **Trails:** at least 10 miles of trail accessible from camping place

RATING: NICOLET NORDIC TRAILS (TRAIL MAP #5). 🌲

🌲 **Solitude:** unlikely to encounter more than 2 other parties per day

NICOLET SIDE
Chequamegon—Nicolet National Forest
South Part

N

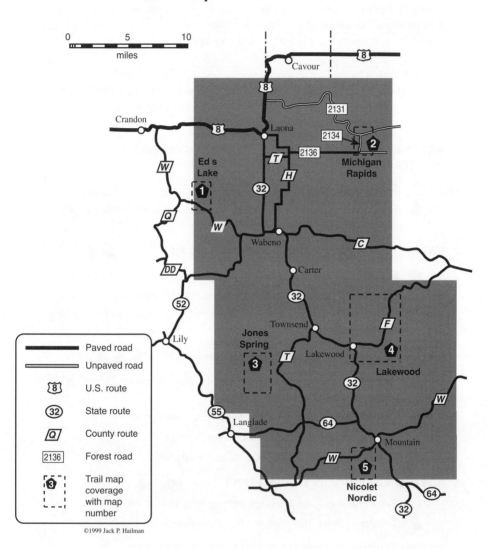

area map

Legend:
- Paved road
- Unpaved road
- ⑧ U.S. route
- ㉜ State route
- Ⓠ County route
- 2136 Forest road
- ❸ Trail map coverage with map number

©1999 Jack P. Hailman

ENTRANCE FEE. Forest Service vehicle sticker (or daily pass) required to park in some forest lots or to use other national forest facilities.

CAMPING. Wilderness camping only on most of the trails covered here. Wilderness camps must be set up at least 50 feet from trails. There are campsites available on Fanny Lake in the Jones Spring area, with tables and open throne toilets; this trail system also has a shelter. There are Forest Service campgrounds (fees charged) at Richardson Lake, Bear Lake, Wheeler Lake, Boot Lake, Boulder Lake, and Bagley Rapids. These public campgrounds have water, but are not close enough to any of the backpacking sites to be on the maps. Water can also be found at the wayside west of Lakewood Trails.

PERMIT AND RESERVATIONS. None needed for wilderness camping, use of the campsites at Fanny Lake, or the trail shelter at Jones Spring.

CONTACT INFORMATION. Lakewood/Laona Ranger Station, Laona Office, Route 1, Box 11B, Laona, WI 54541; phone and TTY: 715/674-4481; fax: 715/674-2545; or, Lakewood/Laona Ranger Station, Lakewood Office, 15085 State Road 32, Lakewood, WI 54138; phone: 715/276-6333; fax: 715/276-3594; TTY: 715/674-4481. *Also,* Forest Supervisor's Office, Chequamegon-Nicolet National Forest, 68 S. Stevens St., Rhinelander, WI 54501; phone: 715/362-1300; fax: 715/362-1359; TTY: 715/362-1383.

FINDING THE TRAIL. To reach the **Michigan Rapids** trailhead, take Forest County Highway H from Laona (on U.S. Highway 8) southeast and then go east on Forest Road 2136. At Forest Road 2134 (Michigan Creek Rd.) go north to the parking area. All of the other trails can be reached from State Highway 32, which goes north-south in Forest and Oconto counties. **Ed's Lake** is west of State 32 on Forest County Highway W. The **Jones Spring** area is reached by turning off State 32 at Townsend onto Oconto County Highway T, then going south to Forest Road 2938 (Fanny Lake Rd.) or Forest Road 2336 (Saul Springs Rd.). The **Lakewood Trails** are east of State 32 near Lakewood off Oconto County Highway F, and the **Nicolet Nordic Trails** are southwest of Mountain (on State 32); take Oconto County Highway W to Forest Road 2311 (McComb Lake Rd.) and go south.

BACKGROUND NOTES. See Nicolet, North part, earlier in this chapter.

OUR TRAIL NOTES. Temperatures were in the lower 40s late in October when we set out from the Fanny Lake parking lot in the Jones Spring area. We hiked north on the loop to the Jones Spring impoundment and around to the Upper and Lower Jones Springs, a marvelously varied route, with elevation changes and many scenic views of the springs and wetlands. When we met a couple of chaps who said they were headed toward the shelter for the night, we returned to Fanny Lake and set up our tent in a campsite. A few snow flurries fell while we were hiking, and that night the temperatures were in the low 30s. We had the lake to ourselves and enjoyed a night of silence broken only by the hooting of a Great Horned Owl.

Flora. We passed through spruce and Red Pine plantations and saw other conifers such as Eastern White Pine and Eastern Hemlock; also a red oak, maples, Bigtooth Aspen, American Beech trees with clinging orange-brown leaves, and Paper Birch. We identified ground pine, sphagnum moss, Red Raspberries, Bunchberry (Dwarf Correl), and Pipsissewa in berry.

Fauna. The only mammal we met was the ubiquitous Red Squirrel, but there was evidence of Beaver from downed trees. Considering the lateness in the fall, we recorded a good number of birds: Great Horned Owl, Ruffed Grouse, Hairy Woodpecker, Gray Jay (the farthest south we have encountered this boreal species on our backpacking trips), Blue Jay, Black-capped Chickadee, Hermit Thrush, American Robin, American Tree Sparrow, and Dark-eyed Junco.

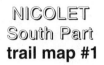

NICOLET
South Part
trail map #1

Ed's Lake National
Recreation Trail

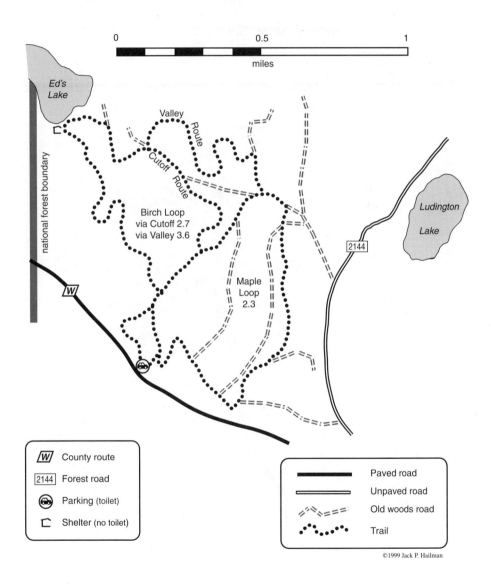

0	**0.5**	**1**

miles

Ed's Lake

national forest boundary

Valley Route

Cutoff Route

Birch Loop
via Cutoff 2.7
via Valley 3.6

Ludington

Lake

2144

Maple
Loop
2.3

W

W	County route
2144	Forest road
🚗	Parking (toilet)
⊏	Shelter (no toilet)

▬▬▬▬	Paved road
═════	Unpaved road
⌇⌇⌇⌇	Old woods road
••••••	Trail

©1999 Jack P. Hailman

183

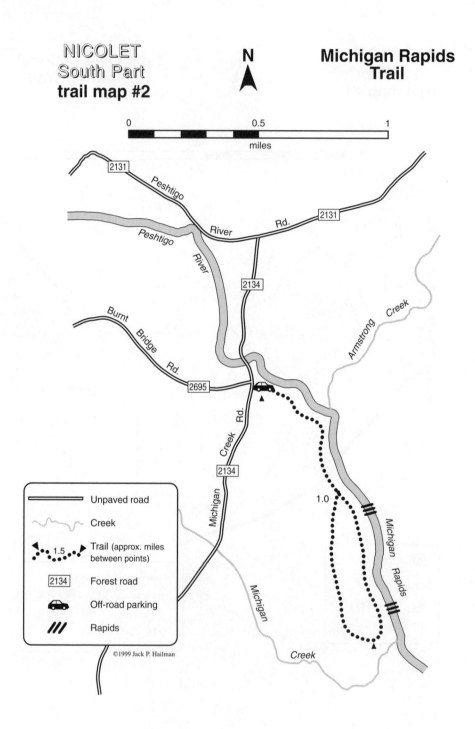

NICOLET
South Part
trail map #2

N

**Michigan Rapids
Trail**

0   0.5   1
miles

2131

Peshtigo   River   Rd.   2131

Peshtigo

River

2134

Burnt

Bridge   Rd.

2695

Armstrong   Creek

Michigan   Creek   Rd.

2134

1.0

Michigan   Rapids

Michigan

Creek

───── Unpaved road

～～～ Creek

•◀•1.5•▶ Trail (approx. miles
         between points)

2134 Forest road

🚗 Off-road parking

/// Rapids

©1999 Jack P. Hailman

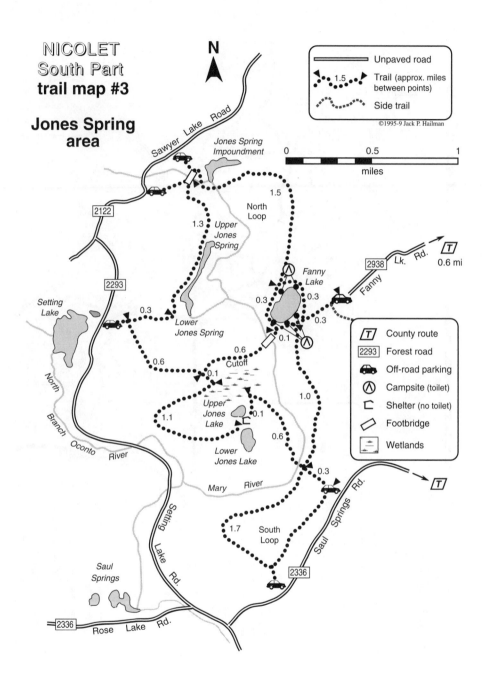

NICOLET
South Part
trail map #3

**Jones Spring
area**

N

Sawyer Lake Road

Jones Spring
Impoundment

2122

North
Loop

1.5

1.3 *Upper
Jones
Spring*

2293

*Setting
Lake*

0.3

*Lower
Jones Spring*

Fanny
Lake

2938   Fanny Lk. Rd.   T
0.6 mi

0.3   0.3

0.3

0.1

0.6
Cutoff

0.6

0.1

*Upper
Jones
Lake*   0.1

1.1

0.6

*Lower
Jones Lake*

1.0

North Branch Oconto River

Setting Lake Rd.

Mary   River

0.3

1.7   South
Loop

Saul Springs Rd.

T

2336

*Saul
Springs*

2336   Rose   Lake   Rd.

0 ——————— 0.5 ——————— 1
miles

Unpaved road

1.5   Trail (approx. miles
between points)

Side trail

©1995-9 Jack P. Hailman

T	County route
2293	Forest road
	Off-road parking
Ⓐ	Campsite (toilet)
⌐	Shelter (no toilet)
	Footbridge
	Wetlands

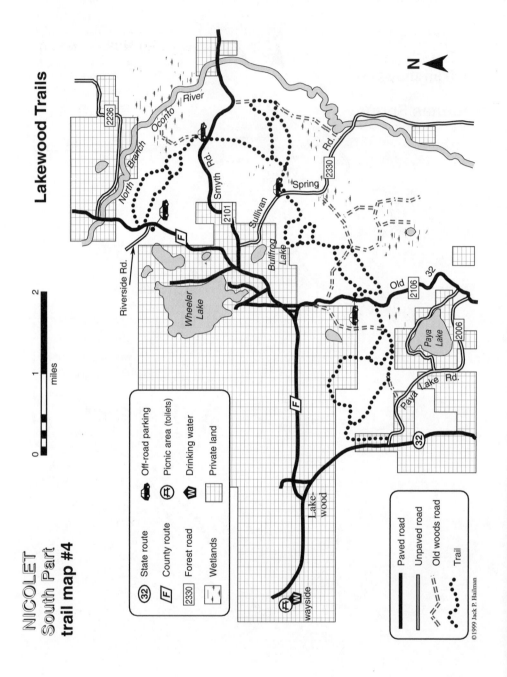

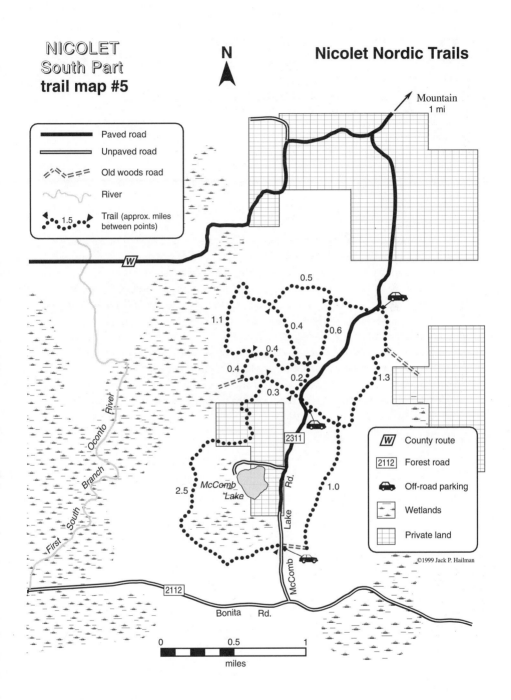

NICOLET
South Part
trail map #5

N

Nicolet Nordic Trails

Mountain
1 mi

Legend:
- Paved road
- Unpaved road
- Old woods road
- River
- 1.5 Trail (approx. miles between points)

W

0.5

1.1

0.4

0.6

0.4

0.4

0.2

0.3

1.3

2311

McComb
Lake

2.5

Lake Rd.

1.0

W County route

2112 Forest road

Off-road parking

Wetlands

Private land

©1999 Jack P. Hailman

Oconto River

South Branch

First

McComb Rd.

2112

Bonita Rd.

0   0.5   1
miles

DOOR, SOUTHWEST, AND SOUTHEAST REGIONS

Although northern Wisconsin regions provide the largest variety of backpacking experiences in the state, the other regions have opportunities that should not be overlooked. Many of the backpacking places treated in this chapter have the advantage of being within easy reach of the metropolitan areas where so many Wisconsinites reside, for example, Governor Dodge and New Glarus Woods State Parks in the Southwest region near Madison, and the South and Lapham Peak Units of Kettle Moraine State Forest in the Southeast region near Milwaukee. The wilds of Black River State Forest in the Southwest region are generally underappreciated. And some places have downright spectacular scenery to offer the backpacker: Rock Island and Newport State Parks in the Door region, and the North Unit of Kettle Moraine State Forest in the Southeast region.

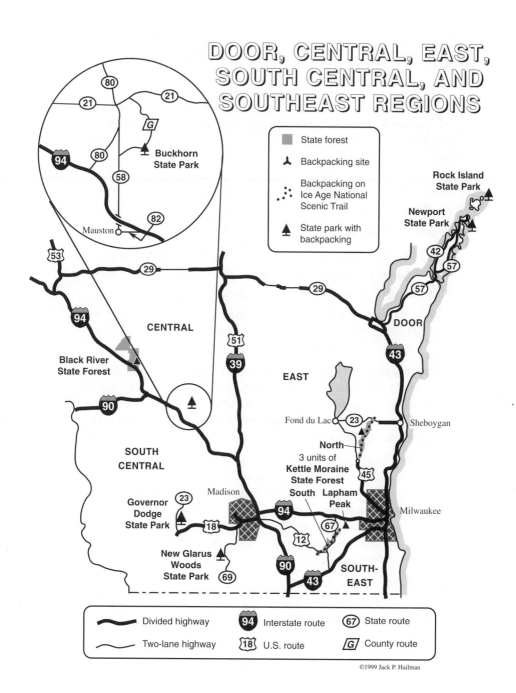

DOOR, CENTRAL, EAST, SOUTH CENTRAL, AND SOUTHEAST REGIONS

80
21
21
G
94
80
58
Buckhorn
State Park
82
Mauston

State forest

Backpacking site

Backpacking on
Ice Age National
Scenic Trail

State park with
backpacking

Rock Island
State Park

Newport
State Park

42
57
57

53
29
29

94
CENTRAL

51
39

DOOR

43

EAST

Black River
State Forest

Fond du Lac
23
Sheboygan

90

North
3 units of
Kettle Moraine
State Forest
South
Lapham
Peak

45

SOUTH
CENTRAL

Governor
Dodge
State Park
23
18

Madison

94

67

Milwaukee

12

New Glarus
Woods
State Park
69

90

43

SOUTH-
EAST

Divided highway	94 Interstate route	67 State route
Two-lane highway	18 U.S. route	G County route

Rock Island State Park

Although it is a car-ferry ride and another boat ride away from the mainland of Door County, Rock Island is still a very popular state park with good reason: it is arguably the most picturesque and interesting park in Wisconsin. No mechanical vehicles, not even bikes, are allowed on the island.

LOCATION. Door region, coordinates J-4/5 on official state highway map (Door County).

RATING. 🌲 🌲 🌲 🌲

🌲 **Scenery:** beautiful location on Rock Island in Lake Michigan

🌲 **Quiet:** can camp a mile or more from nearest paved road

🌲 **Trails:** can camp on circuit of about 5 miles

🌲 **Interest:** "Viking Hall" and stone tower on National Register of Historic Places; first lighthouse in Wisconsin; Lake Michigan shoreline natural history

ENTRANCE FEE. Free parking at the Karfi Ferry parking lot. Because there are no vehicles on the island, there is no vehicle sticker or other entrance fee required for day visitors—the best bargain in the state park system! (If you camp on Rock Island, you pay the usual state park camping fee.)

CAMPING. Only at designated sites (see map); each campsite has a table and fire ring with a pit toilet nearby. The real backpacking sites—the five lettered sites shown on the map—are called "remote sites" by the park. The family campground near the boat dock resembles a large backpacking area in that all are walk-in campsites. There are 40 sites and 2 group campsites; there are no carts for carrying gear. Park is open May 1–December 1.

PERMIT AND RESERVATIONS. Camping permit required for a specific campsite (fee). Obtain your permit at the park office in the booth near the boat dock. Advance reservations of campsites are accepted by the state's phone reservation service at 888/947-2757 (9 A.M. to 10 P.M. weekdays and 9 A.M. to 6 P.M. weekends) or on the web at www.wiparks.net; reservation fee charged. *Note:* Because of the popularity of this park, advance reservations are recommended.

CONTACT INFORMATION. Rock Island State Park, Route 1, Box 118A, Washington Island, WI 54246-9728; phone: 920/847-2235 (no fax); in winter, 920/746–2890 (Potawatomi State Park).

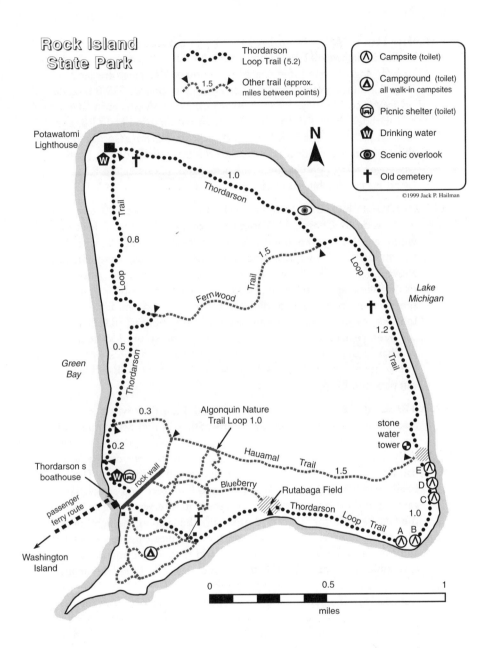

Rock Island State Park

Thordarson Loop Trail (5.2)

Other trail (approx. 1.5 miles between points)

Campsite (toilet)

Campground (toilet) all walk-in campsites

Picnic shelter (toilet)

Drinking water

Scenic overlook

Old cemetery

©1999 Jack P. Hailman

Potawatomi Lighthouse

N

1.0

Thordarson

0.8

Loop

Trail

1.5

Loop

Lake Michigan

Fernwood Trail

1.2

Trail

Green Bay

0.5

Thordarson

0.3

Algonquin Nature Trail Loop 1.0

stone water tower

0.2

Hauamal Trail 1.5

E

Thordarson s boathouse

rock wall

Blueberry

Rutabaga Field

D

C

passenger ferry route

Thordarson Loop Trail

1.0

Washington Island

A B

0 0.5 1

miles

FINDING THE TRAIL. From Sturgeon Bay in Door County go northeast on State Highway 42 to its end at the Northport pier. Take the ferry to Washington Island (fee charged). (Contact Washington Island Ferry Line Inc., Washington Island, WI 54246; phone: 920/847-2546 or, in Wisconsin only, 800/223-2094.) Once on Washington Island, take Lobdell Point Rd. to Main Rd., then go north on Main Rd. and east on Jackson Harbor Rd. to reach Jackson Harbor. Go north a short distance on Indian Point Rd. to the boat dock for the Karfi passenger ferry (fee charged) to Rock Island. (Contact the Rock Island Ferry, Washington Island, WI 54246; phone: 920/847-2252.)

BACKGROUND NOTES. In the early 1900s, the wooded 900-acre island was owned by Chester H. Thordarson, an immigrant from Iceland, who made his fortune in electrical inventions. The huge boathouse that he built of native dolomitic limestone with a large assembly hall above it ("Viking Hall") and the stone water tower on the east side of the island are listed in the National Register of Historic Places. On the northernmost point of the island is the Potawatomi Lighthouse, the oldest lighthouse in Wisconsin, which was built in 1836; its light has been replaced by a nearby light tower. The state of Wisconsin purchased the island from the Thordarson family in 1965. There are interpretive exhibits in the Viking Hall and a nature trail, as well as camping and hiking.

OUR TRAIL NOTES. The trip to Rock Island State Park was a marvelous adventure, aided by good weather in mid-September. We enjoyed both boat rides needed to get to the island, watching gulls winging gracefully over the waters. Our campsite right on the lake had a wonderful view, as well as a table to make life easier. The old boathouse is a spectacle in itself, and the literature and signboards gave a good picture of the history behind it. We were delighted with the hike around the island and especially the stop at the lighthouse. The climb down the steep steps on the dolomite cliffs to the lake and then back up—many stone steps and then 73 wooden ones— was sufficiently challenging to the leg muscles. The loop hike around the island is through lovely woods with many views of the lake (especially in the south), and we learned more history from further interpretive signs. Jack wrote a paragraph about Rock Island for an essay contest sponsored by the Wisconsin Department of Tourism and won first prize, which in this age of grade inflation was actually second place to the grand prize. Rock Island won him a field cap, fleece jacket, day pack, and hiking boots—a delayed bonus from our backpacking trip.

Flora. The forest on the island is mostly deciduous trees, of which there is a large variety. We noted Northern Red Oak, Black

Liz on a boat to Rock Island State Park

Oak, Paper Birch, Yellow Birch, Bigtooth Aspen, Red Maple, Sugar Maple, Eastern Hophornbeam (Ironwood), American Beech, and American Basswood. We also saw an old apple orchard, Northern White-Cedar, or Arborvitae (which is thick in the family campground), a field of rutabaga, ferns, and these flowers: Thimbleberry, Herb-Robert, Harebell, a purple aster, and a goldenrod.

    Fauna. We recorded Monarch Butterflies, snail shells, two Whitetail Deer, a largish bat, and some birds: Double-crested Cormorant, an *Accipiter* hawk, Ring-billed Gull, Downy Woodpecker, Red-eyed Vireo, Blue Jay, American Crow, Black-capped Chickadee, Red-breasted Nuthatch, Brown Creeper, Swainson's Thrush, Chipping Sparrow, White-throated Sparrow, White-crowned Sparrow, and Dark-eyed Junco.

Newport State Park

A great contrast to the bustling of most state parks, and also to the towns in Door County during the summer and fall tourist seasons, is the relatively remote Newport State Park. Declared a wilderness area by the Wisconsin Department of Natural Resources in 1974, the 2,400-acre park has done a good job of preserving a wild atmosphere. Very little of the park is accessible by road, there is no central campground, and the 11 miles of shoreline and the many hiking trails give the visitor a wilderness feeling.

LOCATION.   Door region, coordinates J-5 on official state highway map (Door County).

RATING.   🌲 🌲 🌲 🌲

🌲 **Scenery:** scenic shoreline and hiking trails through woods

🌲 **Quiet:** can camp a mile or more from nearest paved road (but subject to powerboat noise)

🌲 **Trails:** at least 10 miles of trail accessible from camping place

🌲 **Interest:** Lake Michigan shore is special natural history attraction

ENTRANCE FEE.   State vehicle sticker required.

CAMPING.   Only at designated sites (see map). Each tent site has a metal fire ring with grate, a metal food box (use it), a small sitting bench, and a pit toilet nearby. (There is no family campground in this park.) Backpackers must park in lots (see map) and display the carbon copy of their permit on the dashboard. A special, small parking lot is provided off Europe Bay Road for backpackers at sites 14–16. Drinking water is available at the park office, and except in winter also at picnic grounds and on the trail between Europe Bay Rd. and sites 14–16 (see map). Campsite toilets are of two types: a conventional outhouse serving several campsites or a one-sided, roofless stall serving one campsite (toilet paper not provided).

PERMIT AND RESERVATIONS.   Camping permit required for a specific campsite (fee). Obtain your permit at the park office (HQ on the map); when the office is closed, use the self-registration system by the door. Advance reservations for 13 of the 16 campsites are accepted by the state's phone reservation service at 888/947-2757 (9 A.M. to 10 P.M. weekdays and 9 A.M. to 6 P.M. weekends) or on the web at www.wiparks.net; reservation fee charged. *Note:* All campsites are occupied virtually every Friday and Saturday night from early spring to late fall.

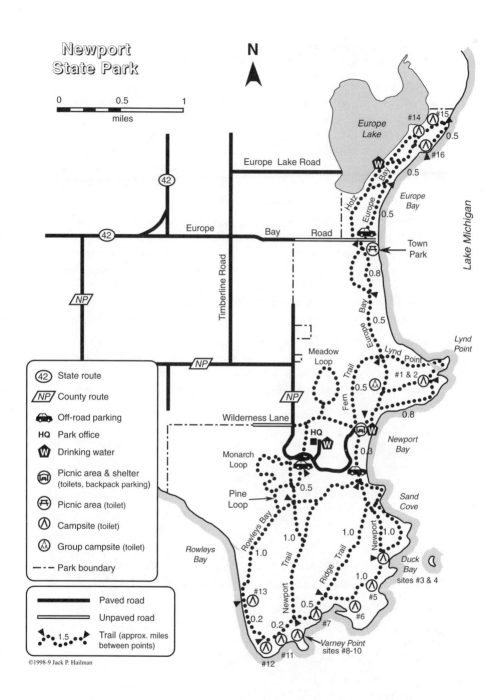

Newport
State Park

N

0   0.5   1
miles

Europe
Lake

#14   #15

0.5

#16

0.5

Europe Lake Road

Europe   Bay   Road

Hotz

Europe Bay

0.5

Europe Bay

0.5

Town
Park

Lake Michigan

42

42

Europe   Bay

Timberline Road

NP

0.8

0.5

Lynd
Point

Meadow
Loop

Fern Trail

Europe Bay

Lynd Point

#1 & 2

NP

0.5

0.8

NP

Wilderness Lane

HQ

W

W

0.3

Newport
Bay

Monarch
Loop

Sand
Cove

Pine
Loop

0.5

Rowleys Bay Trail

1.0

1.0

Newport

1.0

Duck
Bay
sites #3 & 4

Rowleys
Bay

1.0

Newport Trail

1.0

Newport Ridge Trail

1.0

#5

#13

0.5

#6

0.2

0.2   0.2

#7

Varney Point
sites #8-10

#11

#12

Legend

42   State route

NP   County route

Off-road parking

HQ   Park office

W   Drinking water

Picnic area & shelter
(toilets, backpack parking)

Picnic area (toilet)

Campsite (toilet)

Group campsite (toilet)

— · —   Park boundary

━━━   Paved road

══   Unpaved road

•••• 1.5 ••••►   Trail (approx. miles
between points)

©1998-9 Jack P. Hailman

CONTACT INFORMATION.   Newport State Park, 475 Cty. Hwy. NP, Ellison Bay, WI 54210; phone: 920/854-2500; fax: 920/854-1914.

FINDING THE TRAIL.   From Sturgeon Bay take State Highway 42 northeast toward Northport. After going through Ellison Bay, turn right on Door County Highway NP and follow it to the park. The park office is on a signed side road on the left after entering the park. Three parking areas for backpacking sites lie along the main park road, and the one for sites 14–16 is reached by returning to County Highway NP, taking Timberline Rd. north to Europe Bay Rd., and going east to the parking lot near Lake Michigan (see map).

BACKGROUND NOTES.   The natural history of Newport State Park is especially interesting, with the land set upon Silurian-age limestone layers laid down over 100 million years ago as sediment at the bottom of a vast sea. In the last part of the 19th century there was a bustling logging town at Newport, one of the "pier towns" where ships would pick up wood and Christmas trees for large Great Lakes cities.

OUR TRAIL NOTES.   We spent a Sunday night in mid-May because both Friday and Saturday nights of that weekend were already booked by the previous week. On Sunday, we hiked from the picnic grounds out on lovely Lynd Point Trail, up to Europe Bay Road, and back.

Liz walking the trail, Newport State Park

Door, Southwest, and Southeast Regions

The toilet building in the Europe Bay Town (Hotz Memorial) Park was locked. On Gravel Island (directly east of the town park, beyond the map) we could see with binoculars hundreds of gulls, presumably a nesting colony. We saw both Herring and Ring-billed Gulls along the shore.

Later, after parking the car at the lot by the park entrance, we hiked a circuit of Rowleys Bay and Newport Trails along the shoreline, camping at one of the sites and passing by sites 3–13. During the night, a snorting porcupine began roaming our campsite (probably searching for salt, according to the ranger) and Liz twice went out of the tent to chase the intruder away while Jack slept oblivious to the drama. In the morning, Double-crested Cormorants flew over our heads and into Rowleys Bay with empty bills, and also back toward the southeast with sticks, grassy vegetation and other nesting materials. East-southeast of Varney Point is Spider Island (beyond the map), where we could see through binoculars hundreds of cormorants flying among the skeletons of dead trees on the island. We emerged on Monday morning at the parking lot directly east of ours and walked along the large grassy shoulder of the paved road back to our car.

Flora. Along the scenic shoreline of white ledges grow stately Northern White-Cedar (also called Arborvitae) trees, often surprisingly dense. Two principal forest types are encountered inland: lovely open woods dominated by American Beech and Sugar Maple on the one hand, and darker areas of Eastern Hemlock and Paper Birch on the other. On tree trunks are bracket fungi such as Artist's Fungus and Hoof Fungus. Looking down we found mosses on the rocks, at least two species of lycopodium, and various ferns. Lists of wildflowers and birds may be secured at the park office. The wildflowers we found blooming on this trip in the middle of May included Clintonia (Corn-lily, Yellow Beadlily), Nodding Trillium, Large-flowered (White, Large) Trillium, Starry False Solomon's-seal (Starry Solomon's Plume), Large-flowered Bellwort, Dwarf Lake-Iris, Spotted Coralroot, Columbine, Garlic Mustard (a pernicious alien that crowds out native vegetation), Common Strawberry, Fringed Polygala (Gaywings), Downy Yellow Violets and violet violets of various species, Starflower, True Forget-me-not, Common Dandelion, and many others.

Fauna. Birds were equally in evidence: Double-crested Cormorant, Canada Goose, Merlin, Ring-billed Gull, Herring Gull, Caspian Tern, Mourning Dove, Downy Woodpecker, Hairy Woodpecker, Northern Flicker, Red-eyed Vireo, Blue Jay, American Crow, Tree Swallow, Northern Rough-winged Swallow, Black-capped Chickadee, Red-breasted Nuthatch, House Wren, Winter Wren, Hermit Thrush,

197

Wood Thrush, American Robin, Cedar Waxwing, Golden-winged Warbler, Northern Parula, Black-throated Green Warbler, Pine Warbler, American Redstart, Ovenbird, Common Yellowthroat, White-throated Sparrow, Northern Cardinal, Indigo Bunting, and American Goldfinch. The most interesting bird we found was a Northern Mockingbird in the picnic grounds, seen both Sunday and Monday. This species was not on the park's checklist of birds and was well north of its reputed breeding range. Nevertheless, mockers straggle northward irregularly and have been seen previously in Door County by other observers.

We must not forget the porcupine that invaded our campsite. A ranger told us that porcupines are a real problem, a fact not emphasized in the park literature. We were glad to have used the metal box for food (although we do always string up food for the night everywhere we go backpacking). The other mammals we encountered were Whitetail Deer and—you guessed it—Red Squirrel.

Black River State Forest

With no designated campsites, backpacking in the Black River State Forest is a chance to "rough it" on one of the many ski trails or to spend the night at one of the two trail shelters. Situated at the edge of the Driftless Area of relatively high relief in southwestern Wisconsin, the forest has taken advantage of its hills for ski trails and scenic viewpoints along the trails.

LOCATION. Southwest region, coordinates D-7 on official state highway map (Jackson County).

RATING. 🌲 🌲 🌲 🌲

> 🌲 **Scenery:** many scenic viewpoints overlooking forest
>
> 🌲 **Quiet:** can camp a mile or more from nearest paved road
>
> 🌲 **Trails:** can camp on circuit of over 5 miles
>
> 🌲 **Solitude:** unlikely to encounter more than 2 other parties per day

ENTRANCE FEE. State vehicle sticker required for use of parking lots and other state forest facilities.

CAMPING. Wilderness camping or trail shelter. Backpackers must camp at least 1 mile from their vehicles. Use of fire is restricted in the spring owing to high fire danger. There are also state forest campgrounds (fees charged) at Pigeon Creek (on North Settlement Rd.), East Fork (northernmost part of the forest), and Castle Mound Park (on U.S. Highway 12).

PERMIT AND RESERVATIONS. Free camping permit required (1999), but a charge is likely to be instituted in the year 2000. Obtain your permit at the DNR office at 910 Highway 54 East (near Interstate 94) on weekdays; in summer and part of the fall (no set schedule) you may also get permits at the campgrounds mentioned above. For advance permits, write to the forest superintendent (address below), stating the days and area where you wish to camp, number of people, vehicle make and license number, and where you will park.

CONTACT INFORMATION. Black River State Forest, 910 Hwy. 54 East, Black River Falls, WI 54615-9276; phone: 715/284-1400 or 715/284-4103; fax: 715/284-1737.

FINDING THE TRAIL. Exit Interstate 94 on Jackson County Highway O at Millston (southeast of Black River Falls) and proceed east on County O to North Settlement Rd. The Pigeon Creek campground

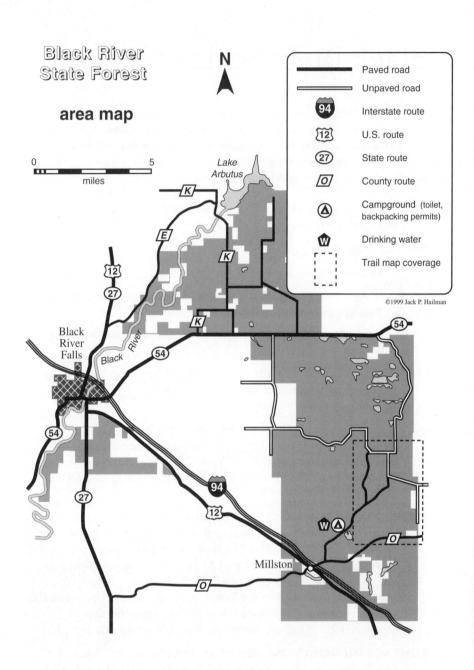

Black River
State Forest

area map

N

	Paved road
	Unpaved road
94	Interstate route
12	U.S. route
27	State route
O	County route
⚊	Campground (toilet, backpacking permits)
W	Drinking water
┆	Trail map coverage

©1999 Jack P. Hailman

0 ────────── 5
miles

Lake
Arbutus

K

E

12
27

K

Black
River
Falls

Black River

K

54

54

54

27

94

12

W ⚊

O

Millston

O

(where you can get a backpacking permit) and the main parking lot are on this road.

BACKGROUND NOTES.   As in many areas of Wisconsin, the Eastern White Pines of the original forest were removed by logging in the 1800s. However, here there has been an effort to replant and encourage Eastern White Pine, in addition to Red and Jack Pine. The resulting forest gives a large area for backpacking and many other recreational activities. The forest was originally conveyed to the state in 1957 by the federal government and has been augmented since. It is located near the edge of a glacial lake bed and overlooks unglaciated buttes and bluffs, which were islands in the lake.

OUR TRAIL NOTES.   Our trip to Black River State Forest was memorable in turning up an extraordinary species of bird. Summer still reigned in Wisconsin the first weekend of September when we backpacked on the ski trails south and east of the parking lot on North Settlement Road. Mosquitoes made us relieved to get into our tent that night on the Ridge Trail, and shorts were the preferred dress the next day. We were happy that we had covered the packs with rain covers overnight—not because it rained but because something ate a hole in one cover without hurting the pack itself. We paused at the many viewpoints with vistas, some of which were

Enjoying the view, Black River State Forest

obscured by the leafy trees; they would be better in the late fall. The second day we had lunch at the shelter, then crossed North Settlement Road at the parking lot and hiked the Red Oak Trail, with a break at the other shelter to cool off from the strain of carrying packs on a hot day, and to put on dry T-shirts. About that extraordinary bird: see the section on fauna below.

Flora. There were many nonflowering plants: ferns, ground pine, two mushrooms we were able to identify (Emetic Russula and Gem-studded Puffball), plus a red mushroom, and the lichen called British Soldiers. Of the flowers, we saw only one that was not in the daisy family: Common Evening-primrose. The representatives of the daisy family were Orange Hawkweed, Rough Blazing-star, Black-eyed Susan, and a goldenrod. The ski trails are in an area of Red Pine, Quaking Aspen, maples, and oaks.

Fauna. While hiking we met up with two remarkably fearless grouse, which resolutely but unhurriedly walked away from us and into the underbrush. Jack sketched the tail of the second bird to disappear: dark feathers on the outer parts. Then we found on the ground a tail feather—dark with a reddish-orange tip—that clinched the identification. The species had never before been recorded in this county, or so far south in Wisconsin: it was the Spruce Grouse, whose populations in eastern North America seem to be declining, for unknown reasons. During our two days on the trail we saw and heard a variety of other birds: Turkey Vulture, Great Horned Owl, Whip-poor-will, Downy Woodpecker, Hairy Woodpecker, Northern Flicker, Pileated Woodpecker, Eastern Wood-Pewee, Red-eyed Vireo, Blue Jay, Black-capped Chickadee, Red-breasted Nuthatch, Swainson's Thrush, American Robin, Scarlet Tanager, Chipping Sparrow, and American Goldfinch. A baby *Peromyscus* mouse and the ubiquitous Red Squirrel were the only mammals; an American Toad hopped across the trail. There were more insects than usual; we heard orthopterans (grasshoppers) calling, and saw dragonflies and three butterflies which we were delighted to able to identify: Monarch, Cloud Sulfur Butterfly, and Spicebush Swallowtail.

Door, Southwest, and Southeast Regions

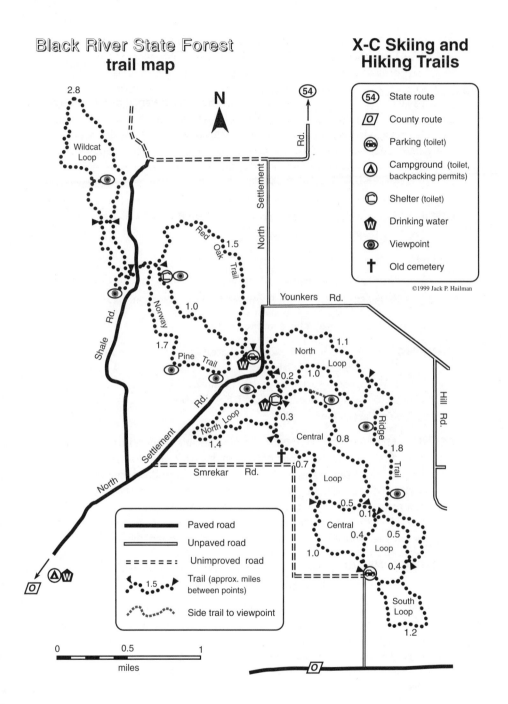

Black River State Forest
trail map

X-C Skiing and Hiking Trails

N

54 Rd.

Legend (X-C Skiing and Hiking Trails):

- 54 State route
- O County route
- Parking (toilet)
- Campground (toilet, backpacking permits)
- Shelter (toilet)
- W Drinking water
- Viewpoint
- Old cemetery

©1999 Jack P. Hailman

2.8

Wildcat Loop

Red Oak Trail

1.5

North Settlement Rd.

Younkers Rd.

1.0

Norway

1.7

Pine Trail

Shale Rd.

North Settlement Rd.

North Loop 1.1

0.2   1.0

North Loop

1.4

0.3

Central Loop

0.8

Ridge Trail

1.8

Hill Rd.

Smrekar Rd.

0.7

Loop

0.5

0.1

Central Loop

0.4

1.0

0.5 Loop

0.4

South Loop

1.2

O   W

O

Legend (bottom box):

- Paved road
- Unpaved road
- Unimproved road
- 1.5 Trail (approx. miles between points)
- Side trail to viewpoint

0   0.5   1

miles

Buckhorn State Park

An unusual type of camping characterizes Buckhorn State Park: "cart-in" camping. For those desiring the relative isolation of a backpacking site without lugging a big pack, putting your gear in a cart and pushing it to a campsite is an easy alternative. There are also sites that can be reached by wheelchair, allowing the disabled to enjoy a backpacking experience. However, you must suffer boat traffic noise at these lakeside campsites.

LOCATION. Southwest region, coordinates E/F-8 on official state highway map (Juneau County).

RATING.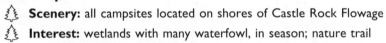

Scenery: all campsites located on shores of Castle Rock Flowage

Interest: wetlands with many waterfowl, in season; nature trail

ENTRANCE FEE. State vehicle sticker required.

CAMPING. Only at one of the 24 designated cart-in sites (see map). All campsites have carts available for transporting goods, as well as tables and toilets nearby. Sites 10–12 have a rain shelter nearby. Campsites must be occupied by 11 P.M. Drinking water is available at the picnic areas (see map).

PERMIT AND RESERVATIONS. Camping permit required for a specific campsite (fee). Obtain your permit at the park entrance station (HQ on the map); self-register when the office is closed, consulting the signboard showing the occupied sites. Advance reservations of campsites accepted by the state's phone reservation service at 888/947-2757 (9 A.M. to 10 P.M. weekdays and 9 A.M. to 6 P.M. weekends) or on the web at www.wiparks.net; reservation fee charged.

CONTACT INFORMATION. Buckhorn State Park, W8450 Buckhorn Park Ave., Necedah, WI 54646-7338; phone: 608/565-2789.

FINDING THE TRAIL. Exit Interstate 90/94 on State Highway 82 at Mauston, and go west to State Highway 58 (formerly Juneau County Highway Q), which you take north about 11 miles to Juneau County Highway G; then go east and follow signs to the park. A map available in the park shows the parking areas for the backpacking sites.

BACKGROUND NOTES. The original vast Eastern White Pine forest of this area was logged heavily in the 1800s after lumbermen were led

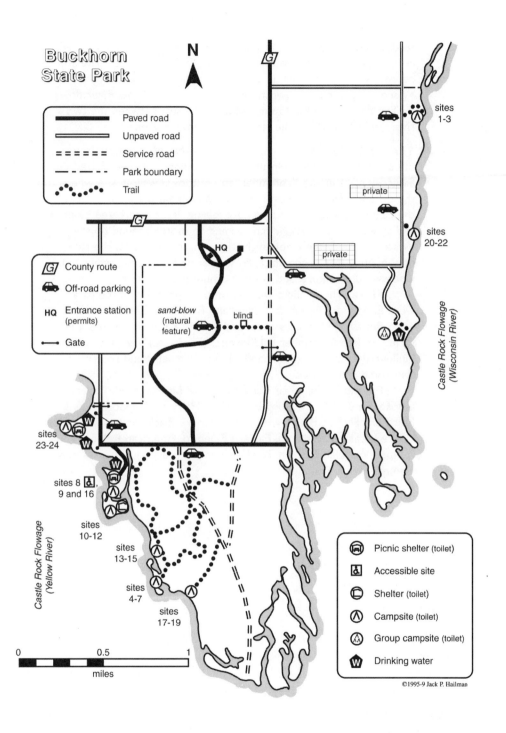

Buckhorn State Park

N

Paved road	
Unpaved road	
Service road	
Park boundary	
Trail	

G	County route
	Off-road parking
HQ	Entrance station (permits)
	Gate

sand-blow (natural feature)

blind

Castle Rock Flowage (Wisconsin River)

Castle Rock Flowage (Yellow River)

sites 1-3

private

sites 20-22

private

sites 23-24

sites 8, 9 and 16

sites 10-12

sites 13-15

sites 4-7

sites 17-19

	Picnic shelter (toilet)
	Accessible site
	Shelter (toilet)
	Campsite (toilet)
	Group campsite (toilet)
W	Drinking water

0   0.5   1
miles

©1995-9 Jack P. Hailman

to the area by the yellow in the Yellow River, which they guessed correctly must be due to the pollen of nearby pine trees. The area became small farms until, in the 1940s, a dam was built on the Wisconsin River just downstream of where the Yellow River flows in. The dam created a flowage with a peninsula between the two rivers, which is where the state park is now located.

OUR TRAIL NOTES. The campsites that are the most remote, toward the south end of the peninsula, were all taken when we arrived on a Saturday night in late September, so we took a walk-in site where the distance was just two-tenths of a mile from the parking lot to the campsite. The lack of a remote feeling was exacerbated by noisy and smelly powerboats, which seemed to motor around on the Wisconsin River the whole night through. In the rest of the park, bow-hunting was taking place, so we hardly felt like hiking around; when we did venture out, we met a hunter soon after.

Flora. The conifers we saw on our short stay in the park were Eastern Redcedar, Jack Pine, and Red Pine. Deciduous trees were Bur Oak, Quaking Aspen, and Yellow Birch. There was a nice variety of late September wildflowers: (Prostrate) Vervain, Common Mullein, Butter-and-eggs (Toadflax), a purple aster and goldenrod; also some ground pine.

Fauna. There were many species of birds around: Canada Goose, Sandhill Crane, Ring-billed Gull, Hairy Woodpecker, Northern Flicker, Blue Jay, American Crow, Black-capped Chickadee, White-breasted Nuthatch, Eastern Bluebird, American Robin, Yellow-rumped Warbler, Eastern Towhee, and Dark-eyed Junco. The only mammal was a Red Squirrel.

Governor Dodge State Park

The backpack sites at this park are less than one-half mile from the parking lot and provide a chance to hike some of the many trails in this park without staying in a family campground.

LOCATION.   Southwest region, coordinates E-10 on official state highway map (Iowa County).

RATING.

 Scenery: campsites in open area with scattered trees; other areas of park are wooded

ENTRANCE FEE.   State vehicle sticker required.

CAMPING.   Only at the six designated sites (see map) near the Hickory Ridge group campsites. Each campsite has a table and fire ring; water and pit toilets are at the parking lot. (A shower building with flush toilets is to be constructed by spring 2000.) There are also two family campgrounds, eight group campsites, and a horse campground (fees charged) in this popular park.

PERMIT AND RESERVATIONS.   Camping permit required for a specific campsite (fee). Obtain permit at park office (HQ on the map). Advance reservations of campsites accepted by the state's phone reservation service at 888/947-2757 (9 A.M. to 10 P.M. weekdays and 9 A.M. to 6 P.M. weekends) or on the web at www.wiparks.net; reservation fee charged. (Trail passes are required for biking and horse trails, but hikers do not require trail passes.)

CONTACT INFORMATION.   Governor Dodge State Park, 4175 State Rd. 23 N, Dodgeville, WI 53533; phone: 608/935-2315; fax: 608/935-3959.

FINDING THE TRAIL.   From Madison, take U.S. Highway 18 west to Dodgeville. Go north on State Highway 23 to the park entrance on the right. Continue straight on the park road past the road to the campgrounds. Turn left at the road up to the group campsites. The trail to the campsites is a dead end, and the only trail accessible from the parking lot is a horse trail. Most of the non-equestrian trails allow mountain bikes, but a few miles of trails just for hikers exist in the Cox Hollow Lake area, to which you must drive from the backpacking sites.

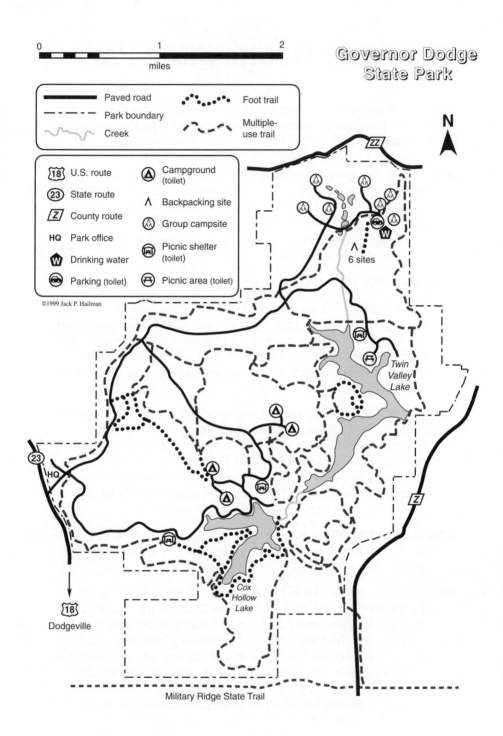

BACKGROUND NOTES.   The park is located in the Driftless Area, the unglaciated southwest region of Wisconsin, which makes it very different from most other areas in this book. Instead of rounded hills and glacial debris, there are steep hills and pronounced valleys. Hiking trails in the park have steep rocky grades in the sandstone cliffs. There is evidence that the area was visited by prehistoric peoples, and Ho-Chunk, Fox, and Sauk Indians have lived here. Europeans came in the 1820s to mine lead and zinc, and later the area was farmed. The park is named for Henry Dodge, who was Wisconsin's first territorial governor. It was created in 1948, when Iowa County gave the state of Wisconsin the 160-acre farm estate of Henry Larson, and was considerably added to over the years; it now contains over 5,000 acres.

OUR TRAIL NOTES.   One rainy weekend in late May we decided to go to Governor Dodge on a "shakedown" trip to test our aging equipment. We were able to secure a site, probably because someone had decided not to use a reservation owing to the bad weather. The short hike in was a bit surprising because it was mostly uphill and, as late as it was in spring, this was our first trip of the season so we were not yet in top hiking shape. That night, our old, small, two-person tent leaked badly. Treatments with waterproofing in our backyard the next week failed to improve it, so we bought a new and more spacious tent (but actually lighter in weight) before a far more strenuous backpacking trip to Rocky Mountain National Park later that summer.

    Flora. Some of the original prairie remains. The woods are oak and hickory; pine and fern are on the ridges.

    Fauna. More than 100 species of birds are on the park list, as well as Whitetail Deer and other mammals.

New Glarus Woods
State Park

The thick woods around the backpack/bicycle campsites in this state park make it pleasant even on a hot day. The sites were established to serve bicyclists on the nearby Sugar River State Trail, and are little more than walk-in sites. Still, there is sufficient mileage of hiking trails to provide a minimal overnight experience.

LOCATION. Southwest region, coordinates F-10 on official state highway map (Green County).

RATING.

 **Interest:** nature trails

ENTRANCE FEE. State vehicle sticker required. (Cyclists must have a trail pass, but this requirement does not apply to hikers.)

CAMPING. Only at 14 designated walk-in sites (see map), which are reservable. Developed mainly for the cyclist, the campsites are also available to the hiker. All are wooded and some are fairly private, each having a fire ring and table; outhouses are nearby. There is also a family campground and six group campsites (fees charged).

PERMIT AND RESERVATIONS. Camping permit required for a specific campsite (fee). Obtain your permit at the park office (HQ on the map). Advance reservations of campsites accepted by the state's phone reservation service at 888/947-2757 (9 A.M. to 10 P.M. weekdays and 9 A.M. to 6 P.M. weekends) or on the web at www.wiparks.net; reservation fee charged.

CONTACT INFORMATION. New Glarus Woods State Park, W5446 Cty. Hwy. NN, New Glarus, WI 53574; phone: 608/527-2335; fax: 608/527-6435.

FINDING THE TRAIL. From Madison take U.S. Highway 18/151 southwest to Verona. Go south on State Highway 69 about 20 miles, through New Glarus. Continue south on State 69 to Green County Highway NN; go west to the park, whose facilities are on the north side of the road.

BACKGROUND NOTES. This area of Wisconsin is well known for its Swiss flavor, as it was settled by Swiss immigrants in the 1840s and has retained their culture and architecture. The immigrants followed

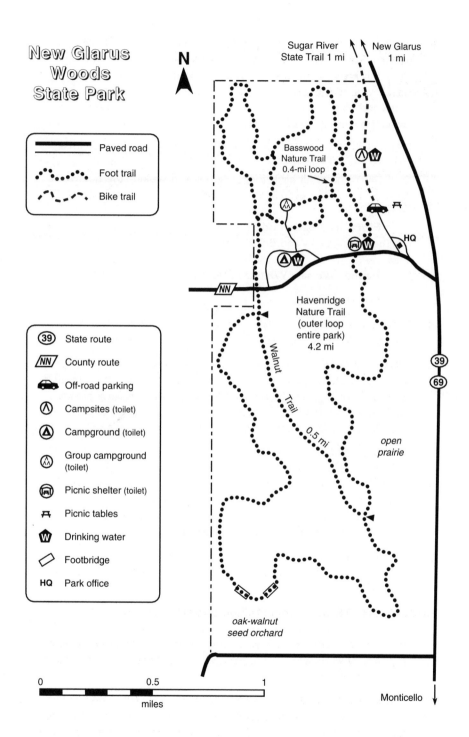

New Glarus Woods State Park

Legend:
- Paved road
- Foot trail
- Bike trail

- **(39)** State route
- **(NN)** County route
- Off-road parking
- **(A)** Campsites (toilet)
- **(▲)** Campground (toilet)
- **(M)** Group campground (toilet)
- **(曲)** Picnic shelter (toilet)
- **日** Picnic tables
- **(W)** Drinking water
- **◇** Footbridge
- **HQ** Park office

N

Sugar River State Trail 1 mi

New Glarus 1 mi

Basswood Nature Trail 0.4-mi loop

HQ

NN

Havenridge Nature Trail (outer loop entire park) 4.2 mi

Walnut Trail 0.5 mi

open prairie

(39)
(69)

oak-walnut seed orchard

0   0.5   1
miles

Monticello

the "Old Lead Road"—which goes through the south part of the park and over which mined lead was carried to Mineral Point—and settled in New Glarus just north of the park. The park has oak/walnut woods and prairie habitat. There are two nature trails, the Basswood Nature Trail, which has interpretive signs, and the much longer Havenridge Nature Trail.

OUR TRAIL NOTES. The thick woods in the campsite are deceptive; State Highway 69 is just to the east, and when we camped there the trucks were noisy all night long. We enjoyed walking the Basswood Nature Trail in the evening and the Havenridge Nature Trail the next morning.

   Flora. The Basswood Trail goes through oak and maple forest. Northern Red Oaks and Black Walnuts are seen on the Havenridge Trail.

   Fauna. We saw Whitetail Deer and a variety of birds.

Kettle Moraine State Forest
North Unit

The North Unit of Kettle Moraine State Forest (hereafter Kettle Moraine North) is surprisingly wild for being so close to three cities, and a pleasant respite from urban life and parks. This unit contains some of the best preserved glacial topography in the entire world. All units of Kettle Moraine State Forest are open year-round and offer many forms of recreation, including backpacking on the Ice Age National Scenic Trail. Kettle Moraine North offers backpacking in another area as well, the Zillmer Ski Trails.

LOCATION. Southeast region, coordinates H/I-8/9 on official state highway map (Fond du Lac, Sheboygan, and Washington Counties).

RATING: ICE AGE NATIONAL SCENIC TRAIL (TRAIL MAPS # 1– 4). 🌲🌲🌲

🌲 **Scenery:** interesting glacial features and beautiful views from ridges

🌲 **Trails:** at least 10 miles of trail accessible from camping places

🌲 **Interest:** trail goes on Parnell Esker, by Greenbush Kettle and other kettles

RATING: ZILLMER TRAILS (TRAIL MAP #2). 🌲🌲

🌲 **Scenery:** varied terrain with pine plantations, marshes, kettles, viewpoints

🌲 **Trails:** can camp on circuit of over 5 miles

ENTRANCE FEE. State vehicle sticker required for use of parking lots and other state forest facilities.

CAMPING. Backpack camping only at six designated shelters, five of which are on the Ice Age Trail and one on the Zillmer Trails. You are not required to stay *in* the three-sided shelter, but must spend the night *at* the shelter (e.g., by pitching your tent in the shelter clearing). The shelters have fire rings, and outhouses nearby. There are also developed campgrounds (fees charged) at Mauthe Lake (trail map #2) and Long Lake (trail map #3), and a group campsite at Greenbush (trail map #4).

PERMIT AND RESERVATIONS. Camping permit required for a specific shelter (fee). You can obtain a same-day permit at the Ice Age Visitor Center on State Highway 67 (trail map #2), at the Kettle

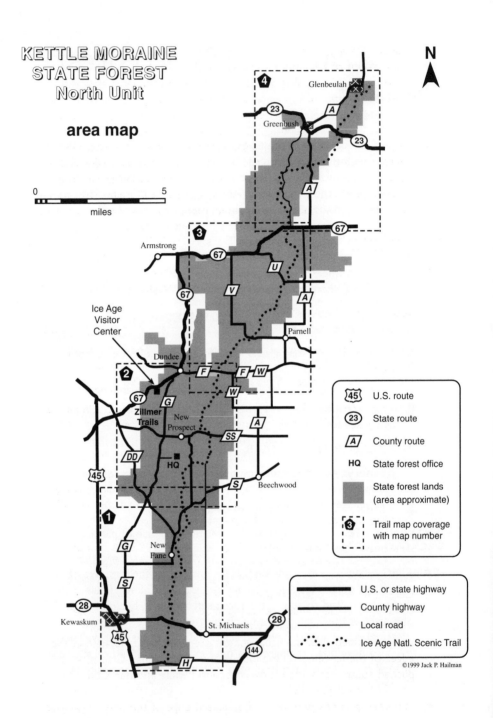

KETTLE MORAINE
STATE FOREST
North Unit

area map

N

0 ——— 5
miles

Glenbeulah

4

23

Greenbush

A

23

67

3

Armstrong

67

U

67

V

A

Ice Age
Visitor
Center

Parnell

Dundee

F

F W

2

W

67

G

A

Zillmer
Trails

New
Prospect

SS

DD

HQ

1

S

Beechwood

45

G

New
Fane

S

28

Kewaskum

St. Michaels

28

45

144

H

45	U.S. route
23	State route
A	County route
HQ	State forest office
	State forest lands (area approximate)
3	Trail map coverage with map number

U.S. or state highway
County highway
Local road
Ice Age Natl. Scenic Trail

©1999 Jack P. Hailman

Moraine State Forest Headquarters off Fond du Lac County Highway G just south of County SS (trail map #2), or at the campground offices at Mauthe Lake (trail map #2) or Long Lake (trail map #3). Advance reservations of campsites are accepted by the state's phone reservation service at 888/947-2757 (9 A.M. to 10 P.M. weekdays and 9 A.M. to 6 P.M. weekends) or on the web at www.wiparks.net; reservation fee charged. *Note:* Kettle Moraine North is immensely popular, and the shelters on the Ice Age Trail are usually reserved weeks or months in advance for weekends from spring to fall. You can sometimes obtain a permit for the Zillmer Trail shelter for the same day (i.e., without advance reservations), even on weekends.

CONTACT INFORMATION. Kettle Moraine State Forest–Northern Unit, N1765 Hwy. G, Campbellsport, WI 53010; phone: 262/626-2116. Ice Age Visitor Center phone: 262/533-8322.

    Ice Age National Scenic Trail. Ice Age Park & Trail Foundation of Wisconsin, Inc., 207 E. Buffalo St., Suite 515, Milwaukee, WI 53202-5712; phone 800/227-0046; e-mail: cthisted@sbtsi.com. The office can put you in touch with the current coordinator of the chapter responsible for this section of trail. *Also,* Ice Age National Scenic Trail, National Park Service, 700 Rayovac Dr., Suite 100, Madison, WI 53711; phone: 608/264-5610.

FINDING THE TRAIL. The southern portion of this linear state forest is located just east of U.S. Highway 45, from which State Highway 67 goes into the northern part. The **Ice Age Trail** crossings and the parking for the **Zillmer Trails** can be reached from roads leading from these highways. Although there are numerous roads crossing the Ice Age Trail, most have no off-road parking so it is best to leave your vehicle in one of the parking lots (trailheads and picnic areas) near the trail, as shown on the trail maps.

BACKGROUND NOTES. Encompassing 28,000 acres, Kettle Moraine North is the largest of the nine units of the Ice Age National Scientific Reserve (see Ice Age National Scenic Trail in the North Central Region). Glacial features here resulted from the last continental glacier, which retreated about 10,000 years ago. The Kettle Moraine is no ordinary moraine, but is higher and more sharply defined than the usual end or lateral moraines formed at the edges of the ice sheets. One lobe of the Wisconsinan Glaciation pushed south into what is now Wisconsin while another lobe enlarged the depression that now holds Lake Michigan. The lateral moraines of these two lobes, the eastern edge of the Wisconsin lobe and the western edge of the Lake Michigan lobe, merged to form the large interlobate moraine we see today.

A stop at the Henry S. Reuss Ice Age Visitor Center on State Highway 67 (trail map #2) is a fine way to learn the geological history of the area. Here in Kettle Moraine North you can find glacial topographic features such as kames (conical hills), eskers (ridges resulting from deposits in underground streams), and kettles (depressions formed from earth-covered pockets of ice from which the ice melted), the last giving its name to the interlobate moraine. The visitor center has a loop trail over the morainal deposit on which it is located. Nearby cross-county ski loops of the Zillmer Trails offer the backpacker an alternative to the linear Ice Age Trail, where you have to retrace your steps unless you have two vehicles.

OUR TRAIL NOTES. At the visitor center on a Saturday in mid-September we were able to get a permit for trail shelter #6 on the Zillmer Trails; not surprising, all the Ice Age Trail shelters had been taken. Shortly after leaving the trailhead on County Highway SS, we came to a stone with a plaque honoring the trails' namesake, Raymond T. Zillmer, who originated the concept of the Ice Age Trail. We walked east on the red trail into a pine plantation, then a spruce plantation, and across a mowed meadow. In less than half an hour we reached the shelter after detouring on the green trail. The shelter had sleeping platforms, an outhouse, and a bench to sit on, but no table. In the evening we were visited first by two young men and a young woman from Sheboygan who apparently came to the fire ring to have a cigarette. The visitor center personnel had warned us that forest rangers sometimes issued permits for the Zillmer shelter without checking first, and sure enough a nice young couple arrived as we were taking an after-dinner walk. They had just been issued a permit by a ranger, so we invited them to share the shelter with us, but they decided against that and departed in the failing light. Still later, we met a family with four children on the dark trails and began to feel as if we were in Grand Central Station. The hike out (by a different route) the next day led down to a marsh in a kettle hole, then into the woods, and out into a long section of open area where we walked through unmowed grass. On this otherwise uneventful hike the highlight of the trip suddenly occurred when a Mink crossed the trail in front of us near a small ditch with running water.

Flora. Much of the trail is in planted Red Pine with scattered Eastern White Pine plantations and a spruce plantation. Some other trees in the woods were Eastern Redcedar, Red Maple, Paper Birch, and American Beech. Near the wet area where we saw the Mink was ground pine. In the open areas were Staghorn Sumac, milkweed with

216

seed pods, and a few members of the daisy family: Yarrow, a little white aster, and a goldenrod.

Fauna. We saw a nice variety of birds for late fall: Canada Goose, Red-shouldered Hawk, Sandhill Crane, a Barred Owl during the night, Downy Woodpecker, Eastern Wood-Pewee, Blue Jay, American Crow, Black-capped Chickadee, Red- and White-breasted Nuthatches, American Robin, Gray Catbird, Northern Cardinal, and American Goldfinch. We heard the frog Spring Peeper singing, and grasshoppers chirping. A baby toad hopped over the path, and we saw a Monarch Butterfly. In addition to the Mink the only other mammal was our old friend, the ubiquitous Red Squirrel.

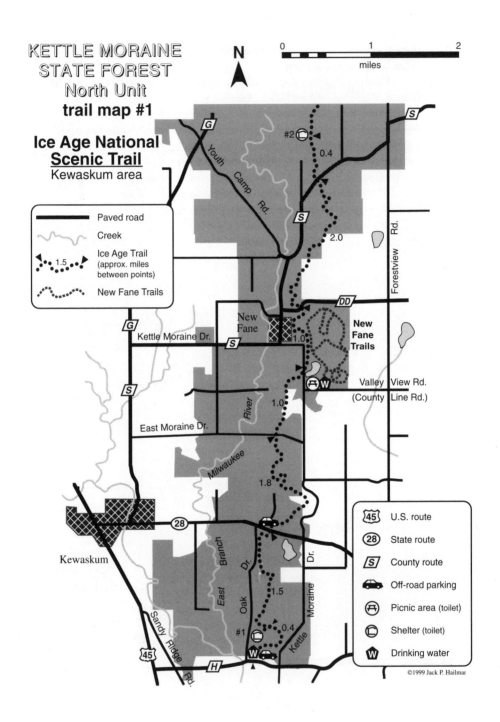

KETTLE MORAINE
STATE FOREST
North Unit
trail map #1

**Ice Age National
<u>Scenic Trail</u>**
Kewaskum area

N

0   1   2
miles

Legend

━━━ Paved road

Creek

Ice Age Trail
(approx. miles
between points)

New Fane Trails

Youth Camp Rd.

#2 0.4

S 2.0

Forestview Rd.

DD

New
Fane

New
Fane
Trails

Kettle Moraine Dr.

G

S

S

1.0

W

Valley View Rd.
(County Line Rd.)

East Moraine Dr.

River

Milwaukee

1.0

1.8

28

Kewaskum

East Branch Dr.

Oak Dr.

Kettle Moraine Dr.

1.5

#1 0.4

W

Sandy Ridge Rd.

45

H

Legend (routes)

45   U.S. route

28   State route

S   County route

🚗 Off-road parking

Picnic area (toilet)

Shelter (toilet)

W   Drinking water

©1999 Jack P. Hailmar

218

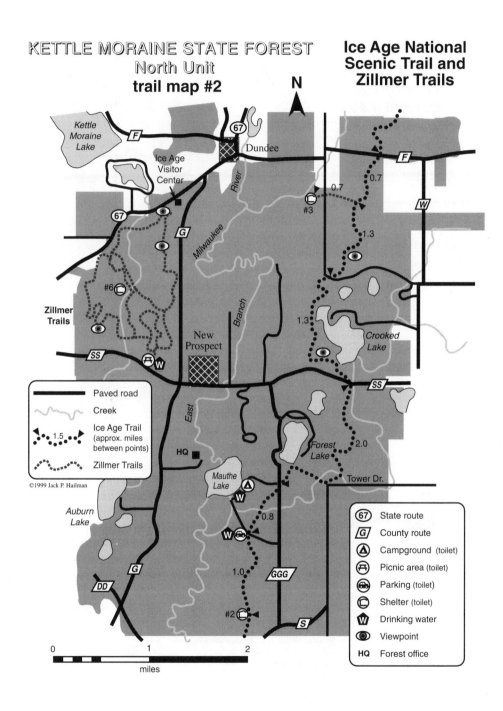

KETTLE MORAINE STATE FOREST
North Unit
trail map #2

N

Ice Age National Scenic Trail and Zillmer Trails

Kettle Moraine Lake

F

67

Dundee

Ice Age Visitor Center

67

G

Milwaukee River

F

W

0.7

0.7

#3

0.7

1.3

#6

Zillmer Trails

New Prospect

1.3

Crooked Lake

SS

W

SS

	Paved road
	Creek
1.5	Ice Age Trail (approx. miles between points)
	Zillmer Trails

©1999 Jack P. Hailman

East Branch

HQ

Forest Lake

2.0

Tower Dr.

Auburn Lake

Mauthe Lake

W

0.8

W

G

1.0

GGG

DD

#2

S

67	State route
G	County route
▲	Campground (toilet)
	Picnic area (toilet)
	Parking (toilet)
	Shelter (toilet)
W	Drinking water
◉	Viewpoint
HQ	Forest office

0   1   2

miles

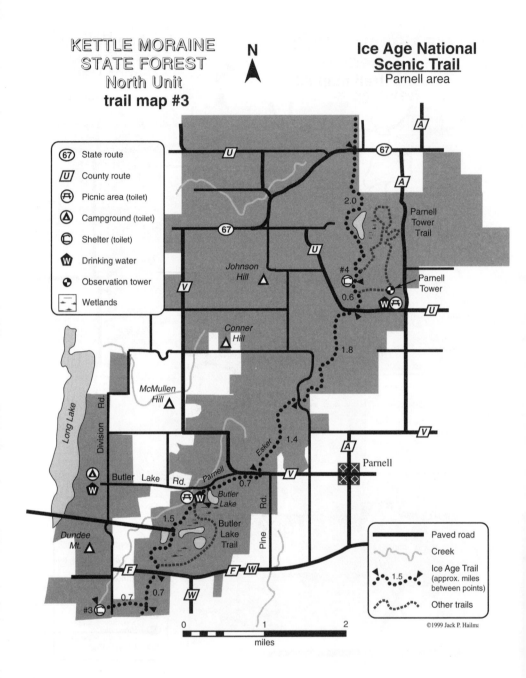

KETTLE MORAINE
STATE FOREST
North Unit
trail map #3

N

Ice Age National
Scenic Trail
Parnell area

67 State route
U County route
Picnic area (toilet)
Campground (toilet)
Shelter (toilet)
Drinking water
Observation tower
Wetlands

Parnell
Tower
Trail

Parnell
Tower

Johnson
Hill

Conner
Hill

McMullen
Hill

Long Lake

Division Rd.

Butler Lake Rd.

Parnell

Esker

Parnell

Butler
Lake

Butler
Lake
Trail

Pine Rd.

Dundee
Mt.

Paved road
Creek
Ice Age Trail
(approx. miles
between points)
Other trails

©1999 Jack P. Hailma

0   1   2
miles

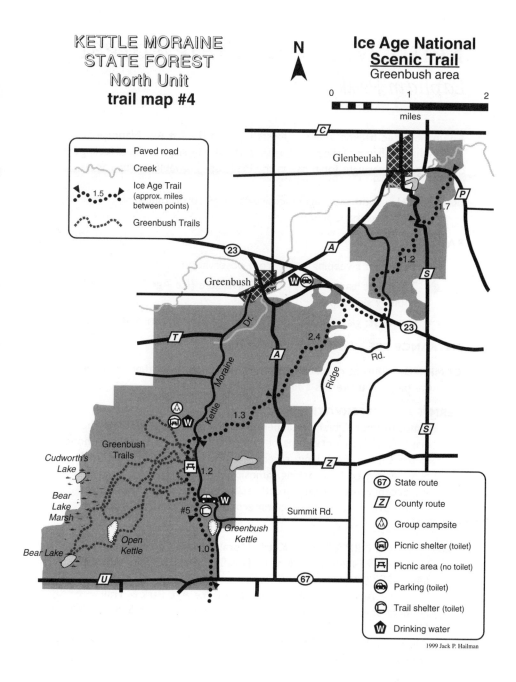

Kettle Moraine State Forest
Lapham Peak Unit

An unpublicized backpacking site exists right off the Ice Age National Scenic Trail in this small unit of the state forest. It has a surprisingly isolated feeling and offers a good overnight for those in the Madison–Milwaukee urban areas.

LOCATION.   Southeast region, coordinates H-10 on official state highway map (Waukesha County).

RATING.   🌲 🌲

🌲 **Scenery:** sweeping views from observation tower

🌲 **Trails:** at least 10 miles of trail available (Ice Age Trail and cross-country ski loops)

🌲 **Interest:** glacial features typical of Kettle Moraine State Forest

ENTRANCE FEE.   State vehicle sticker required.

CAMPING.   Only at one designated site (see map); no other camping in the park. The site has a fire ring and picnic table.

PERMIT AND RESERVATIONS.   Camping permit required for the campsite (fee). Obtain your permit at the park office (HQ on the map). Advance reservations of campsite accepted by mail and phone to the Lapham Peak Unit; reservation fee charged. *Note:* This is the only designated backpacking campsite in a state park or forest that still accepts reservations directly at the unit; all others have been turned over to a commercial enterprise under contract from the state.

CONTACT INFORMATION.   Kettle Moraine State Forest–Lapham Peak Unit, W329 N846, Cty. Hwy. C, Delafield, WI 53018; phone: 262/646-3025.

   Ice Age National Scenic Trail. Ice Age Park & Trail Foundation of Wisconsin, Inc., 207 E. Buffalo St., Suite 515, Milwaukee, WI 53202-5712; phone: 800/227-0046; e-mail: cthisted@sbtsi.com. The office can put you in touch with the current coordinator of the chapter responsible for this section of trail. *Also,* Ice Age National Scenic Trail, National Park Service, 700 Rayovac Dr., Suite 100, Madison, WI 53711; phone: 608/264-5610.

FINDING THE TRAIL.   Lapham Peak is located a little south of Interstate 94 at Delafield on the east side of Waukesha County Highway C.

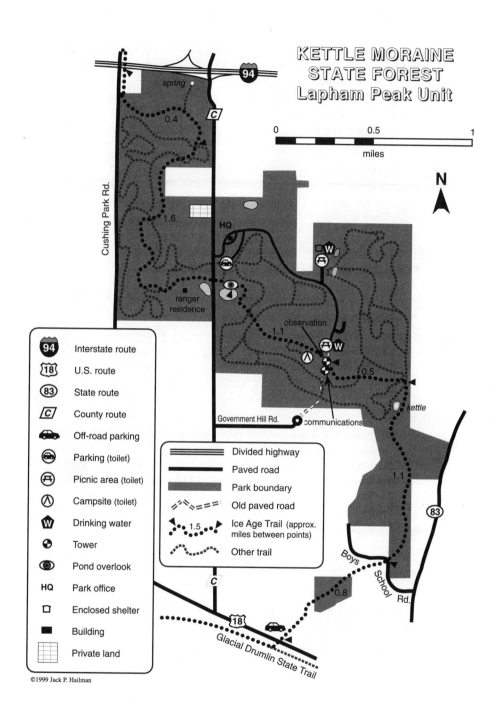

KETTLE MORAINE
STATE FOREST
Lapham Peak Unit

spring

0.4

C

Cushing Park Rd.

1.6

HQ

W

ranger
residence

observation

1.1

W

0.5

kettle

Government Hill Rd.   communications

1.1

94   Interstate route

18   U.S. route

83   State route

C   County route

🚗   Off-road parking

🚗   Parking (toilet)

🚻   Picnic area (toilet)

⛺   Campsite (toilet)

W   Drinking water

🛆   Tower

👁   Pond overlook

HQ   Park office

▢   Enclosed shelter

■   Building

▦   Private land

©1999 Jack P. Hailman

Divided highway

Paved road

Park boundary

Old paved road

1.5   Ice Age Trail (approx.
miles between points)

Other trail

C

83

Boys

School

Rd.

1.1

0.8

18

Glacial Drumlin State Trail

0   0.5   1

miles

N

223

To reach the trail to the backpacking site you can park at the **Evergreen Trail** parking lot (to the right, just after entering the park) or at the observation tower. The **Ice Age Trail** is accessed from the Evergreen parking lot by going south on a connecting trail; the trail goes right by the observation tower. Walking southeast from the Evergreen parking lot or northwest from the tower, look for a side trail to the campsite.

BACKGROUND NOTES.   Increase Lapham was a scientist, author, and conservationist who lived in Milwaukee in the 18th century. He pressured Congress to start the U.S. Weather Bureau (now Weather Service) but would not accept the post of chief because the bureau was at the time in the Department of War and he was a Quaker. He also established a weather relay station on what we now call Lapham Peak, from which information was sent to Chicago and used in weather forecasts to aid shipping on the Great Lakes. This unit of the Kettle Moraine State Forest occupies 1,006 acres and, at 1,233 feet, the top of the hill is the highest point in Waukesha County.

OUR TRAIL NOTES.   There was a small but steady stream of visitors to the observation tower, which we climbed to get a sense for the lay of the land. Then we hiked on the Ice Age Trail, returning along the west side of County Highway C, and enjoyed the crisp fall air. This was the latest we had camped in Wisconsin, the second week of November, and we found the problem was not the cold (it being a mild weekend), but the darkness. After setting up our tent before 6 P.M., we were in complete darkness, so we went back to the car and drove to a mall for some early Christmas shopping! The overnight was a stopover on our way to an event in Milwaukee the next day.

    Flora. On the Ice Age Trail around the observation tower we saw Eastern White Pine, Eastern Redcedar, White Oak, Quaking and Bigtooth Aspen, and the introduced invasive species European Buckthorn. Along the highway were planted the nonnative Blue Spruce and Weeping Willow. We also saw Post Oak; there were no flowers of any kind.

    Fauna. Our early November trip netted mostly permanent-resident birds: Canada Goose, American Black Duck, Mallard, Mourning Dove, Great Horned Owl, Blue Jay, American Crow, Black-capped Chickadee, White-breasted Nuthatch, Dark-eyed Junco (a wintering species that breeds in the north), and Northern Cardinal.

Kettle Moraine State Forest
South Unit

The South Unit of Kettle Moraine State Forest (hereafter Kettle Moraine South) is the forest most accessible to metropolitan areas, yet despite its popularity, it offers a surprisingly wild feel on the 30-plus miles of the Ice Age National Scenic Trail that run through it. The relatively high relief of the area provides scenic beauty, and its early settlement left a legacy of historically interesting sites.

LOCATION. Southeast region, coordinates H-10 on official state highway map (Waukesha, Jefferson, and Walworth Counties).

**RATING: ICE AGE NATIONAL SCENIC TRAIL
(TRAIL MAPS #1–4).** 🌲 🌲 🌲

🌲 **Scenery:** occasional views, especially at shelters, of glacial and varied terrain

🌲 **Trails:** at least 10 miles of trail accessible from camping places

🌲 **Interest:** trail goes by visitor center with natural history and regional history displays

ENTRANCE FEE. State vehicle sticker required for use of parking lots and other state forest facilities.

CAMPING. Backpack camping only at three designated shelters (trail maps #2–4). You are not required to stay *in* the three-sided shelter, but must spend the night *at* the shelter (e.g., by pitching your tent in the shelter clearing). The shelters have outhouses nearby. There are also developed campgrounds (fees charged) at Whitewater Lake (trail map #1), Pine Woods (trail map #3), and Ottawa Lake (trail map #4); group campsites are at Hickory Woods (trail map #1) and within the Pine Woods campground (trail map #3).

PERMIT AND RESERVATIONS. Camping permit required for a specific shelter (fee). You can obtain a same-day permit for an unreserved shelter at Forest Headquarters and Visitor Center on State Highway 59 (trail map #3), or at the Ottawa Lake Campground (trail map #4). Advance reservations of campsites are accepted by the state's phone reservation service at 888/947-2757 (9 A.M. to 10 P.M. weekdays and 9 A.M. to 6 P.M. weekends) or on the web at www.wiparks.net; reservation fee charged. *Note:* Kettle Moraine State Forest is immensely popular, and the shelters on the Ice Age Trail are usually reserved weeks or months in advance for weekends from spring to fall.

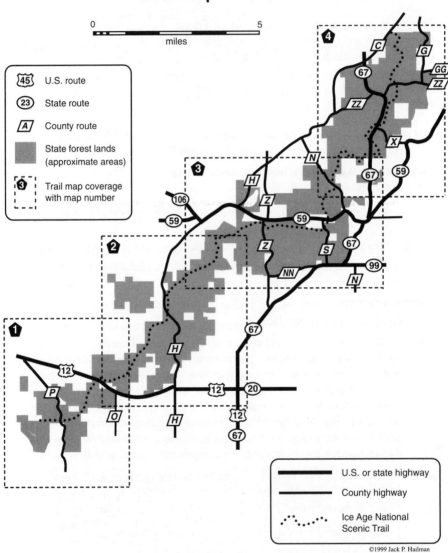

KETTLE MORAINE STATE FOREST
South Unit

area map

N

0 ——— 5
miles

45 U.S. route

23 State route

A County route

State forest lands
(approximate areas)

3 Trail map coverage
with map number

——— U.S. or state highway

——— County highway

········ Ice Age National
Scenic Trail

©1999 Jack P. Hailman

CONTACT INFORMATION. Kettle Moraine State Forest–South Unit, S91 W39091 Hwy. 59, Eagle, WI 53119; phone: 262/594-6200 (headquarters) or 262/594-6220 (Ottawa Lake Campground); fax: 262/594-6222; e-mail: morgec@dnr.state.wi.us.

Ice Age National Scenic Trail. Ice Age Park & Trail Foundation of Wisconsin, Inc., 207 E. Buffalo St., Suite 515, Milwaukee, WI 53202-5712; phone: 800/227-0046; e-mail: cthisted@sbtsi.com. The office can put you in touch with the current coordinator of the chapter responsible for this section of trail. *Also,* Ice Age National Scenic Trail, National Park Service, 700 Rayovac Dr., Suite 100, Madison, WI 53711; phone: 608/264-5610.

FINDING THE TRAIL. Kettle Moraine South is west-southwest of Milwaukee and mostly northeast of U.S. Highway 12, along State Highways 67 and 59. Numerous county highways and other roads crisscross the forest lands, providing access to the **Ice Age Trail.** You can also reach the trail from the visitors' center (HQ on trail map #3), but it is a little tricky getting there. If you follow the nature trail that leaves from the left side of the building, eventually you will climb a ridge and meet a T-junction. Turn right and go downhill to find the nearby Ice Age Trail. Or, from the parking lot follow the old woods road that is marked as the trail to the shelter; in a short distance this old road crosses the Ice Age Trail and heads uphill to shelter #2.

BACKGROUND NOTES. The South Unit of the Kettle Moraine is a continuation of the same geologic formation as the North Unit and contains less dramatic forms of the same geological features, such as kettles and moraines. There is evidence here of settlements as long ago as 6000 B.C., and there were Potawatomi villages in the area when European Americans arrived in the 1830s. There continues to be a great deal of activity here, as a glance at the Department of Natural Resources map of the forest shows: picnicking, camping, nature trails, hunting, boating, lake swimming, hiking, biking, horseback riding, skiing, snowmobiling, dog trial grounds, a sports center, and historic sites. The Ice Age Trail is 32 miles long in the park and goes by two state natural areas, the Bald Bluff Natural Area and the Scuppernong Prairie. The Scuppernong Springs Nature Trail is an interesting combination of natural springs and historic structures, and there are three other nature trails.

OUR TRAIL NOTES. "A room with a view" is what we had when we stayed at shelter #2 on the Ice Age Trail, high on a ridge near the visitors' center. We had to make our reservation in June for a September weekend, but it was worth waiting for. It was hard to believe

Our tent by shelter #2, Kettle Moraine State Forest, South Unit

that the weather in mid-September for our long-planned trip would be hot, but the temperature was near 90°F, so we strolled without packs on some shady trails and later cooked a leisurely dinner in a city park. The temperature was still in the upper 80s when approaching sunset dictated that we don our packs and head to the shelter. We were rewarded with a wonderful view to the west with a quiet stream far below, and watched the sun set in this idyllic spot. The next morning the temperature had gone down to the low 60s, which made for a more pleasant walk out, treading on acorns and Black Walnuts and creating a crunching noise that we preferred to the rampant gunshots that broke the Sunday morning quiet.

Flora. At the beginning of the trail from the parking lot were Black and White Oak. We passed some sumac with bright red leaves, Eastern Redcedar, Shagbark Hickory, and Bigtooth Aspen on the way out. The only flowers were False Solomon's Seal (Solomon's Plume) in red berry and White Snakeroot in flower.

Fauna. It is amazing what one can hear from inside a tent! During the night, we heard a Great Horned Owl and a Whip-poor-will, and in the morning before unzipping the tent we added to our list: Canada Goose, Sandhill Crane, Blue Jay, Northern Cardinal, and American Goldfinch. We also heard the chattering of a chipmunk. From outside the tent we listed Wood Duck pairs flying by, White-breasted Nuthatch, American Robin, and Cedar Waxwing.

228

Door, Southwest, and Southeast Regions

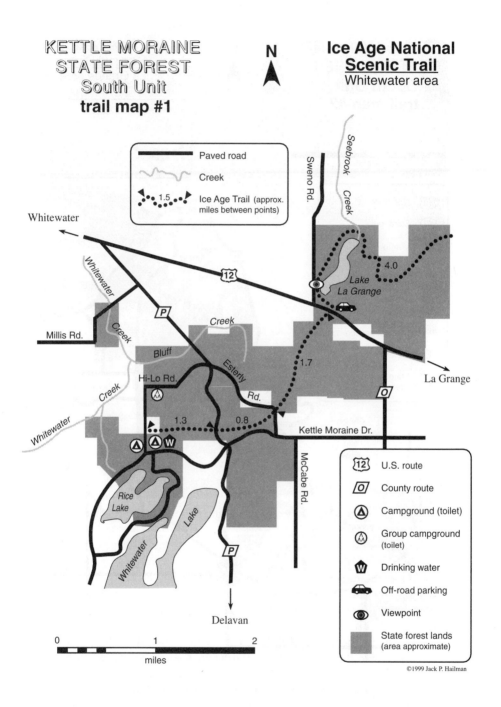

KETTLE MORAINE
STATE FOREST
South Unit
trail map #1

N

**Ice Age National
Scenic Trail**
Whitewater area

Paved road

Creek

1.5 Ice Age Trail (approx.
miles between points)

Whitewater

Sweno Rd.

Seebrook Creek

12

Lake
La Grange

4.0

Whitewater Creek

P

Millis Rd.

Creek

Bluff

Esterly

1.7

Creek

Hi-Lo Rd.

Rd.

La Grange

O

1.3   0.8

Whitewater

Kettle Moraine Dr.

W

McCabe Rd.

Rice
Lake

Whitewater   Lake

P

Delavan

12	U.S. route
O	County route
⚠	Campground (toilet)
⚠	Group campground (toilet)
W	Drinking water
🚗	Off-road parking
👁	Viewpoint
	State forest lands (area approximate)

0   1   2
miles

©1999 Jack P. Hailman

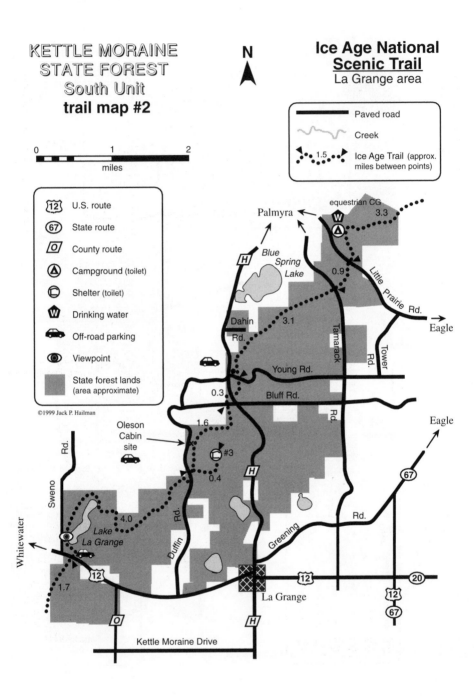

KETTLE MORAINE STATE FOREST South Unit trail map #2

N

Ice Age National Scenic Trail
La Grange area

Legend:
- ▬▬▬ Paved road
- ～～～ Creek
- ◄•••1.5•••► Ice Age Trail (approx. miles between points)

0   1   2
miles

Map legend:
- (12) U.S. route
- (67) State route
- ◻O County route
- ⓐ Campground (toilet)
- ⓒ Shelter (toilet)
- Ⓦ Drinking water
- 🚗 Off-road parking
- ◉ Viewpoint
- State forest lands (area approximate)

©1999 Jack P. Hailman

equestrian CG   3.3

Palmyra

Blue Spring Lake

H

0.9

Little Prairie Rd.

Eagle

Dahin Rd.   3.1

Tamarack Rd.

Tower Rd.

Young Rd.

0.3   Bluff Rd.

Rd.

Eagle

1.6

Oleson Cabin site

ⓒ #3

0.4

H

(67)

Sweno Rd.

4.0

Duffin Rd.

Greening Rd.

Whitewater

Lake La Grange

1.7

(12)

La Grange

(12) (20)

(12)
(67)

◻O   Kettle Moraine Drive   H

230

KETTLE MORAINE STATE FOREST
South Unit
trail map #3

Ice Age National
Scenic Trail
Palmyra-Eagle area

©1999 Jack P. Hailman

Legend:
- 67 State route
- County route
- Campground (toilet)
- Picnic area (toilet)
- Shelter (toilet)
- Drinking water
- Off-road parking
- Viewpoint
- HQ Forest office and visitor center
- State forest lands (area approximate)

- Paved road
- Creek
- Ice Age Trail (approx. miles between points)

N

miles
0   1   2

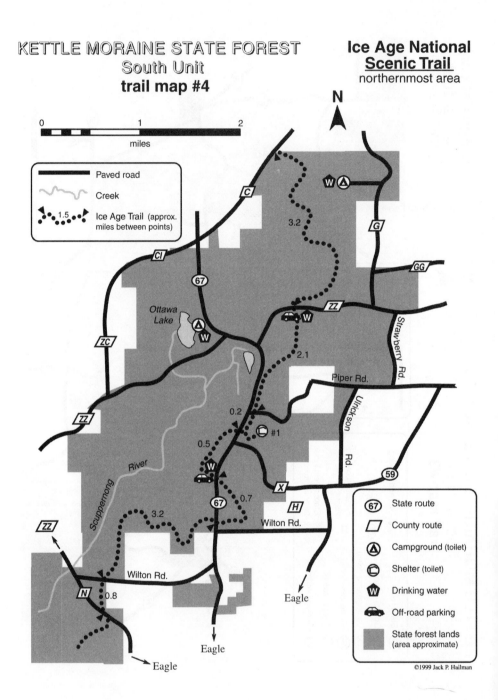

KETTLE MORAINE STATE FOREST
South Unit
trail map #4

Ice Age National
Scenic Trail
northernmost area

N

0   1   2
miles

Paved road

Creek

1.5 Ice Age Trail (approx. miles between points)

C

3.2

G

CI

GG

67

ZZ

Ottawa
Lake

ZC

W

Strawberry Rd.

2.1

Piper Rd.

ZZ

Ulrickson Rd.

0.2

0.5

#1

59

River

Scuppernong

W

X

67

0.7

H

3.2

Wilton Rd.

ZZ

Eagle

Wilton Rd.

N 0.8

Eagle

Eagle

Eagle

67	State route
▱	County route
▲	Campground (toilet)
⬢	Shelter (toilet)
W	Drinking water
🚗	Off-road parking
▨	State forest lands (area approximate)

©1999 Jack P. Hailman

232

APPENDIXES

FURTHER READING

INDEX

APPENDIX A

Quasi-backpacking Places

"Quasi-backpacking place" is a term we invented for areas where one can hike at least 10 miles and camp in a campground on or near the trail. These areas do not meet the minimum requirements for an account in the body of this book because campgrounds are accessible by motor vehicles, and many of the trails lack interesting natural history features. Nevertheless, readers may sometimes choose quasi-backpacking because they find an area conveniently located, they want to test equipment on a shakedown hike, or they want a first experience in a more civilized setting.

Quasi-backpacking areas in Wisconsin are of two major types: trails that both forbid trailside camping and lack designated campsites away from vehicular access, and campgrounds located on a network of hiking trails. Backpacking areas given separate accounts elsewhere are not repeated here even if they have quasi-backpacking potential in addition to true backpacking opportunities. We have not visited many of the trails and parks listed here, but instead have relied primarily upon brochures and other published information. For that reason we strongly suggest that you contact the supervising authority for up-to-date information before planning a trip to any of the quasi-backpacking places. Finally, the lists here are representative rather than comprehensive.

LINEAR HIKING TRAILS NEAR CAMPGROUNDS

At least four types of linear hiking trails exist in Wisconsin: (1) completed segments of national scenic trails outside of those areas that are suitable for backpacking, (2) another kind of national trail that does not allow backpacking, (3) state hike-bike trails, which are mainly old railroad grades surfaced for biking, and (4) other long trails, especially hike-bike trails that are not part of the state system. The linear trails are geographically attractive for the backpacker because most lie in the southern half of the state, where true backpacking opportunities are scarce.

Use of all state hike-bike trails is free to hikers, but cyclists must purchase trail permits. The Department of Natural Resources lists two state trails as offering "backpack camping" (Elroy-Sparta and Glacial Drumlin) and two others as having such camping "located nearby" (Military and Red Cedar). Those four are listed below along with some other state trails that qualify for quasi-backpacking but are not so listed by the DNR.

The map that is near the front of this book names the regions that we defined to locate backpacking areas. Those regional names are used in the entries here for purposes of general location, but these trails are not shown on the region map. For inclusion here a trail must pass within 5 miles of a public campground (roughly a 2-hour walk with a full pack). We have excluded trails known to us to be surfaced with asphalt or other pavement and those that allow use by horses or motorized vehicles when not snow covered; many trails listed do allow snowmobiles in winter. Trails are listed alphabetically.

400 State Trail

This trail is in our Southwest backpacking region (Juneau and Sauk Counties). The trail runs for 22 miles between Elroy and Reedsburg, thus connecting in Elroy with the Elroy-Sparta Trail (see below). There are public campgrounds near the trail at Elroy, Wink, and Reedsburg. The trail is sometimes advertised as also being for equestrian use, but actually the 7-mile horse trail is separate from the hike-bike trail. *Contact:* The 400 State Trail, Reedsburg Chamber, P.O. Box 142, Reedsburg, WI 53959; phone: 608/524-2850 or 800/844-3507.

Bearskin State Trail

Crossing between our North Central and Northeast regions, south of Minocqua (Oneida County), this trail runs north-south for 18 miles over a former railroad route, and appears to be about 5 miles from a campground in Northern Highland–American Legion State Forest. A DNR brochure says that privately owned "campgrounds are also available near either end of the trail." *Contact:* Superintendent, Bearskin State Park Trail, Trout Lake Forestry Headquarters, 4125 Cty. Hwy. M, Boulder Junction, WI 54512; phone: 715/385-2727. *Also,* Minocqua Chamber of Commerce, P.O. Box 1006, Minocqua, WI 54548; phone: 715/356-5266 or 800/NORTH; or Northwoods Store, Hwy. 51 and K, Tomahawk, WI 54487; phone: 715/282-5696.

Elroy-Sparta State Trail

Located in our Southwest region (Monroe and Juneau Counties), the Elroy-Sparta State Trail is believed to be the first hike-bike trail in the United States created from an abandoned rail line. This east-west, 32-mile trail over an old Chicago and Northwestern Railroad bed passes through three tunnels. Elroy-Sparta is one of two state trails listed by the Department of Natural Resources as offering backpacking; the DNR maintains primitive bike campgrounds at the trail's ends in Elroy and Sparta. The villages of Norwalk, Wilson, Kendall, and Elroy on the trail also have municipal campgrounds. *Contact:* Elroy-Sparta State Trail Headquarters, P.O. Box 297, Kendall, WI 54638; phone: 608/463-7109.

Glacial Drumlin State Trail

This trail runs east-west in the Southeast region (Dane, Jefferson, and Waukesha Counties). This 47-mile hike-bike trail has a 4-mile gap near the town of

Jefferson, dividing the trail into roughly equal eastern and western halves. The eastern half is one of two state trails listed by the Department of Natural Resources as offering backpacking, apparently based solely on the fact that the trail passes just south of the Lapham Peak Unit of Kettle Moraine State Forest (see account in main body). The closest public camping on the western half of the trail is at Sandhill Station State Campground, about a mile from the trail, south of the town of Lake Mills. *Contact:* Glacial Drumlin Trail–East, 280H Cty. Hwy. C, Delafield, WI 53018; phone: 262/646-3025; and Glacial Drumlin Trail–West, 1213 S. Main St., Lake Mills, WI 53551; phone: 920/648-8774.

Great River State Trail

The Great River State Trail is in the Southwest region (La Crosse and Trempealeau Counties). The trail runs for 24 miles along the Mississippi River over an old railroad bed but next to a rail route still in use. There is a campground at Perrot State Park, which the trail passes, and private camping at the communities of Midway and Onalaska at the southeastern end of the trail. *Contact:* Great River State Trail Friends, 800 Oak Forest Dr., Onalaska, WI 54650; phone: 608/781-9570 or 608/534-6409.

Ice Age National Scenic Trail

This trail is wholly within Wisconsin, with completed segments in all backpacking regions. Segments suitable for true backpacking are included in the main body of the book. Many short, and a few long, segments are completed through public land such as county forests and state wildlife areas; other completed segments run mainly through private lands. As the trail is under construction, new quasi-backpacking (as well as true backpacking) areas will continue to appear. *Contact:* Ice Age Park & Trail Foundation, 207 E. Buffalo St., Suite 515, Milwaukee, WI 53202-5712; phone: 800/227-0046; e-mail: cthisted@sbtsi.com. *Also,* Ice Age National Scenic Trail, National Park Service, 700 Rayovac Dr., Suite 100, Madison, WI 53711; phone: 608/264-5610.

La Crosse River State Trail

Located in our Southwest region (La Crosse and Monroe Counties), this 21.5-mile trail parallels the La Crosse River, running between Medary (near La Crosse) in the west and Sparta in the east. The trail thus connects with the Elroy-Sparta Trail and very nearly with the Great River Trail (see entries above). There are public and/or private campgrounds on or near the trail at Medary, West Salem, and Sparta. *Contact:* La Crosse River Trail, Trail Headquarters, 111 Milwaukee St., Sparta, WI 54656; phone: 608/269-4123.

Military Ridge State Trail

Running east-west in the Southwest region, from near Madison to Dodgeville, in Dane and Iowa Counties, the trail is 39.6 miles long, and it is one of two state trails listed by the Department of Natural Resources as having backpack camping "located nearby." This designation is based on the fact that the trail passes just south of Blue Mound State Park (a side trail leads to the park and its campground) and also passes within a few miles of Governor Dodge State Park (see account in main body). *Contact:* Military Ridge State Trail, c/o Blue Mound State Park, 4350 Mounds Park Rd., P.O. Box 98, Blue Mounds, WI 53517; phone: 608/437-7393.

North Country National Scenic Trail

When completed this trail will run through the North Central and Northwest regions (Iron, Ashland, Bayfield, and Douglas Counties). The longest of the nine national scenic trails, the North Country Trail runs through seven states from North Dakota to New York. The trail actually originated in Wisconsin; the section going across the top of the Chequamegon side of the Chequamegon-Nicolet National Forest was a preexisting pathway called the North Country Trail. The trail's segments in Brule River State Forest, Chequamegon, Copper Falls State Park, and Iron County are treated in the body of the book. More trail is under development in the state forest and in Iron County and may be opened in the year 2000. *Contact:* North Country National Scenic Trail Association, Wisconsin State Coordinator, Gaylord Yost, 2925 W. Bradley Rd., River Hills, WI 53217-1719; phone: 262/354-8987; e-mail: gaylyost@aol.com. *Also,* North Country Trail Association, 49 Monroe Center NW, Suite 200B, Grand Rapids, MI 49503; phone: 616/454-5506; web site: www.northcountrytrail.org; and National Park Service, North Country National Scenic Trail, 700 Rayovac Dr., Suite 100, Madison, WI 53711; phone: 608/264-5610; web site: www.nps.gov/noco.

Pine Line

This is a locally maintained, north-south hike-bike trail in the North Central region (Price and Taylor Counties). The route is currently 26.2 miles, but the trail will likely be extended into downtown Prentice and Medford. Pine Line is named for the Eastern White Pines taken out of here on the Wisconsin Central Railroad for more than a century, beginning in 1876. The closest public camping is in Medford's city park, an attractive strip park along the Black River about one-half mile from the southern terminus of the trail. *Contact:* Price-Taylor Rail Trail Association, c/o Sue Minks, N4217 West Rd., Kennan, WI 54537; phone: 715/474-2234. *Also,* Price County Tourism Department, Price County Courthouse, Phillips, WI 54555; phone: 800/269-4505 or 715/339-4505; and Taylor

County Tourism Council, P.O. Box 172, Medford, WI 55451; phone: 800/257-4729 or 715/748-4729.

Red Cedar State Trail

A 14.5-mile, north-south hike-bike trail in the Southwest region (Dunn County), the trail is one of two listed by the Department of Natural Resources as having backpack camping "located nearby," but the literature on the trail published by the DNR says only "Please DO NOT . . . Camp overnight." Perhaps the county park located near the southern terminus of the trail has a campground. *Contact:* Red Cedar State Trail, Department of Natural Resources, Route 6, Box 1, Menomonie, WI 54751; phone: 715/232-2631. *Also,* Greater Menomonie Area Chamber of Commerce, 700 Wolske Bay Rd., Suite 200, Menomonie, WI 54751; phone: 715/235-9087.

Sugar River State Trail

The Sugar River State Trail runs 23 miles from New Glarus southeastward to Brodhead in the Southwest region (Green County). The trail is included here by virtue of the fact that its northwestern terminus is only 1.5 miles north of New Glarus Woods State Park (see account in main body). *Contact:* Sugar River Trail, P.O. Box 781, New Glarus, WI 53574; phone: 608/527-2334.

Timm's Hill National Trail

Located in the North Central region (Price and Taylor Counties), Timm's Hill is the highest point in Wisconsin (elevation 1,951.5 feet). This north-south, 10-mile trail connects the high point with the Ice Age National Scenic Trial to its south and is maintained by the local chapter of the Ice Age Park and Trail Foundation. There is a primitive campsite open to the public about a mile south of where the Timm's Hill Trail intersects with the Ice Age Trail. The closest public campground appears to be at Wood Lake in Taylor County Forest, about 3 miles from the trail. *Contact:* Ice Age Park & Trail Foundation, 207 E. Buffalo St., Suite 515, Milwaukee, WI 53202-5712; phone: 800/227-0046; e-mail: cthisted@sbtsi.com. *Also,* Price County Tourism Department, Price County Courthouse, Phillips, WI 54555; phone: 800/269-4505 or 715/339-4505; and Taylor County Tourism Council, P.O. Box 172, Medford, WI 55451; phone: 800/257-4729 or 715/748-4729.

Wild Goose State Trail

Found in the Southeast region (Dodge and Fond du Lac Counties), this was the first "cooperative" trail in the state. The 34-mile, north-south corridor of the abandoned Chicago and Northwestern Railroad is owned by the state, whereas the trail itself is maintained and managed by the counties. The trail is named for the Canada Geese that gather by the tens of thousands each autumn on nearby

Horicon National Wildlife Refuge. The closest public campground is Horicon Ledge County Park, about 4 miles east of the trail near Horicon. The Playful Goose Campground, 2.5 miles east of the trail south of Horicon, appears to be commercial. *Contact:* Friends of the Recreation Trail (F.O.R.T.), c/o Virginia Seaholm, copresident, P.O. Box 72, Juneau, WI 53039; phone: 262/485-2917. *Also,* Dodge County Planning & Development, 127 East Oak St., Juneau, WI 53039-1329; phone: 262/386-3705; and Fond du Lac County Planning & Parks, City/County Government Center, 160 South Macy St., Fond du Lac, WI 54935; phone: 262/929-3135.

CAMPGROUNDS AT TRAIL COMPLEXES

The list below is of campgrounds that lie in a complex with at least 10 miles of trail. We found only certain state parks and forests that qualified; county and town parks with camping always had too little trail mileage for inclusion, as was true of some state parks as well. State units given full accounts earlier in the book are omitted here even if they also qualify as quasi-backpacking places.

The parks and forests listed here may prove especially useful for shakedown trips. You can hike most of the day with a full pack and camp in the campground as if it were a backcountry site, using only equipment and food carried in your pack. Like the linear trails above, the parks and forests here have the geographic advantage of tending to be in the southern half of the state, where proper backpacking opportunities are few and scattered. Although these trails do not "go" anywhere, as the linear trails do, park trails are generally far shadier than wide bike paths, and often more scenic. The map that is located near the front of this book names the regions that we defined to locate backpacking areas. Those regional names are used in the entries here for purposes of general location, but these parks are not shown on the region map. The list is alphabetical.

Big Bay State Park

On Madeline Island—the only Apostle Island not in the national lakeshore—Big Bay State Park offers 10 miles of trail including 1.5 miles along the Lake Superior shoreline (North Central region, Bayfield County). There are a few walk-in campsites in the campground. *Contact:* Big Bay State Park, Box 589, Bayfield, WI 54814-0589; phone: 715/747-6425 in summer, 715/779-4020 off season.

Devil's Lake State Park

Composed of more than 9,000 acres, Devil's Lake State Park is located in our Southwest backpacking region (Sauk County). The park's 22.9 miles of trail provide some of the most scenic hiking in the state as you ascend either the east or west bluff overlooking the lake. Furthermore, the Ice Age National Scenic Trail has a long section within the park, regrettably without designated trail campsites. Along with Peninsula State Park (below), this is the most popular park in Wisconsin. *Contact:* Devil's Lake State Park, S5975 Park Rd., Baraboo, WI 53913-9299; phone: 608/356-8301.

Hartman Creek State Park

More than 1,400 acres, Hartman Creek State Park lies in the Southeast backpacking region (Portage County). This quiet park has 13.7 miles of hiking trails, including a section of the Ice Age Trail. *Contact:* Hartman Creek State Park, N2480 Hartman Creek Rd., Waupaca, WI 54981-9727; phone: 715/258-2372.

Interstate State Park

Composed of more than 1,300 acres, Interstate State Park is located on the Minnesota border in the Northwest region (Polk County). Wisconsin's oldest state park, situated on a narrow gorge of the St. Croix River, offers precisely 10 miles of trail, including the western terminus of the Ice Age Trail. *Contact:* Interstate State Park, P.O. Box 703, St. Croix Falls, WI 54024; phone: 715/483-3747.

Lake Wissota State Park

Across the flowage lake from Chippewa Falls, at the extreme southwest corner of our North Central backpacking region (Chippewa County), Lake Wissota State Park consists of about 1,000 acres. Especially attractive to boaters and fishermen, the park has 22.3 miles of trail to beckon the hiker. *Contact:* Lake Wissota State Park, 18127 Cty. Hwy. O, Chippewa Falls, WI 54729; phone: 715/382-4574.

Mirror Lake State Park

Mirror Lake State Park, 2,000 acres, is in the Southwest region (Sauk County). A picturesque site on a bluff-lined lake, the park contains 20 miles of trail. *Contact:* Mirror Lake State Park, E10320 Fern Dell Rd., Baraboo, WI 53913; phone: 608/254-2333.

Peninsula State Park

The more than 3,700 acres of Peninsula State Park lie along the shore of Green Bay in Door County (Door region). This is a somewhat "civilized" place (with a golf course and summer theater) in a heavily touristic area. Nevertheless, it offers 20 miles of trail to the hiker. Along with Devil's Lake State Park (above), this is the most popular park in Wisconsin. *Contact:* Peninsula State Park, 9462 Shore Rd., Box 218, Fish Creek, WI 54212-0218; phone: 920/868-3258.

Perrot State Park

This 1,200-acre park on the Mississippi River is in the Southwest region (Trempealeau County). The scenic confluence of the Trempealeau and Mississippi Rivers with 500-foot bluffs adds spice to the park's 14.5 miles of trail. *Contact:* Perrot State Park, W26247 Sullivan Rd., P.O. Box 407, Trempealeau, WI 54661-0407; phone: 608/534-6409.

Point Beach State Forest

Nearly 3,000 acres, Point Beach State Forest occupies a 6-mile stretch of Lake Michigan beach in our Southeast region (Manitowoc County). The park has 11.5 miles of trail in addition to the miles of shoreline if you like beach walking. *Contact:* Point Beach State Forest, 9400 Cty. Hwy. O, Two Rivers, WI 54241; phone: 920/794-7480.

Potawatomi State Park

The 1,200 acres of Potawatomi State Park are near Sturgeon Bay in Door County (Door region). Climb the observation tower to see clear across Green Bay, stroll the 2 miles of shoreline, or hike the 16.8 miles of trail, including the eastern terminus of the Ice Age Trail. *Contact:* Potawatomi State Park, 3740 Park Dr., Sturgeon Bay, WI 54235; phone: 920/746-2890.

Wildcat Mountain State Park

A whopping 3,500 acres, Wildcat Mountain State Park is in the Southwest region (Vernon County). Overlooking the Kickapoo River, the park offers 25.8 miles of scenic hiking trails. *Contact:* Wildcat Mountain State Park, Hwy. 33E, Box 90, Ontario, WI 54651; phone: 608/337-4775.

Willow River State Park

Composed of nearly 3,000 acres, this park offers 13 miles of trail including trails to a lovely waterfall (Northwest region, St. Croix County). Still listed in 1999 DNR literature as having backpacking, the backcountry campsites were actually bulldozed away in the spring of 1999, and the only camping is now in the campground. *Contact:* Willow River State Park, 1034 Cty. Rd. A, Hudson, WI 54016; phone: 715/386-5931.

Wyalusing State Park

The more than 2,000 acres of Wyalusing State Park can be found in the Southwest region (Grant County). Located where the Wisconsin River flows into the mighty Mississippi, this is one of the state's oldest parks. It contains 22.2 miles of trail, much of it with scenic views to the rivers below. *Contact:* Wyalusing State Park, 13081 State Park Ln., Bagley, WI 53801; phone: 608/996-2261.

Yellowstone Lake State Park

Yellowstone Lake State Park, 885 acres, is located in the Southwest region (Lafayette County). The impounded lake attracts mainly swimmers, boaters, and fishermen, but the park also offers 10 miles of trail. *Contact:* Yellowstone Lake State Park, 7896 Lake Rd., Blanchardville, WI 53516; phone: 608/523-4427.

APPENDIX B

Fee Schedules

Any information about backpacking is subject to change, but fees are perhaps the only data virtually guaranteed to change. The data provided here were the latest available, but as they rise you may wish to pencil in the new values.

STATE PARKS, FORESTS, AND HIKE-BIKE TRAILS

The Bureau of Parks and Recreation of the Wisconsin Department of Natural Resources is responsible for administering fees (set by the governor and the legislature) in state parks, state forests, and certain state trails for biking, horseback riding, and cross-country skiing. (A trail pass is *not* required for hiking.) For information on current fees contact the bureau at P.O. Box 7921, Madison, WI 53707-7921; phone: 608/266-2181; TTY: 608/267-2752; e-mail: wiparks@dnr.state.wi.us.

Admission Stickers

A vehicle that stops in any state park or forest must display a current admission sticker. Stickers are available for a calendar year, for the day, or in some parks and forests for one hour. *Note:* Although park and forest offices, as well as park entrance stations, theoretically sell stickers, these offices are often closed (especially forest offices on weekends, when visitation is highest). If you make at least four visits to state parks and forests in a given calendar year, it is worth purchasing an annual sticker, which can be obtained by mail from the DNR at the address given above. The rate schedule for 1999 was:

> *Nonresident:* $25 annual, $7 daily, and (where available) $3 hourly.
> *Resident:* $18 annual, $5 daily, $3 hourly.
> *Resident Senior (65 and older):* $9 annual, $3 daily, $3 hourly.

Camping Fees

Wisconsin parks are unusual in charging the same fee for backpacking as for use of campgrounds, with discounts for weekdays (Sunday through Thursday) and off season (after Labor Day and before Memorial Day). All backpacking in state parks is restricted to designated campsites, use of which requires paying the campground fee. The charges also apply to designated campsites within state forests but *not* to wilderness camping in state forests where that is allowed. Campgrounds are rated as class A or B, and (curiously) the backpacking campsite fee always matches the campground rate when the park or forest also has a campground. There is no discount for senior citizens. The rate schedule for class A campgrounds in 1999 was:

Nonresident: $12 Friday and Saturday (Memorial Day through Labor Day), $10 weeknights and off season.

Resident: $10 Friday and Saturday (Memorial Day through Labor Day), $8 weeknights and off season.

Class B campgrounds are slightly less expensive:

Nonresident: $11 Friday and Saturday (Memorial Day through Labor Day), $9 weeknights and off season.

Resident: $9 Friday and Saturday (Memorial Day through Labor Day), $7 weeknights and off season.

Reservation Fees

Advance reservations of backpacking campsites are handled by the same commercial reservation service that the state hired beginning in 1999 to handle campground reservations. Reservations are accepted by phone at 888/947-2757 (9 A.M. to 10 P.M. weekdays and 9 A.M. to 6 P.M. weekends) or on the web at www.wiparks.net. In 1999, the reservation fee was $9.50 and the cancellation fee was $8.50. The only exception we know of is the Lapham Peak Unit of Kettle Moraine State Forest, which handles its own reservations for its one backpacking site ($4 reservation fee in 1999); see the Lapham Peak account in main body for contact information.

FEDERAL PASSPORTS

Three kinds of federal "passports" are issued that give the holder specified discounts in certain federal recreation areas such as national forests and national parks. The Golden Access Passport (free lifetime pass) is not relevant for backpacking. The Golden Eagle Passport (1999 cost, $50 for the 12 months following purchase) does not gain the holder a discount for any backpacking area in this book (although it does provide half-price campground fees in all national forests). The Golden Age Passport can be purchased by anyone at least 62 years of age (1999 cost, $10) and is a lifetime pass. The Golden Age Passport (but *not* the Golden Eagle) entitles the holder to a 50% discount on the purchase of an annual vehicle sticker for national forests, so it is useful for backpacking seniors in Wisconsin. These passports can be obtained at any national park entrance station and at the National Park Service Office, 700 Rayovac Dr., Suite 100, Madison, WI 53711; phone: 608/264-5610.

NATIONAL LAKESHORE

The Apostle Islands National Lakeshore has no entrance fee. The 1999 camping fee was $15, good for 14 days. Because it is called a special use permit rather than a camping permit, the national lakeshore refuses to allow discounts to holders of the federal golden passports. Advanced camping registration (no extra cost) can be obtained by mail or phone from Apostle Islands National Lakeshore, Route 1, Box 4, Bayfield, WI 54814; phone: 715/779-3397.

NATIONAL FORESTS

The U.S. Forest Service is responsible for fees in national forests. For information on current fees contact the Forest Supervisor's Office, Chequamegon-Nicolet National Forest, 1170 4th Avenue S., Park Falls, WI 54522; phone: 715/752-2461; fax: 715/762-5179; TTY: 715/762-5701. *Also,* Forest Supervisor's Office, Chequamegon-Nicolet National Forest, 58 South Stevens St., Rhinelander, WI 54501; phone: 715/362-1300; fax: 715/362-1359; TTY: 715/362-1383.

Parking Sticker

National forests do not have entrance fees (as they are not restricted-access areas like national parks). Instead, to park in Forest Service lots in Wisconsin—which provide access to trails and other recreational facilities—you must have a parking sticker on the vehicle. The sticker is valid for the Chequamegon-Nicolet National Forest but not for forests elsewhere in the country. The 1999 fees were:

Yearly (March to March): $10
Daily: $3

These permits can be obtained at any ranger district office (see section on contacts in each trail account in this book) or by mail to either of the above addresses. The Golden Age and Golden Access (but *not* Golden Eagle) Passports give the holder a 50% discount on the parking fee.

Camping Fees

The national forest in Wisconsin does not charge for backpack camping, including use of shelters and established campsites. (Fees are charged in campgrounds.)

Checklist for Backpacks

USUALLY DEEMED ESSENTIAL

backpack
small flashlight
whistle
minimal first-aid kit
food
cup and utensils
water bottles
stove, fuel, and cook kit
matches or fire starter
tent with fly, stakes, and poles
sleeping bag in stuff sack and pad
straps or rope for lashing things to pack
raincoat or poncho
hiking boots
change of clothing
toilet paper
pocket knife
small sewing kit
moleskin, duct tape, or Spenco for blisters
identification sheet with name and address of backpacker, medications and relevant health conditions, identifying marks
map and compass
required medications
water filter or treatment chemicals

GENERALLY CONSIDERED DESIRABLE

tent liner or ground cloth
rain pants
backpack rain cover
trowel for digging "cat hole"
lightweight rain tarp for making a shelter

potentially useful medicines (prescription, antidiarrheal, pain killers, cold remedies)
nylon cord
plastic garbage bags (I for trash, I for putting food in to tie up)
moccasins or sandals for around camp
small towel and soap
sponge and biodegradable dishwashing detergent
bandana (for drying dishes, use as a potholder, tying back hair)
unbreakable plate
toothbrush, toothpaste, comb
waterproof map case
candle
sun hat
sunscreen and bug repellent
hat, gloves
warm jacket
tissues or handkerchief
some cash or a wallet
paper and pen or pencil
signaling mirror
tent repair material

OPTIONAL

recreational reading material
special cookware (Outback Oven, coffee pot)
small thermos
fanny pack or small day pack
GPS receiver
camera, binoculars
fishing line
air mattress and pump
stove repair kit
nature guides
small plastic bowl, for washing

Trail, Outdoor, and Conservation Organizations

Get involved in securing foot trails and wild places for today and the future by joining with those wonderful people who are already involved. These and other such organizations need and deserve your support.

American Hiking Society
P.O. Box 20160, Washington, D.C. 20041-2160; phone: 301/565-6704; web site: www.americanhiking.org.

Hoofers Outing Club
University of Wisconsin, Memorial Union, 800 Langdon St., Madison, WI 53706; phone: 608/262-1630; web site: www.hoofers.org.

Ice Age Park and Trail Foundation of Wisconsin, Inc.
207 E. Buffalo St., Suite 515, Milwaukee, WI 53202-5712; phone: 800/227-0046; e-mail: cthisted@sbtsi.com; web site: www.iceagetrail.org/.

The Nature Conservancy
International Headquarters, 4245 North Fairfax Dr., Suite 100, Arlington, VA 22203-1606; phone: 703/841-5300; web site: www.tnc.org. *Also,* Wisconsin Chapter, 633 West Main St., Madison, WI 53703; phone: 608/251-8140; fax: 608/251-8535.

North Country Trail Association
49 Monroe Center, Suite 200B, Grand Rapids, MI 49503; phone: 616/454-5506; e-mail: NCTAssoc@aol.com; web site: www.northcountrytrail.org. *Also,* Wisconsin State Coordinator, Gaylord Yost, 2925 W. Bradley Rd., River Hills, WI 53217-1719; phone: 262/354-8987; e-mail: gaylyost@aol.com.

Sierra Club
85 Second St., San Francisco, CA 94105; phone: 415/977-5500 *or* 800/477-2627. Web site: www.sierraclub.org. *Also,* Wisconsin Chapter, 222 S. Hamilton St., Suite 1, Madison, WI 53703; phone: 608/256-0565.

Further Reading

BACKPACKING, HIKING, AND CAMPING

Berger, Karen. *Advanced Backpacking, a Trailside Guide.* New York: W. W. Norton & Co., 1998. [Part of a series; long distance hiking, expedition planning, food resupply, high country, cold weather, guided treks.]

Berger, Karen. *Hiking and Backpacking, a Complete Guide.* New York: W. W. Norton & Co., 1995. [Part of a series; first aid, planning, leave-no-trace camping, food preparation.]

Boga, Steve. *Camping and Backpacking with Children.* Mechanicsburg, Penn.: Stackpole Books, 1995. [Suggestions for making backpacking with children an enjoyable experience.]

Bryson, Bill. *A Walk in the Woods.* New York: Broadway Books, 1998. [Hilarious account of the author's experiences while hiking the Appalachian Trail; if this isn't the funniest book ever written about backpacking, Jack claims he'll eat it, page by page.]

Fleming, June. *The Well-Fed Backpacker.* 3rd ed. New York: Vintage Books, 1986. [Meal planning, recipes, drying food, packaging, gourmet cooking, baking, winter outdoors.]

Fletcher, Colin. *The Complete Walker III.* New York: Alfred A. Knopf, 1984. [If any handbook on backpacking deserves the approbation "classic," this is the one; Fletcher has probably interested more people in backpacking than has any other individual, through both the editions of this book and his other classic, *The Man Who Walked Through Time.*]

Hall, Adrienne. *Backpacking: A Woman's Guide.* Camden, Me.: Ragged Mountain Press, 1998. [Considerations especially for women such as locating a pack and safety, and write-ups by women about their experiences.]

Harmon, Will. *Wild Country Companion: The Ultimate Guide to No-Trace Outdoor Recreation and Wilderness Safety.* Helena, Mont.: Falcon Publ. Co., 1994. [Probably the most complete and accessible handbook yet on environmental and safety concerns.]

Hodgson, Michael. *Basic Essentials of Minimizing Impact on the Wilderness.* Merrillville, Ind.: ICS Books, 1991. [One of the first books devoted to leave-no-trace recreation in the out-of-doors.]

Manning, Harvey. *Backpacking One Step at a Time.* 4th ed. New York: Vintage Books, 1986. [An old standby that has seen generations through backpacking; how to walk, equipment, food, finding the route, winter camping.]

Meyer, Kathleen. *How to Shit in the Woods: An Environmentally Sound Approach to a Lost Art.* 2nd ed. Berkeley, Calif.: Ten Speed Press, 1994. [Despite the attention-getting title this is a serious book on backcountry sanitation; covers the "pack-it-out" policy of some river corridors and gives instructions on a "one-sit-hole."]

Simer, Peter, and John Sullivan. *The National Outdoor Leadership School's Wilderness Guide.* New York: Simon and Schuster, 1985. [The N.O.L.S. continues to train new generations in survival techniques and environmental ethics; this book collects much of the lore.]

Sobey, Ed. *The Whole Backpacker's Catalog.* Camden, Me.: Ragged Mountain Press, 1999. [Advice on gear and techniques plus comprehensive lists of resources for the backpacker including books, maps, web sites, e-mail addresses, addresses and phone numbers of manufacturers of equipment, stores, organizations, and regional hiking places.]

Townsend, Chris. *Backpacker's Handbook.* Camden, Me.: International Marine/Ragged Mountain Press, 1997. [Highly acclaimed guide to choosing equipment, footwear, dressing for the wilderness, skills, hazards, backpacking abroad; extensive coverage of equipment with evaluations.]

Waterman, Laura and Guy. *Backwoods Ethics,* 2nd ed. Woodstock, Vt.: Countryman Press, 1993. [Arguably the most widely read book on its subject; let us hope it will continue to be updated in new editions.]

TRAILS

Crawford, Bob. *Walking Trails of Eastern and Central Wisconsin.* Madison: University of Wisconsin Press, 1997. [Trails in Kettle Moraine North, on the Lake Michigan shoreline, and elsewhere.]

Crawford, Bob. *Walking Trails of Southern Wisconsin.* 2nd ed. Madison: University of Wisconsin Press, 2000. [Trails in Kettle Moraine South, Lapham Peak, and elsewhere; an appendix in Lyme disease.]

Davenport, Don. *A Traveler's Guide to Wisconsin State Parks and Forests.* Madison: Wisconsin Natural Resources Magazine, 1989. [A publication of the Wisconsin Department of Natural Resources with official information and many photographs, but badly out of date.]

Hintz, Martin. *Hiking Wisconsin.* Champaign, Ill.: Human Kinetics, 1997. [Guide to trail difficulty, road maps and annotated trail maps.]

Hutchins, Byron and Margaret. *The North Country Trail Through Wisconsin's Chequamegon National Forest and the Old Portage Trail in Brule River State Park.* Rev. ed. Rockford, Ill.: Hutchins Guidebooks, 1996. [A detailed guide with every creek crossing and trail junction, based on the authors' backpacking trips.]

McGrath, Chad. *Great Wisconsin Walks.* Madison: Wisconsin Trails, 1997. ["Forty-five strolls, rambles, hikes and treks."]

Reuss, Henry S. *On the Trail of the Ice Age.* Rev. ed. Sheboygan, Wis.: Ice Age Park and Trail Foundation, Inc., 1995. ["A Guide for Wisconsin Hikers, Bikers and Motorists"; covers Ice Age National Scientific Reserve and the Ice Age Trail.]

Umhoeffer, Jim. *Guide to Wisconsin Outdoors.* Minnetonka, Minn.: NorthWord Press, Inc., 1990. [Sections about most of the state and national areas listed in this backpacking guide.]

GEOLOGY, GEOGRAPHY, AND MAPS

Martin, Lawrence. *The Physical Geography of Wisconsin.* 3rd ed. Madison: University of Wisconsin Press, 1965. [Glacial geology, geography by provinces.]

Paull, Rachel K., and Richard A. Paull. *Wisconsin and Upper Michigan.* Dubuque, Iowa: Kendall/Hunt Publishing Company, 1980. [A field guide in the K/H Geology Field Guide Series with text organized by interstate and U.S. highways.]

Robinson, Arthur, and Jerry Culver. *The Atlas of Wisconsin.* Madison: University of Wisconsin Press, 1974. [Sectional geographical maps, city maps, and gazetteer; alphabetical listing of place names.]

Wisconsin Atlas and Gazetteer. Freeport, Me.: DeLorme Mapping Company, 1988. [Divides the state into 85 detailed 7-½ minute by 7-½ minute maps.]

PLANTS

Brockman, C. Frank. *A Guide to Field Identification: Trees of North America.* New York: Golden Press, 1968. [Major native and introduced species north of Mexico, maps and colored plates with tree shape, twigs, leaves, and fruit.]

Courtenay, Booth, and James Hall Zimmerman. *Wildflowers and Weeds: A Field Guide in Full Color.* New York: Van Nostrand Reinhold Co., [1972]. Paperback repr. Englewood Cliffs, N.J.: Prentice Hall, 1990. [A guide to common flowering plants of the Great Lakes region; our recommended book for identifying Wisconsin wildflowers.]

Fassett, Norman C. *Spring Flora of Wisconsin*. 4th ed., rev. by faculty of the University of Wisconsin's Botany Department. Madison: University of Wisconsin Press, 1976. [Classic, technical, comprehensive.]

Peterson, Roger Tory, and Margaret McKenny. *A Field Guide to Wildflowers: Northeastern and North-central North America*. Boston: Houghton Mifflin Co., 1968. [Mostly black-and-white illustrations with habitats, flowering dates, and pointers for distinguishing field characteristics.]

Platt, Rutherford. *A Pocket Guide to the Trees*. New York: Pocket Books, Inc., 1952. [Native and introduced species, photos, sketches of leaves, absolutely delightful text.]

Shuttleworth, Floyd S., and Herbert S. Zim. *Non-Flowering Plants*. New York: Golden Press. 1967. [A Golden Field Guide to ferns, mosses, lichens, mushrooms and other fungi.]

Venning, Frank D. *Wildflowers of North America: A Guide to Field Identification*. New York: Golden Press, 1984. [Colored illustrations, covers huge area, organized by genera.]

ANIMALS

American Ornithologists' Union. *The A.O.U. Check-list of North American Birds*. 7th ed. Washington, D.C.: Allen Press, Inc., 1988. [The standard for names maintained by one of the continent's most venerable scientific societies.]

Burt, William Henry, and Richard Philip Grossenheider. *A Field Guide to the Mammals*. 2nd ed. Boston: Houghton Mifflin Co., 1964. [A guide in the Peterson series with distinguishing characteristics, range maps, habits, and habitats.]

Conant, Roger. *A Field Guide to Reptiles and Amphibians of Eastern and Central North America*. Boston: Houghton Mifflin Co., 1975. [Identification, habitat, range maps.]

Gromme, Owen. *Birds of Wisconsin*. Rev. ed. Madison: University of Wisconsin Press, 1998. [Gorgeous color portraits of the state's birds by a world-famous Wisconsin wildlife artist, distribution maps and datelines, with an introduction by Samuel Robbins.]

Jackson, Hartley H. T. *Mammals of Wisconsin*. Madison: University of Wisconsin Press, 1961. [Standard reference work.]

Mitchell, Robert T., and Herbert S. Zim. *Butterflies and Moths.* New Y
Golden Press, 1964. [A Golden Field Guide to the more common
American species with over 400 color illustrations.]

Peterson, Roger Tory. *A Field Guide to the Birds of Eastern and Central North
America.* 4th ed. Boston: Houghton Mifflin Co., 1980. [Illustrations with
arrows to critical field characteristics, range maps; the most recent
edition of the book that pioneered modern field guides by the late
Roger Tory Peterson.]

Robbins, Chandler S., Bertel Bruun, and Herbert S. Zim. *A Guide to Field
Identification: Birds of North America.* Rev. ed. New York: Golden Press,
1983. [A Golden Field Guide with illustrations, short descriptions, range
maps, and sonographs of vocal sounds.]

Robbins, Samuel D., Jr. *Wisconsin Birdlife: Population and Distribution Past and
Present.* Madison: University of Wisconsin Press, 1991. [Abundance,
distribution, habitat, breeding dates, and discussion of every bird reliably
seen in Wisconsin.]

Smith, Hobart M. *A Guide to Field Identification: Amphibians of North America.*
New York: Golden Press, 1978. [A Golden Field Guide to frogs, toads,
and other amphibians, with information for hobbyists, keys to
identification, range maps, and habitats.]

Smith, Hobart M., and Edmund D. Brodie, Jr. *A Guide to Field Identification:
Reptiles of North America.* New York: Golden Press, 1982. [A Golden
Field Guide to reptiles north of Mexico with information for hobbyists,
keys to identification, range maps, and habitats.]

Temple, Stanley A., John R. Cary, and Robert E. Rolley. *Wisconsin Birds:
A Seasonal and Geographical Guide.* 2nd ed. Madison: University of
Wisconsin Press, 1997. [Maps and graphs of abundance by month of the
common bird species.]

PERIODICALS

Backpacker, 33 E. Minor St., Emmaus, PA 18098; phone: 800/666-3434; web
site: www.bpbasecamp.com. [Advice, latest information, ads on
equipment and destinations.]

Silent Sports, 717 Tenth Street, P.O. Box 152, Waupaca, WI 54981; phone
715/258-5546; fax: 715/258-8162; e-mail: info@silentsports.net; web site:
www.silentsports.net. [Monthly magazine focusing on nonmotorized
sports in the upper Midwest.]

Wisconsin Trails, Trails Media Group Inc., P.O. Box 5650, 6225 University
Ave., Madison, WI 53705; phone: 800/236-8088; fax: 608/231-1557;
e-mail: info@wistrails.com; web site: www.wistrails.com. [Bimonthly
magazine of life in Wisconsin.]

Index

Page numbers in *italics* denote maps. (Not indexed: addresses, map contents, terminal references, photograph captions, highways, roads, and streets.)